MY WORKING BIBLE

The Guideposts Bible Study Program

GUIDEPOSTS ®

Carmel   New York   10512

D1414220

THE GUIDEPOSTS BIBLE STUDY PROGRAM
Judges, Ruth, 1 & 2 Samuel
  1. Discovering Judges, Ruth, 1 & 2 Samuel
  2. MY WORKING BIBLE
  3. Knowing More About Judges, Ruth, 1 & 2 Samuel

Copyright © 1988 by GUIDEPOSTS ASSOCIATES, INC.
Carmel, N.Y. 10512

All rights reserved. No part of this program or publications within this program may be reproduced, stored in a retrieval system, or transmitted in any form by any means, electronic, mechanical, photocopying, recording or otherwise, without the written permission of the publisher, Guideposts Associates, Inc., Carmel, New York 10512.

All Scripture verses referenced herein are from the King James Version of the Bible.

Printed in the United States of America.

Introduction

Your Working Bible contains the text (KJV) of the Books of Judges, Ruth, and 1 & 2 Samuel and is designed to be used with the Discovering Judges, Ruth, and 1 & 2 Samuel study book.

It's called a "working" Bible because that's exactly what you can do in it—work. Space and lines are provided for you to jot down notes, emphasize points you'll want to remember, make comparisons, record your questions. The Scriptures are clearly keyed to the Lessons in the study book so you cannot lose track of where you are. All in all, your Working Bible is a convenient, practical workbook that will help you in your study of God's Word.

LESSON 1

JUDGES 1:1–9:57
Judgments Which Lead to Faith

1 NOW AFTER the death of Josh'u-a it came to pass, that the children of Is'ra-el asked the Lord, saying, Who shall go up for us against the Ca'naan-ites first, to fight against them?

2 And the Lord said, Ju'dah shall go up: behold, I have delivered the land into his hand.

3 And Ju'dah said unto Sim'e-on his brother, Come up with me into my lot, that we may fight against the Ca'naan-ites; and I likewise will go with thee into thy lot. So Sim'e-on went with him.

4 And Ju'dah went up; and the Lord delivered the Ca'naan-ites and the Per'iz-zites into their hand: and they slew of them in Be'zek ten thousand men.

5 And they found A-don'i-be'zek in Be'zek: and they fought against him, and they slew the Ca'-naan-ites and the Per'iz-zites.

6 But A-don'i-be'zek fled; and they pursued after him, and caught him, and cut off his thumbs and his great toes.

7 And A-don'i-be'zek said, Threescore and ten kings, having their thumbs and their great toes cut off, gathered *their meat* under my table: as I have done, so God hath requited me. And they brought him to Je-ru'sa-lem, and there he died.

Judges and History

_____

_____

_____

The Themes in Judges

_____

_____

Israel Moves to Occupy Canaan (1:1–2:5)

_____

Successes and Failures

_____

_____

_____

_____

_____

_____

5

8 Now the children of Ju'dah had fought against Je-ru'sa-lem, and had taken it, and smitten it with the edge of the sword, and set the city on fire.

9 And afterward the children of Ju'dah went down to fight against the Ca'naan-ites, that dwelt in the mountain, and in the south, and in the valley.

10 And Ju'dah went against the Ca'naan-ites that dwelt in He'bron: (now the name of He'-bron before *was* Kir'jath-ar'ba:) and they slew She'shai, and A-hi'man, and Tal'mai.

11 And from thence he went against the inhabitants of De'bir: and the name of De'bir before *was* Kir'jath-se'pher:

12 And Ca'leb said, He that smiteth Kir'jath-se'pher, and taketh it, to him will I give Ach'sah my daughter to wife.

13 And Oth'ni-el the son of Ke'naz, Ca'leb's younger brother, took it: and he gave him Ach'sah his daughter to wife.

14 And it came to pass, when she came *to him,* that she moved him to ask of her father a field; and she lighted from off *her* ass; and Ca'leb said unto her, What wilt thou?

15 And she said unto him, Give me a blessing: for thou hast given me a south land; give me also springs of water. And Ca'leb gave her the upper springs and the nether springs.

16 And the children of the Ken'ite, Mo'ses' father in law, went up out of the city of palm trees with the children of Ju'dah into the wilderness of Ju'dah, which *lieth* in the south of A'rad; and they went and dwelt among the people.

17 And Ju'dah went with Sim'e-on his brother, and they slew the Ca'naan-ites that inhabited Ze'-

phath, and utterly destroyed it. And the name of the city was called Hor'mah.

18 Also Ju'dah took Ga'za with the coast thereof, and As'ke-lon with the coast thereof, and Ek'ron with the coast thereof.

19 And the LORD was with Ju'dah; and he drave out *the inhabitants of* the mountain; but could not drive out the inhabitants of the valley, because they had chariots of iron.

20 And they gave He'bron unto Ca'leb, as Mo'ses said: and he expelled thence the three sons of A'nak.

21 And the children of Ben'ja-min did not drive out the Jeb'u-sites that inhabited Je-ru'sa-lem; but the Jeb'u-sites dwell with the children of Ben'ja-min in Je-ru'sa-lem unto this day.

22 And the house of Jo'seph, they also went up against Beth'-el: and the LORD *was* with them.

23 And the house of Jo'seph sent to descry Beth'-el. (Now the name of the city before *was* Luz.)

24 And the spies saw a man come forth out of the city, and they said unto him, Shew us, we pray thee, the entrance into the city, and we will shew thee mercy.

25 And when he shewed them the entrance into the city, they smote the city with the edge of the sword; but they let go the man and all his family.

26 And the man went into the land of the Hit'-tites, and built a city, and called the name thereof Luz: which *is* the name thereof unto this day.

27 Neither did Ma-nas'seh drive out *the inhabitants of* Beth-she'an and her towns, nor Ta'a-nach and her towns, nor the inhabitants of Dor and her towns, nor the inhabitants of Ib'le-am and her

The Canaanite Religion

7

The Occupation Is Incomplete
Because of Disobedience

towns, nor the inhabitants of Me-gid'do and her towns: but the Ca'naan-ites would dwell in that land.

28 And it came to pass, when Is'ra-el was strong, that they put the Ca'naan-ites to tribute, and did not utterly drive them out.

29 Neither did E'phra-im drive out the Ca'naan-ites that dwelt in Ge'zer; but the Ca'naan-ites dwelt in Ge'zer among them.

30 Neither did Zeb'u-lun drive out the inhabitants of Kit'-ron, nor the inhabitants of Na'ha-lol; but the Ca'naan-ites dwelt among them, and became tributaries.

31 Neither did Ash'er drive out the inhabitants of Ac'cho, nor the inhabitants of Zi'don, nor of Ah'lab, nor of Ach'zib, nor of Hel'bah, nor of A'phik, nor of Re'hob:

32 But the Ash'er-ites dwelt among the Ca'naan-ites, the inhabitants of the land: for they did not drive them out.

33 Neither did Naph'ta-li drive out the inhabitants of Beth-she'mesh, nor the inhabitants of Beth-a'nath; but he dwelt among the Ca'naan-ites, the inhabitants of the land: nevertheless the inhabitants of Beth-she'mesh and of Beth-a'nath became tributaries unto them.

34 And the Am'or-ites forced the children of Dan into the mountain: for they would not suffer them to come down to the valley:

35 But the Am'or-ites would dwell in mount He'res in Aij'a-lon, and in Sha-al'bim: yet the hand of the house of Jo'seph prevailed, so that they became tributaries.

36 And the coast of the Am'or-ites _was_ from the going up to A-krab'bim, from the rock, and upward.

2 AND AN angel of the LORD came up from Gil'-gal to Bo'chim, and said, I made you to go up out of E'gypt, and have brought you unto the land which I sware unto your fathers; and I said, I will never break my covenant with you.

2 And ye shall make no league with the inhabitants of this land; ye shall throw down their altars: but ye have not obeyed my voice: why have ye done this?

3 Wherefore I also said, I will not drive them out from before you; but they shall be *as thorns* in your sides, and their gods shall be a snare unto you.

4 And it came to pass, when the angel of the LORD spake these words unto all the children of Is'ra-el, that the people lifted up their voice, and wept.

5 And they called the name of that place Bo'-chim: and they sacrificed there unto the LORD.

6 And when Josh'u-a had let the people go, the children of Is'ra-el went every man unto his inheritance to possess the land.

7 And the people served the LORD all the days of Josh'u-a, and all the days of the elders that outlived Josh'u-a, who had seen all the great works of the LORD, that he did for Is'ra-el.

8 And Josh'u-a the son of Nun, the servant of the LORD, died, *being* an hundred and ten years old.

9 And they buried him in the border of his inheritance in Tim'nath-he'res, in the mount of E'phra-im, on the north side of the hill Ga'ash.

10 And also all that generation were gathered unto their fathers: and there arose another generation after them, which knew not the LORD, nor yet the works which he had done for Is'ra-el.

Israel's Cycle of History
(2:6–3:4)
The Need for Strong Leadership

Israel Falls Away from God

11 And the children of Is'ra-el did evil in the sight of the LORD, and served Ba'al-im:

12 And they forsook the LORD God of their fathers, which brought them out of the land of E'gypt, and followed other gods, of the gods of the people that *were* round about them, and bowed themselves unto them, and provoked the LORD to anger.

13 And they forsook the LORD, and served Ba'al and Ash'ta-roth.

Judgment for Israel's Disobedience

14 And the anger of the LORD was hot against Is'ra-el, and he delivered them into the hands of spoilers that spoiled them, and he sold them into the hands of their enemies round about, so that they could not any longer stand before their enemies.

15 Whithersoever they went out, the hand of the LORD was against them for evil, as the LORD had said, and as the LORD had sworn unto them: and they were greatly distressed.

Israel's Deliverance

16 Nevertheless the LORD raised up judges, which delivered them out of the hand of those that spoiled them.

17 And yet they would not hearken unto their judges, but they went a whoring after other gods, and bowed themselves unto them: they turned quickly out of the way which their fathers walked in, obeying the commandments of the LORD; *but* they did not so.

18 And when the LORD raised them up judges, then the LORD was with the judge, and delivered them out of the hand of their enemies all the days of the judge: for it repented the LORD because of their groanings by reason of them that oppressed them and vexed them.

19 And it came to pass, when the judge was dead, *that* they returned, and corrupted *themselves* more than their fathers, in following other gods to serve them, and to bow down unto them; they ceased not from their own doings, nor from their stubborn way.

20 And the anger of the LORD was hot against Is'ra-el; and he said, Because that this people hath transgressed my covenant which I commanded their fathers, and have not hearkened unto my voice;

21 I also will not henceforth drive out any from before them of the nations which Josh'u-a left when he died:

22 That through them I may prove Is'ra-el, whether they will keep the way of the LORD to walk therein, as their fathers did keep *it,* or not.

23 Therefore the LORD left those nations, without driving them out hastily; neither delivered he them into the hand of Josh'u-a.

3 NOW THESE *are* the nations which the LORD left, to prove Is'ra-el by them, *even* as many *of Is'ra-el* as had not known all the wars of Ca'naan;

2 Only that the generations of the children of Is'ra-el might know, to teach them war, at the least such as before knew nothing thereof;

3 *Namely,* five lords of the Phi-lis'tines, and all the Ca'naan-ites, and the Si-do'ni-ans, and the Hi'vites that dwelt in mount Leb'a-non, from mount Ba'al-her'mon unto the entering in of Ha'math.

4 And they were to prove Is'ra-el by them, to know whether they would hearken unto the com-

Israel's Pattern of Falling Away

_____
_____
_____
_____
_____
_____
_____
_____
_____
_____
_____
_____
_____
_____
_____
_____
_____

Not an Easy Way

_____
_____

11

_____

_____

_____

_____

_____

_____

_____

Othniel, Caleb's Nephew

_____

_____

_____

_____

_____

_____

_____

_____

_____

_____

mandments of the LORD, which he commanded their fathers by the hand of Mo'ses.

5 And the children of Is'ra-el dwelt among the Ca'naan-ites, Hit'tites, and Am'or-ites, and Per'iz-zites, and Hi'vites, and Jeb'u-sites:

6 And they took their daughters to be their wives, and gave their daughters to their sons, and served their gods.

7 And the children of Is'ra-el did evil in the sight of the LORD, and forgat the LORD their God, and served Ba'al-im and the groves.

8 Therefore the anger of the LORD was hot against Is'ra-el, and he sold them into the hand of Chu'shan-rish-a-tha'im king of Mes-o-po-ta'-mi-a: and the children of Is'ra-el served Chu'shan-rish-a-tha'im eight years.

9 And when the children of Is'ra-el cried unto the LORD, the LORD raised up a deliverer to the children of Is'ra-el, who delivered them, *even* Oth'ni-el the son of Ke'naz, Ca'leb's younger brother.

10 And the Spirit of the LORD came upon him, and he judged Is'ra-el, and went out to war: and the LORD delivered Chu'shan-rish-a-tha'im king of Mes-o-po-ta'mi-a into his hand; and his hand prevailed against Chu'shan-rish-a-tha'im.

11 And the land had rest forty years. And Oth'ni-el the son of Ke'naz died.

12 And the children of Is'ra-el did evil again in the sight of the LORD: and the LORD strengthened Eg'lon the king of Mo'ab against Is'ra-el, because they had done evil in the sight of the LORD.

13 And he gathered unto him the children of Am'mon and Am'a-lek, and went and smote Is'ra-el, and possessed the city of palm trees.

14 So the children of Is'ra-el served Eg'lon the king of Mo'ab eighteen years.

15 But when the children of Is'ra-el cried unto the LORD, the LORD raised them up a deliverer, E'hud the son of Ge'ra, a Ben'ja-mite, a man left-handed: and by him the children of Is'ra-el sent a present unto Eg'lon the king of Mo'ab.

16 But E'hud made him a dagger which had two edges, of a cubit length; and he did gird it under his raiment upon his right thigh.

17 And he brought the present unto Eg'lon king of Mo'ab: and Eg'lon *was* a very fat man.

18 And when he had made an end to offer the present, he sent away the people that bare the present.

19 But he himself turned again from the quarries that *were* by Gil'gal, and said, I have a secret errand unto thee, O king: who said, Keep silence. And all that stood by him went out from him.

20 And E'hud came unto him; and he was sitting in a summer parlour, which he had for himself alone. And E'hud said, I have a message from God unto thee. And he arose out of *his* seat.

21 And E'hud put forth his left hand, and took the dagger from his right thigh, and thrust it into his belly:

22 And the haft also went in after the blade; and the fat closed upon the blade, so that he could not draw the dagger out of his belly; and the dirt came out.

23 Then E'hud went forth through the porch, and shut the doors of the parlour upon him, and locked them.

24 When he was gone out, his servants came; and when they saw that, behold, the doors of the

Ehud, the Benjamite

13

parlour *were* locked, they said, Surely he covereth his feet in his summer chamber.

25 And they tarried till they were ashamed: and, behold, he opened not the doors of the parlour; therefore they took a key, and opened *them:* and, behold, their lord *was* fallen down dead on the earth.

26 And E'hud escaped while they tarried, and passed beyond the quarries, and escaped unto Se'i-rath.

27 And it came to pass, when he was come, that he blew a trumpet in the mountain of E'phra-im, and the children of Is'ra-el went down with him from the mount, and he before them.

28 And he said unto them, Follow after me: for the LORD hath delivered your enemies the Mo'ab-ites into your hand. And they went down after him, and took the fords of Jor'dan toward Mo'ab, and suffered not a man to pass over.

29 And they slew of Mo'ab at that time about ten thousand men, all lusty, and all men of valour; and there escaped not a man.

30 So Mo'ab was subdued that day under the hand of Is'ra-el. And the land had rest four-score years.

Shamgar and His Strange Weapon

31 And after him was Sham'gar the son of A'nath, which slew of the Phi-lis'tines six hundred men with an ox goad: and he also delivered Is'ra-el.

Victory Through Courageous and Faithful Women (4:1–5:31)

4 AND THE children of Is'ra-el again did evil in the sight of the LORD, when E'hud was dead.

2 And the LORD sold them into the hand of Ja'bin king of Ca'naan, that reigned in Ha'zor; the captain

of whose host *was* Sis'e-ra, which dwelt in Ha-ro'sheth of the Gen'tiles.

3 And the children of Is'ra-el cried unto the LORD: for he had nine hundred chariots of iron; and twenty years he mightily oppressed the children of Is'ra-el.

4 And Deb'o-rah, a prophetess, the wife of Lap'i-doth, she judged Is'ra-el at that time.

5 And she dwelt under the palm tree of Deb'o-rah between Ra'mah and Beth'-el in mount E'phra-im: and the children of Is'ra-el came up to her for judgment.

6 And she sent and called Ba'rak the son of A-bin'o-am out of Ke'desh-naph'ta-li, and said unto him, Hath not the LORD God of Is'ra-el commanded, *saying,* Go and draw toward mount Ta'bor, and take with thee ten thousand men of the children of Naph'ta-li and of the children of Zeb'u-lun?

7 And I will draw unto thee to the river Ki'shon Sis'e-ra, the captain of Ja'bin's army, with his chariots and his multitude; and I will deliver him into thine hand.

8 And Ba'rak said unto her, If thou wilt go with me, then I will go: but if thou wilt not go with me, *then* I will not go.

9 And she said, I will surely go with thee: notwithstanding the journey that thou takest shall not be for thine honour; for the LORD shall sell Sis'e-ra into the hand of a woman. And Deb'o-rah arose, and went with Ba'rak to Ke'desh.

10 And Ba'rak called Zeb'u-lun and Naph'ta-li to Ke'-desh; and he went up with ten thousand men at his feet: and Deb'o-rah went up with him.

11 Now He'ber the Ken'ite, *which was* of the children of Ho'bab the father in law of Mo'ses, had

A Woman Chosen by God

Deborah, the Exception to the Rule

Deborah Confers with Barak

Barak Attempts to Assemble an Army

15

severed himself from the Ken'ites, and pitched his tent unto the plain of Za-a-na'im, which *is* by Ke'-desh.

12 And they shewed Sis'e-ra that Ba'rak the son of A-bin'o-am was gone up to mount Ta'-bor.

13 And Sis'e-ra gathered together all his chariots, *even* nine hundred chariots of iron, and all the people that *were* with him, from Ha-ro'sheth of the Gen'tiles unto the river of Ki'shon.

14 And Deb'o-rah said unto Ba'rak, Up; for this *is* the day in which the LORD hath delivered Sis'e-ra into thine hand: is not the LORD gone out before thee? So Ba'rak went down from mount Ta'bor, and ten thousand men after him.

15 And the LORD discomfited Sis'e-ra, and all *his* chariots, and all *his* host, with the edge of the sword before Ba'rak; so that Sis'e-ra lighted down off *his* chariot, and fled away on his feet.

16 But Ba'rak pursued after the chariots, and after the host, unto Ha-ro'sheth of the Gen'-tiles: and all the host of Sis'e-ra fell upon the edge of the sword; *and* there was not a man left.

17 Howbeit Sis'e-ra fled away on his feet to the tent of Ja'el the wife of He'ber the Ken'ite: for *there was* peace between Ja'bin the king of Ha'zor and the house of He'ber the Ken'ite.

18 And Ja'el went out to meet Sis'e-ra, and said unto him, Turn in, my lord, turn in to me; fear not. And when he had turned in unto her into the tent, she covered him with a mantle.

19 And he said unto her, Give me, I pray thee, a little water to drink; for I am thirsty. And she opened a bottle of milk, and gave him drink, and covered him.

20 Again he said unto her, Stand in the door of the tent, and it shall be, when any man doth come

and enquire of thee, and say, Is there any man here? that thou shalt say, No.

21 Then Ja'el He'ber's wife took a nail of the tent, and took an hammer in her hand, and went softly unto him, and smote the nail into his temples, and fastened it into the ground: for he was fast asleep and weary. So he died.

22 And, behold, as Ba'rak pursued Sis'e-ra, Ja'el came out to meet him, and said unto him, Come, and I will shew thee the man whom thou seekest. And when he came into her *tent,* behold, Sis'e-ra lay dead, and the nail *was* in his temples.

23 So God subdued on that day Ja'bin the king of Ca'naan before the children of Is'ra-el.

24 And the hand of the children of Is'ra-el prospered, and prevailed against Ja'bin the king of Ca'-naan, until they had destroyed Ja'bin king of Ca'-naan.

5 THEN SANG Deb'o-rah and Ba'rak the son of A-bin'o-am on that day, saying,

2 Praise ye the LORD for the avenging of Is'ra-el, when the people willingly offered themselves.

3 Hear, O ye kings; give ear, O ye princes; I, *even* I, will sing unto the LORD; I will sing *praise* to the LORD God of Is'ra-el.

4 LORD, when thou wentest out of Se'ir, when thou marchedst out of the field of E'dom, the earth trembled, and the heavens dropped, the clouds also dropped water.

5 The mountains melted from before the LORD, *even* that Si'nai from before the LORD God of Is'ra-el.

6 In the days of Sham'gar the son of A'nath, in the days of Ja'el, the highways were unoccupied, and the travellers walked through byways.

7 *The inhabitants of* the villages ceased, they ceased in Is'ra-el, until that I Deb'o-rah arose, that I arose a mother in Is'ra-el.

8 They chose new gods; then *was* war in the gates: was there a shield or spear seen among forty thousand in Is'ra-el?

9 My heart *is* toward the governors of Is'ra-el, that offered themselves willingly among the people. Bless ye the LORD.

10 Speak, ye that ride on white asses, ye that sit in judgment, and walk by the way.

11 *They that are delivered* from the noise of archers in the places of drawing water, there shall they rehearse the righteous acts of the LORD, *even* the righteous acts *toward the inhabitants* of his villages in Is'ra-el: then shall the people of the LORD go down to the gates.

12 Awake, awake, Deb'o-rah: awake, awake, utter a song: arise, Ba'rak, and lead thy captivity captive, thou son of A-bin'o-am.

13 Then he made him that remaineth have dominion over the nobles among the people: the LORD made me have dominion over the mighty.

14 Out of E'phra-im *was there* a root of them against Am'a-lek; after thee, Ben'ja-min, among thy people; out of Ma'chir came down governors, and out of Zeb'u-lun they that handle the pen of the writer.

15 And the princes of Is'sa-char *were* with Deb'o-rah; even Is'sa-char, and also Ba'rak: he was sent on foot into the valley. For the divisions of Reu'ben *there were* great thoughts of heart.

16 Why abodest thou among the sheepfolds, to hear the bleatings of the flocks? For the divisions of Reu'ben *there were* great searchings of heart.

17 Gil'e-ad abode beyond Jor'dan: and why did Dan remain in ships? Ash'er continued on the sea shore, and abode in his breaches.

18 Zeb'u-lun and Naph'ta-li *were* a people *that* jeoparded their lives unto the death in the high places of the field.

19 The kings came *and* fought, then fought the kings of Ca'naan in Ta'a-nach by the waters of Me-gid'do; they took no gain of money.

The Battle

20 They fought from heaven; the stars in their courses fought against Sis'e-ra.

21 The river of Ki'shon swept them away, that ancient river, the river Ki'shon. O my soul, thou hast trodden down strength.

22 Then were the horsehoofs broken by the means of the pransings, the pransings of their mighty ones.

23 Curse ye Me'roz, said the angel of the LORD, curse ye bitterly the inhabitants thereof; because they came not to the help of the LORD, to the help of the LORD against the mighty.

24 Blessed above women shall Ja'el the wife of He'ber the Ken'ite be, blessed shall she be above women in the tent.

A Gruesome Aftermath

25 He asked water, *and* she gave *him* milk; she brought forth butter in a lordly dish.

26 She put her hand to the nail, and her right hand to the workmen's hammer; and with the hammer she smote Sis'e-ra, she smote off his head, when she had pierced and stricken through his temples.

19

27 At her feet he bowed, he fell, he lay down: at her feet he bowed, he fell: where he bowed, there he fell down dead.

28 The mother of Sis'e-ra looked out at a window, and cried through the lattice, Why is his chariot *so* long in coming? why tarry the wheels of his chariots?

29 Her wise ladies answered her, yea, she returned answer to herself,

30 Have they not sped? have they *not* divided the prey; to every man a damsel *or* two; to Sis'e-ra a prey of divers colours, a prey of divers colours of needlework, of divers colours of needlework on both sides, *meet* for the necks of *them that take* the spoil?

Total Victory

31 So let all thine enemies perish, O LORD: but *let* them that love him *be* as the sun when he goeth forth in his might. And the land had rest forty years.

Transforming Weakness Into Strength (6:1–8:32) A New Kind of Difficulty

6 AND THE children of Is'ra-el did evil in the sight of the LORD: and the LORD delivered them into the hand of Mid'i-an seven years.

2 And the hand of Mid'i-an prevailed against Is'ra-el: *and* because of the Mid'i-an-ites the children of Is'ra-el made them the dens which *are* in the mountains, and caves, and strong holds.

3 And *so* it was, when Is'ra-el had sown, that the Mid'i-an-ites came up, and the Am'a-lek-ites, and the children of the east, even they came up against them;

4 And they encamped against them, and destroyed the increase of the earth, till thou come unto Ga'za, and left no sustenance for Is'ra-el, neither sheep, nor ox, nor ass.

5 For they came up with their cattle and their tents, and they came as grasshoppers for multitude; *for* both they and their camels were without number: and they entered into the land to destroy it.

6 And Is'ra-el was greatly impoverished because of the Mid'i-an-ites; and the children of Is'ra-el cried unto the LORD.

7 And it came to pass, when the children of Is'ra-el cried unto the LORD because of the Mid'i-an-ites,

8 That the LORD sent a prophet unto the children of Is'ra-el, which said unto them, Thus saith the LORD God of Is'ra-el, I brought you up from E'gypt, and brought you forth out of the house of bondage;

9 And I delivered you out of the hand of the E-gyp'tians, and out of the hand of all that oppressed you, and drave them out from before you, and gave you their land;

10 And I said unto you, I *am* the LORD your God; fear not the gods of the Am'or-ites, in whose land ye dwell: but ye have not obeyed my voice.

11 And there came an angel of the LORD, and sat under an oak which *was* in Oph'rah, that *pertained* unto Jo'ash the A'bi-ez'rite: and his son Gid'e-on threshed wheat by the winepress, to hide *it* from the Mid'i-an-ites.

12 And the angel of the LORD appeared unto him, and said unto him, The LORD *is* with thee, thou mighty man of valour.

13 And Gid'e-on said unto him, Oh my Lord, if the LORD be with us, why then is all this befallen us? and where *be* all his miracles which our fathers told us of, saying, Did not the LORD bring us up from E'gypt? but now the LORD hath forsaken us, and delivered us into the hands of the Mid'i-an-ites.

A Message from God

Finding God's Will

The Angel of the Lord Speaks

Gideon Is Assured of God's Presence

21

_____

_____

_____

_____

_____

_____

_____

_____

_____

_____

_____

_____

_____

_____

_____

_____

14 And the Lord looked upon him, and said, Go in this thy might, and thou shalt save Is'ra-el from the hand of the Mid'i-an-ites: have not I sent thee?

15 And he said unto him, Oh my Lord, wherewith shall I save Is'ra-el? behold, my family *is* poor in Ma-nas'seh, and I *am* the least in my father's house.

16 And the Lord said unto him, Surely I will be with thee, and thou shalt smite the Mid'i-an-ites as one man.

17 And he said unto him, If now I have found grace in thy sight, then shew me a sign that thou talkest with me.

18 Depart not hence, I pray thee, until I come unto thee, and bring forth my present, and set *it* before thee. And he said, I will tarry until thou come again.

19 And Gid'e-on went in, and made ready a kid, and unleavened cakes of an ephah of flour: the flesh he put in a basket, and he put the broth in a pot, and brought *it* out unto him under the oak, and presented *it.*

20 And the angel of God said unto him, Take the flesh and the unleavened cakes, and lay *them* upon this rock, and pour out the broth. And he did so.

21 Then the angel of the Lord put forth the end of the staff that *was* in his hand, and touched the flesh and the unleavened cakes; and there rose up fire out of the rock, and consumed the flesh and the unleavened cakes. Then the angel of the Lord departed out of his sight.

22 And when Gid'e-on perceived that he *was* an angel of the Lord, Gid'e-on said, Alas, O Lord God! for because I have seen an angel of the Lord face to face.

23 And the LORD said unto him, Peace *be* unto thee; fear not: thou shalt not die.

24 Then Gid'e-on built an altar there unto the LORD, and called it Je-ho'vah-sha'lom: unto this day it *is* yet in Oph'rah of the A'bi-ez'rites.

25 And it came to pass the same night, that the LORD said unto him, Take thy father's young bullock, even the second bullock of seven years old, and throw down the altar of Ba'al that thy father hath, and cut down the grove that *is* by it:

26 And build an altar unto the LORD thy God upon the top of this rock, in the ordered place, and take the second bullock, and offer a burnt sacrifice with the wood of the grove which thou shalt cut down.

27 Then Gid'e-on took ten men of his servants, and did as the LORD had said unto him: and *so* it was, because he feared his father's household, and the men of the city, that he could not do *it* by day, that he did *it* by night.

28 And when the men of the city arose early in the morning, behold, the altar of Ba'al was cast down, and the grove was cut down that *was* by it, and the second bullock was offered upon the altar *that was* built.

29 And they said one to another, Who hath done this thing? And when they enquired and asked, they said, Gid'e-on the son of Jo'ash hath done this thing.

30 Then the men of the city said unto Jo'ash, Bring out thy son, that he may die: because he hath cast down the altar of Ba'al, and because he hath cut down the grove that *was* by it.

31 And Jo'ash said unto all that stood against him, Will ye plead for Ba'al? will ye save him? he

that will plead for him, let him be put to death whilst *it is yet* morning: if he *be* a god, let him plead for himself, because *one* hath cast down his altar.

32 Therefore on that day he called him Je-rub'-ba-al, saying, Let Ba'al plead against him, because he hath thrown down his altar.

33 Then all the Mid'i-an-ites and the Am'a-lek-ites and the children of the east were gathered together, and went over, and pitched in the valley of Jez're-el.

34 But the Spirit of the LORD came upon Gid'e-on, and he blew a trumpet; and A'bi-e'zer was gathered after him.

35 And he sent messengers throughout all Ma-nas'seh; who also was gathered after him: and he sent messengers unto Ash'er, and unto Zeb'u-lun, and unto Naph'ta-li; and they came up to meet them.

36 And Gid'e-on said unto God, If thou wilt save Is'ra-el by mine hand, as thou hast said,

37 Behold, I will put a fleece of wool in the floor; *and* if the dew be on the fleece only, and *it be* dry upon all the earth *beside,* then shall I know that thou wilt save Is'ra-el by mine hand, as thou hast said.

38 And it was so: for he rose up early on the morrow, and thrust the fleece together, and wringed the dew out of the fleece, a bowl full of water.

39 And Gid'e-on said unto God, Let not thine anger be hot against me, and I will speak but this once: let me prove, I pray thee, but this once with the fleece; let it now be dry only upon the fleece, and upon all the ground let there be dew.

40 And God did so that night: for it was dry upon the fleece only, and there was dew on all the ground.

7 THEN JE-RUB'BA-AL, who *is* Gid'e-on, and all the people that *were* with him, rose up early, and pitched beside the well of Ha'rod: so that the host of the Mid'i-an-ites were on the north side of them, by the hill of Mo'-reh, in the valley.

2 And the LORD said unto Gid'e-on, The people that *are* with thee *are* too many for me to give the Mid'i-an-ites into their hands, lest Is'ra-el vaunt themselves against me, saying, Mine own hand hath saved me.

3 Now therefore go to, proclaim in the ears of the people, saying, Whosoever *is* fearful and afraid, let him return and depart early from mount Gil'e-ad. And there returned of the people twenty and two thousand; and there remained ten thousand.

4 And the LORD said unto Gid'e-on, The people *are* yet *too* many; bring them down unto the water, and I will try them for thee there: and it shall be, *that* of whom I say unto thee, This shall go with thee, the same shall go with thee; and of whomsoever I say unto thee, This shall not go with thee, the same shall not go.

5 So he brought down the people unto the water: and the LORD said unto Gid'e-on, Every one that lappeth of the water with his tongue, as a dog lappeth, him shalt thou set by himself; likewise every one that boweth down upon his knees to drink.

6 And the number of them that lapped, *putting* their hand to their mouth, were three hundred men: but all the rest of the people bowed down upon their knees to drink water.

7 And the LORD said unto Gid'e-on, By the three hundred men that lapped will I save you, and deliver the Mid'i-an-ites into thine hand: and let all the *other* people go every man unto his place.

Winning the Victory

25

8 So the people took victuals in their hand, and their trumpets: and he sent all *the rest of* Is'ra-el every man unto his tent, and retained those three hundred men: and the host of Mid'i-an was beneath him in the valley.

9 And it came to pass the same night, that the LORD said unto him, Arise, get thee down unto the host; for I have delivered it into thine hand.

10 But if thou fear to go down, go thou with Phu'rah thy servant down to the host:

11 And thou shalt hear what they say; and afterward shall thine hands be strengthened to go down unto the host. Then went he down with Phu'rah his servant unto the outside of the armed men that *were* in the host.

12 And the Mid'i-an-ites and the Am'a-lek-ites and all the children of the east lay along in the valley like grasshoppers for multitude; and their camels *were* without number, as the sand by the sea side for multitude.

13 And when Gid'e-on was come, behold, *there was* a man that told a dream unto his fellow, and said, Behold, I dreamed a dream, and, lo, a cake of barley bread tumbled into the host of Mid'i-an, and came unto a tent, and smote it that it fell, and overturned it, that the tent lay along.

14 And his fellow answered and said, This *is* nothing else save the sword of Gid'e-on the son of Jo'ash, a man of Is'ra-el: *for* into his hand hath God delivered Mid'i-an, and all the host.

The Battle Strategy

15 And it was *so,* when Gid'e-on heard the telling of the dream, and the interpretation thereof, that he worshipped, and returned into the host of Is'ra-el, and said, Arise; for the LORD hath delivered into your hand the host of Mid'i-an.

16 And he divided the three hundred men *into* three companies, and he put a trumpet in every man's hand, with empty pitchers, and lamps within the pitchers.

17 And he said unto them, Look on me, and do likewise: and, behold, when I come to the outside of the camp, it shall be *that,* as I do, so shall ye do.

18 When I blow with a trumpet, I and all that *are* with me, then blow ye the trumpets also on every side of all the camp, and say, *The sword* of the Lord, and of Gid'e-on.

19 So Gid'e-on, and the hundred men that *were* with him, came unto the outside of the camp in the beginning of the middle watch; and they had but newly set the watch: and they blew the trumpets, and brake the pitchers that *were* in their hands.

20 And the three companies blew the trumpets, and brake the pitchers, and held the lamps in their left hands, and the trumpets in their right hands to blow *withal:* and they cried, The sword of the Lord, and of Gid'e-on.

21 And they stood every man in his place round about the camp: and all the host ran, and cried, and fled.

22 And the three hundred blew the trumpets, and the Lord set every man's sword against his fellow, even throughout all the host: and the host fled to Beth-shit'tah in Zer'e-rath, *and* to the border of A'bel-me-ho'lah, unto Tab'bath.

23 And the men of Is'ra-el gathered themselves together out of Naph'ta-li, and out of Ash'er, and out of all Ma-nas'seh, and pursued after the Mid'i-an-ites.

24 And Gid'e-on sent messengers throughout all mount E'phra-im, saying, Come down against the

Mid'i-an-ites, and take before them the waters unto Beth-ba'rah and Jor'dan. Then all the men of E'phra-im gathered themselves together, and took the waters unto Beth-ba'rah and Jor'dan.

25 And they took two princes of the Mid'i-an-ites, O'reb and Ze'eb; and they slew O'reb upon the rock O'reb, and Ze'eb they slew at the winepress of Ze'eb, and pursued Mid'i-an, and brought the heads of O'reb and Ze'eb to Gid'e-on on the other side Jor'dan.

8 AND THE men of E'phra-im said unto him, Why hast thou served us thus, that thou calledst us not, when thou wentest to fight with the Mid'i-an-ites? And they did chide with him sharply.

2 And he said unto them, What have I done now in comparison of you? *Is* not the gleaning of the grapes of E'phra-im better than the vintage of A'bi-e'zer?

3 God hath delivered into your hands the princes of Mid'i-an, O'reb and Ze'eb: and what was I able to do in comparison of you? Then their anger was abated toward him, when he had said that.

4 And Gid'e-on came to Jor'dan, *and* passed over, he, and the three hundred men that *were* with him, faint, yet pursuing *them.*

5 And he said unto the men of Suc'coth, Give, I pray you, loaves of bread unto the people that follow me; for they *be* faint, and I am pursuing after Ze'bah and Zal-mun'na, kings of Mid'i-an.

6 And the princes of Suc'-coth said, *Are* the hands of Ze'-bah and Zal-mun'na now in thine hand, that we should give bread unto thine army?

7 And Gid'e-on said, Therefore when the Lord hath delivered Ze'bah and Zal-mun'na into mine hand, then I will tear your flesh with the thorns of the wilderness and with briers.

8 And he went up thence to Pe-nu'el, and spake unto them likewise: and the men of Pe-nu'el answered him as the men of Suc'coth had answered *him.*

9 And he spake also unto the men of Pe-nu'el, saying, When I come again in peace, I will break down this tower.

10 Now Ze'bah and Zal-mun'na *were* in Kar'kor, and their hosts with them, about fifteen thousand *men,* all that were left of all the hosts of the children of the east: for there fell an hundred and twenty thousand men that drew sword.

11 And Gid'e-on went up by the way of them that dwelt in tents on the east of No'bah and Jog'be-hah, and smote the host: for the host was secure.

12 And when Ze'bah and Zal-mun'na fled, he pursued after them, and took the two kings of Mid'i-an, Ze'bah and Zal-mun'na, and discomfited all the host.

13 And Gid'e-on the son of Jo'ash returned from battle before the sun *was up,*

14 And caught a young man of the men of Suc'-coth, and enquired of him: and he described unto him the princes of Suc'coth, and the elders thereof, *even* threescore and seventeen men.

15 And he came unto the men of Suc'coth, and said, Behold Ze'bah and Zal-mun'na, with whom ye did upbraid me, saying, *Are* the hands of Ze'bah and Zal-mun'na now in thine hand, that we should give bread unto thy men *that are* weary?

29

16 And he took the elders of the city, and thorns of the wilderness and briers, and with them he taught the men of Suc'coth.

17 And he beat down the tower of Pe-nu'el, and slew the men of the city.

18 Then said he unto Ze'-bah and Zal-mun'na, What manner of men *were they* whom ye slew at Ta'bor? And they answered, As thou *art,* so *were* they; each one resembled the children of a king.

19 And he said, They *were* my brethren, *even* the sons of my mother: *as* the LORD liveth, if ye had saved them alive, I would not slay you.

20 And he said unto Je'ther his firstborn, Up, *and* slay them. But the youth drew not his sword: for he feared, because he *was* yet a youth.

21 Then Ze'bah and Zal-mun'na said, Rise thou, and fall upon us: for as the man *is, so is* his strength. And Gid'e-on arose, and slew Ze'bah and Zal-mun'na, and took away the ornaments that *were* on their camels' necks.

Failure Following Victory

22 Then the men of Is'ra-el said unto Gid'e-on, Rule thou over us, both thou, and thy son, and thy son's son also: for thou hast delivered us from the hand of Mid'i-an.

23 And Gid'e-on said unto them, I will not rule over you, neither shall my son rule over you: the LORD shall rule over you.

24 And Gid'e-on said unto them, I would desire a request of you, that ye would give me every man the earrings of his prey. (For they had golden earrings, because they *were* Ish'ma-el-ites.)

25 And they answered, We will willingly give *them.* And they spread a garment, and did cast therein every man the earrings of his prey.

26 And the weight of the golden earrings that he requested was a thousand and seven hundred *shekels* of gold; beside ornaments, and collars, and purple raiment that *was* on the kings of Mid'i-an, and beside the chains that *were* about their camels' necks.

27 And Gid'e-on made an ephod thereof, and put it in his city, *even* in Oph'rah: and all Is'ra-el went thither a whoring after it: which thing became a snare unto Gid'e-on, and to his house.

28 Thus was Mid'i-an subdued before the children of Is'ra-el, so that they lifted up their heads no more. And the country was in quietness forty years in the days of Gid'e-on.

29 And Je-rub'ba-al the son of Jo'ash went and dwelt in his own house.

30 And Gid'e-on had threescore and ten sons of his body begotten: for he had many wives.

31 And his concubine that *was* in She'chem, she also bare him a son, whose name he called A-bim'e-lech.

32 And Gid'e-on the son of Jo'ash died in a good old age, and was buried in the sepulchre of Jo'ash his father, in Oph'rah of the A'bi-ez'rites.

Rebellion Against God
(8:33–9:57)

33 And it came to pass, as soon as Gid'e-on was dead, that the children of Is'ra-el turned again, and went a whoring after Ba'al-im, and made Ba'al-be'rith their god.

34 And the children of Is'ra-el remembered not the Lord their God, who had delivered them out of the hands of all their enemies on every side:

God's Ultimate Goal

35 Neither shewed they kindness to the house of Je-rub'ba-al, *namely,* Gid'e-on, according to all the goodness which he had shewed unto Is'ra-el.

9 AND A-BIM'E-LECH the son of Je-rub'ba-al went to She'chem unto his mother's brethren, and communed with them, and with all the family of the house of his mother's father, saying,

2 Speak, I pray you, in the ears of all the men of She'chem, Whether *is* better for you, either that all the sons of Je-rub'ba-al, *which are* threescore and ten persons, reign over you, or that one reign over you? remember also that I *am* your bone and your flesh.

3 And his mother's brethren spake of him in the ears of all the men of She'chem all these words: and their hearts inclined to follow A-bim'e-lech; for they said, He *is* our brother.

4 And they gave him threescore and ten *pieces* of silver out of the house of Ba'al-be'rith, wherewith A-bim'e-lech hired vain and light persons, which followed him.

5 And he went unto his father's house at Oph'-rah, and slew his brethren the sons of Je-rub'ba-al, *being* threescore and ten persons, upon one stone: notwithstanding yet Jo'tham the youngest son of Je-rub'ba-al was left; for he hid himself.

6 And all the men of She'-chem gathered together, and all the house of Mil'lo, and went, and made A-bim'e-lech king, by the plain of the pillar that *was* in She'chem.

7 And when they told *it* to Jo'tham, he went and stood in the top of mount Ger'i-zim, and lifted up his voice, and cried, and said unto them, Hearken unto me, ye men of She'chem, that God may hearken unto you.

8 The trees went forth *on a time* to anoint a king over them; and they said unto the olive tree, Reign thou over us.

9 But the olive tree said unto them, Should I leave my fatness, wherewith by me they honour God and man, and go to be promoted over the trees?

10 And the trees said to the fig tree, Come thou, *and* reign over us.

11 But the fig tree said unto them, Should I forsake my sweetness, and my good fruit, and go to be promoted over the trees?

12 Then said the trees unto the vine, Come thou, *and* reign over us.

13 And the vine said unto them, Should I leave my wine, which cheereth God and man, and go to be promoted over the trees?

14 Then said all the trees unto the bramble, Come thou, *and* reign over us.

15 And the bramble said unto the trees, If in truth ye anoint me king over you, *then* come *and* put your trust in my shadow: and if not, let fire come out of the bramble, and devour the cedars of Leb'a-non.

16 Now therefore, if ye have done truly and sincerely, in that ye have made A-bim'e-lech king, and if ye have dealt well with Je-rub'ba-al and his house, and have done unto him according to the deserving of his hands;

17 (For my father fought for you, and adventured his life far, and delivered you out of the hand of Mid'i-an:

18 And ye are risen up against my father's house this day, and have slain his sons, threescore and ten persons, upon one stone, and have made A-bim'e-lech, the son of his maidservant, king over the men of She'chem, because he *is* your brother;)

19 If ye then have dealt truly and sincerely with Je-rub'ba-al and with his house this day, *then* rejoice ye in A-bim'e-lech, and let him also rejoice in you:

20 But if not, let fire come out from A-bim'e-lech, and devour the men of She'chem, and the house of Mil'lo; and let fire come out from the men of She'chem, and from the house of Mil'lo, and devour A-bim'e-lech.

21 And Jo'tham ran away, and fled, and went to Be'er, and dwelt there, for fear of A-bim'e-lech his brother.

22 When A-bim'e-lech had reigned three years over Is'ra-el,

23 Then God sent an evil spirit between A-bim'e-lech and the men of She'chem; and the men of She'chem dealt treacherously with A-bim'e-lech:

24 That the cruelty *done* to the threescore and ten sons of Je-rub'ba-al might come, and their blood be laid upon A-bim'e-lech their brother, which slew them; and upon the men of She'chem, which aided him in the killing of his brethren.

25 And the men of She'chem set liers in wait for him in the top of the mountains, and they robbed all that came along that way by them: and it was told A-bim'e-lech.

26 And Ga'al the son of E'bed came with his brethren, and went over to She'chem: and the men of She'chem put their confidence in him.

27 And they went out into the fields, and gathered their vineyards, and trode *the grapes,* and made merry, and went into the house of their god, and did eat and drink, and cursed A-bim'e-lech.

28 And Ga'al the son of E'bed said, Who *is* A-bim'e-lech, and who *is* She'chem, that we

should serve him? *is* not *he* the son of Je-rub'ba-al? and Ze'bul his officer? serve the men of Ha'mor the father of She'chem: for why should we serve him?

29 And would to God this people were under my hand! then would I remove A-bim'e-lech. And he said to A-bim'e-lech, Increase thine army, and come out.

30 And when Ze'bul the ruler of the city heard the words of Ga'al the son of E'bed, his anger was kindled.

31 And he sent messengers unto A-bim'e-lech privily, saying, Behold, Ga'al the son of E'bed and his brethren be come to She'chem; and, behold, they fortify the city against thee.

32 Now therefore up by night, thou and the people that *is* with thee, and lie in wait in the field:

33 And it shall be, *that* in the morning, as soon as the sun is up, thou shalt rise early, and set upon the city: and, behold, *when* he and the people that *is* with him come out against thee, then mayest thou do to them as thou shalt find occasion.

34 And A-bim'e-lech rose up, and all the people that *were* with him, by night, and they laid wait against She'chem in four companies.

35 And Ga'al the son of E'bed went out, and stood in the entering of the gate of the city: and A-bim'e-lech rose up, and the people that *were* with him, from lying in wait.

36 And when Ga'al saw the people, he said to Ze'bul, Behold, there come people down from the top of the mountains. And Ze'bul said unto him, Thou seest the shadow of the mountains as *if they were* men.

37 And Ga'al spake again and said, See there come people down by the middle of the land, and

another company come along by the plain of Me-on'e-nim.

38 Then said Ze'bul unto him, Where *is* now thy mouth, wherewith thou saidst, Who *is* A-bim'e-lech, that we should serve him? *is* not this the people that thou hast despised? go out, I pray now, and fight with them.

39 And Ga'al went out before the men of She'-chem, and fought with A-bim'e-lech.

40 And A-bim'e-lech chased him, and he fled before him, and many were overthrown *and* wounded, *even* unto the entering of the gate.

41 And A-bim'e-lech dwelt at A-ru'mah: and Ze'bul thrust out Ga'al and his brethren, that they should not dwell in She'chem.

42 And it came to pass on the morrow, that the people went out into the field; and they told A-bim'e-lech.

43 And he took the people, and divided them into three companies, and laid wait in the field, and looked, and, behold, the people *were* come forth out of the city; and he rose up against them, and smote them.

44 And A-bim'e-lech, and the company that *was* with him, rushed forward, and stood in the entering of the gate of the city: and the two *other* companies ran upon all *the people* that *were* in the fields, and slew them.

45 And A-bim'e-lech fought against the city all that day; and he took the city, and slew the people that *was* therein, and beat down the city, and sowed it with salt.

46 And when all the men of the tower of She'-chem heard *that,* they entered into an hold of the house of the god Be'rith.

47 And it was told A-bim'e-lech, that all the men of the tower of She'chem were gathered together.

48 And A-bim'e-lech gat him up to mount Zal'mon, he and all the people that *were* with him; and A-bim'e-lech took an ax in his hand, and cut down a bough from the trees, and took it, and laid *it* on his shoulder, and said unto the people that *were* with him, What ye have seen me do, make haste, *and* do as I *have done.*

49 And all the people likewise cut down every man his bough, and followed A-bim'e-lech, and put *them* to the hold, and set the hold on fire upon them; so that all the men of the tower of She'-chem died also, about a thousand men and women.

50 Then went A-bim'e-lech to The'bez, and encamped against The'bez, and took it.

51 But there was a strong tower within the city, and thither fled all the men and women, and all they of the city, and shut *it* to them, and gat them up to the top of the tower.

52 And A-bim'e-lech came unto the tower, and fought against it, and went hard unto the door of the tower to burn it with fire.

53 And a certain woman cast a piece of a millstone upon A-bim'e-lech's head, and all to brake his skull.

54 Then he called hastily unto the young man his armourbearer, and said unto him, Draw thy sword, and slay me, that men say not of me, A woman slew him. And his young man thrust him through, and he died.

55 And when the men of Is'ra-el saw that A-bim'e-lech was dead, they departed every man unto his place.

56 Thus God rendered the wickedness of A-bim'e-lech, which he did unto his father, in slaying his seventy brethren:

57 And all the evil of the men of She'chem did God render upon their heads: and upon them came the curse of Jo'tham the son of Je-rub'ba-al.

LESSON 2

JUDGES 10:1–21:25
Failures That Lead to Victory

10 AND AFTER A-bim'e-lech there arose to defend Is'ra-el To'la the son of Pu'ah, the son of Do'do, a man of Is'sa-char; and he dwelt in Sha'mir in mount E'phra-im.

2 And he judged Is'ra-el twenty and three years, and died, and was buried in Sha'mir.

3 And after him arose Ja'ir, a Gil'e-ad-ite, and judged Is'ra-el twenty and two years.

4 And he had thirty sons that rode on thirty ass colts, and they had thirty cities, which are called Ha'voth-ja'ir unto this day, which *are* in the land of Gil'e-ad.

5 And Ja'ir died, and was buried in Ca'mon.

6 And the children of Is'ra-el did evil again in the sight of the LORD, and served Ba'al-im, and Ash'ta-roth, and the gods of Syr'i-a, and the gods of Zi'don, and the gods of Mo'ab, and the gods of the children of Am'mon, and the gods of the Phi-lis'tines, and forsook the LORD, and served not him.

7 And the anger of the LORD was hot against Is'ra-el, and he sold them into the hands of the Phi-lis'tines, and into the hands of the children of Am'mon.

8 And that year they vexed and oppressed the children of Is'ra-el: eighteen years, all the children

Consequences of
Thoughtless
Commitments (10:1–12:7)

Little Known But Faithful

_____

_____

_____

_____

_____

_____

_____

_____

_____

_____

_____

_____

_____

_____

_____

of Is'ra-el that *were* on the other side Jor'dan in the land of the Am'or-ites, which *is* in Gil'e-ad.

9 Moreover the children of Am'mon passed over Jor'dan to fight also against Ju'dah, and against Ben'ja-min, and against the house of E'phra-im; so that Is'ra-el was sore distressed.

A Time for Repenting

10 And the children of Is'ra-el cried unto the Lord, saying, We have sinned against thee, both because we have forsaken our God, and also served Ba'al-im.

11 And the Lord said unto the children of Is'ra-el, *Did* not *I deliver you* from the E-gyp'tians, and from the Am'or-ites, from the children of Am'mon, and from the Phi-lis'tines?

12 The Zi-do'ni-ans also, and the Am'a-lek-ites, and the Ma'on-ites, did oppress you; and ye cried to me, and I delivered you out of their hand.

13 Yet ye have forsaken me, and served other gods: wherefore I will deliver you no more.

14 Go and cry unto the gods which ye have chosen; let them deliver you in the time of your tribulation.

15 And the children of Is'ra-el said unto the Lord, We have sinned: do thou unto us whatsoever seemeth good unto thee; deliver us only, we pray thee, this day.

16 And they put away the strange gods from among them, and served the Lord: and his soul was grieved for the misery of Is'ra-el.

17 Then the children of Am'-mon were gathered together, and encamped in Gil'e-ad. And the children of Is'ra-el assembled themselves together, and encamped in Miz'peh.

18 And the people *and* princes of Gil'e-ad said one to another, What man *is he* that will begin to

fight against the children of Am'-mon? he shall be head over all the inhabitants of Gil'e-ad.

11 NOW JEPH'THAH the Gil'e-ad-ite was a mighty man of valour, and he *was* the son of an harlot: and Gil'e-ad begat Jeph'thah.

2 And Gil'e-ad's wife bare him sons; and his wife's sons grew up, and they thrust out Jeph'thah, and said unto him, Thou shalt not inherit in our father's house; for thou *art* the son of a strange woman.

3 Then Jeph'thah fled from his brethren, and dwelt in the land of Tob: and there were gathered vain men to Jeph'thah, and went out with him.

4 And it came to pass in process of time, that the children of Am'mon made war against Is'ra-el.

5 And it was so, that when the children of Am'mon made war against Is'ra-el, the elders of Gil'e-ad went to fetch Jeph'thah out of the land of Tob:

6 And they said unto Jeph'thah, Come, and be our captain, that we may fight with the children of Am'mon.

7 And Jeph'thah said unto the elders of Gil'e-ad, Did not ye hate me, and expel me out of my father's house? and why are ye come unto me now when ye are in distress?

8 And the elders of Gil'e-ad said unto Jeph'thah, Therefore we turn again to thee now, that thou mayest go with us, and fight against the children of Am'mon, and be our head over all the inhabitants of Gil'e-ad.

9 And Jeph'thah said unto the elders of Gil'e-ad, If ye bring me home again to fight against the chil-

The Price of Prejudice

Jephthah's Response

41

dren of Am'mon, and the LORD deliver them before me, shall I be your head?

10 And the elders of Gil'e-ad said unto Jeph'-thah, the LORD be witness between us, if we do not so according to thy words.

11 Then Jeph'thah went with the elders of Gil'e-ad, and the people made him head and captain over them: and Jeph'thah uttered all his words before the LORD in Miz'peh.

12 And Jeph'thah sent messengers unto the king of the children of Am'mon, saying, What hast thou to do with me, that thou art come against me to fight in my land?

13 And the king of the children of Am'mon answered unto the messengers of Jeph'thah, Because Is'ra-el took away my land, when they came up out of E'gypt, from Ar'non even unto Jab'bok, and unto Jor'dan: now therefore restore those *lands* again peaceably.

14 And Jeph'thah sent messengers again unto the king of the children of Am'mon:

15 And said unto him, Thus saith Jeph'thah, Is'ra-el took not away the land of Mo'ab, nor the land of the children of Am'mon:

16 But when Is'ra-el came up from E'gypt, and walked through the wilderness unto the Red sea, and came to Ka'desh;

17 Then Is'ra-el sent messengers unto the king of E'dom, saying, Let me, I pray thee, pass through thy land: but the king of E'dom would not hearken *thereto.* And in like manner they sent unto the king of Mo'ab: but he would not *consent:* and Is'ra-el abode in Ka'desh.

18 Then they went along through the wilderness, and compassed the land of E'dom, and the

land of Mo'ab, and came by the east side of the land of Mo'ab, and pitched on the other side of Ar'non, but came not within the border of Mo'ab: for Ar'non *was* the border of Mo'ab.

19 And Is'ra-el sent messengers unto Si'hon king of the Am'or-ites, the king of Hesh'-bon; and Is'ra-el said unto him, Let us pass, we pray thee, through thy land into my place.

20 But Si'hon trusted not Is'ra-el to pass through his coast: but Si'hon gathered all his people together, and pitched in Ja'haz, and fought against Is'ra-el.

21 And the LORD God of Is'ra-el delivered Si'hon and all his people into the hand of Is'ra-el, and they smote them: so Is'ra-el possessed all the land of the Am'or-ites, the inhabitants of that country.

22 And they possessed all the coasts of the Am'or-ites, from Ar'non even unto Jab'bok, and from the wilderness even unto Jor'dan.

23 So now the LORD God of Is'ra-el hath dispossessed the Am'or-ites from before his people Is'ra-el, and shouldest thou possess it?

24 Wilt not thou possess that which Che'mosh thy god giveth thee to possess? So whomsoever the LORD our God shall drive out from before us, them will we possess.

25 And now *art* thou any thing better than Ba'lak the son of Zip'por, king of Mo'ab? did he ever strive against Is'ra-el, or did he ever fight against them,

26 While Is'ra-el dwelt in Hesh'bon and her towns, and in Ar'o-er and her towns, and in all the cities that *be* along by the coasts of Ar'non, three hundred years? why therefore did ye not recover *them* within that time?

43

27 Wherefore I have not sinned against thee, but thou doest me wrong to war against me: the Lord the Judge be judge this day between the children of Is'ra-el and the children of Am'mon.

28 Howbeit the king of the children of Am'mon hearkened not unto the words of Jeph'thah which he sent him.

29 Then the Spirit of the Lord came upon Jeph'-thah, and he passed over Gil'e-ad, and Ma-nas'seh, and passed over Miz'peh of Gil'e-ad, and from Miz'peh of Gil'e-ad he passed over *unto* the children of Am'mon.

30 And Jeph'thah vowed a vow unto the Lord, and said, If thou shalt without fail deliver the children of Am'mon into mine hands,

31 Then it shall be, that whatsoever cometh forth of the doors of my house to meet me, when I return in peace from the children of Am'mon, shall surely be the Lord's, and I will offer it up for a burnt offering.

32 So Jeph'thah passed over unto the children of Am'mon to fight against them; and the Lord delivered them into his hands.

33 And he smote them from Ar'o-er, even till thou come to Min'nith, *even* twenty cities, and unto the plain of the vineyards, with a very great slaughter. Thus the children of Am'mon were subdued before the children of Is'ra-el.

34 And Jeph'thah came to Miz'peh unto his house, and, behold, his daughter came out to meet him with timbrels and with dances: and she *was his* only child; beside her he had neither son nor daughter.

35 And it came to pass, when he saw her, that he rent his clothes, and said, Alas, my daughter! thou hast brought me very low, and thou art one

of them that trouble me: for I have opened my mouth unto the Lord, and I cannot go back.

36 And she said unto him, My father, *if* thou hast opened thy mouth unto the Lord, do to me according to that which hath proceeded out of thy mouth; forasmuch as the Lord hath taken vengeance for thee of thine enemies, *even* of the children of Am'mon.

37 And she said unto her father, Let this thing be done for me: let me alone two months, that I may go up and down upon the mountains, and bewail my virginity, I and my fellows.

38 And he said, Go. And he sent her away *for* two months: and she went with her companions, and bewailed her virginity upon the mountains.

39 And it came to pass at the end of two months, that she returned unto her father, who did with her *according* to his vow which he had vowed: and she knew no man. And it was a custom in Is'ra-el,

40 *That* the daughters of Is'ra-el went yearly to lament the daughter of Jeph'thah the Gil'e-ad-ite four days in a year.

12 AND THE men of E'phra-im gathered themselves together, and went northward, and said unto Jeph'thah, Wherefore passedst thou over to fight against the children of Am'mon, and didst not call us to go with thee? we will burn thine house upon thee with fire.

2 And Jeph'thah said unto them, I and my people were at great strife with the children of Am'mon; and when I called you, ye delivered me not out of their hands.

3 And when I saw that ye delivered *me* not, I put my life in my hands, and passed over against the

_____

_____

_____

_____

_____

_____

_____

_____

_____

_____

_____

_____

_____

_____

_____

*** The Weakness of Strength
(12:8–16:31)***
*Offering Our Differing
Strengths*

_____

_____

_____

_____

_____

children of Am'mon, and the LORD delivered them into my hand: wherefore then are ye come up unto me this day, to fight against me?

4 Then Jeph'thah gathered together all the men of Gil'e-ad, and fought with E'phra-im: and the men of Gil'e-ad smote E'phra-im, because they said, Ye Gil'e-ad-ites *are* fugitives of E'phra-im among the E'phra-im-ites, *and* among the Ma-nas'-sites.

5 And the Gil'e-ad-ites took the passages of Jor'dan before the E'phra-im-ites: and it was *so,* that when those E'phra-im-ites which were escaped said, Let me go over; that the men of Gil'e-ad said unto him, *Art* thou an E'phra-im-ite? If he said, Nay;

6 Then said they unto him, Say now Shib'bo-leth: and he said Sib'bo-leth: for he could not frame to pronounce *it* right. Then they took him, and slew him at the passages of Jor'dan: and there fell at that time of the E'phra-im-ites forty and two thousand.

7 And Jeph'thah judged Is'ra-el six years. Then died Jeph'thah the Gil'e-ad-ite, and was buried in *one of* the cities of Gil'e-ad.

8 And after him Ib'zan of Beth'-le-hem judged Is'ra-el.

9 And he had thirty sons, and thirty daughters, *whom* he sent abroad, and took in thirty daughters from abroad for his sons. And he judged Is'ra-el seven years.

10 Then died Ib'zan, and was buried at Beth'-le-hem.

11 And after him E'lon, a Zeb'u-lon-ite, judged Is'ra-el; and he judged Is'ra-el ten years.

12 And E'lon the Zeb'u-lon-ite died, and was buried in Aij'a-lon in the country of Zeb'u-lun.

13 And after him Ab'don the son of Hil'lel, a Pir'a-thon-ite, judged Is'ra-el.

14 And he had forty sons and thirty nephews, that rode on threescore and ten ass colts: and he judged Is'ra-el eight years.

15 And Ab'don the son of Hil'lel the Pir'a-thon-ite died, and was buried in Pir'a-thon in the land of E'phra-im, in the mount of the Am'a-lek-ites.

13 AND THE children of Is'ra-el did evil again in the sight of the LORD; and the LORD delivered them into the hand of the Phi-lis'tines forty years.

Human Weakness and the Power of God

2 And there was a certain man of Zo'rah, of the family of the Dan'ites, whose name *was* Ma-no'ah; and his wife *was* barren, and bare not.

3 And the angel of the LORD appeared unto the woman, and said unto her, Behold now, thou *art* barren, and bearest not: but thou shalt conceive, and bear a son.

4 Now therefore beware, I pray thee, and drink not wine nor strong drink, and eat not any unclean *thing:*

5 For, lo, thou shalt conceive, and bear a son; and no razor shall come on his head: for the child shall be a Naz'a-rite unto God from the womb: and he shall begin to deliver Is'ra-el out of the hand of the Phi-lis'tines.

6 Then the woman came and told her husband, saying, A man of God came unto me, and his countenance *was* like the countenance of an angel of God, very terrible: but I asked him not whence he *was,* neither told he me his name:

7 But he said unto me, Behold, thou shalt conceive, and bear a son; and now drink no wine nor

47

strong drink, neither eat any unclean *thing:* for the child shall be a Naz'a-rite to God from the womb to the day of his death.

8 Then Ma-no'ah intreated the LORD, and said, O my Lord, let the man of God which thou didst send come again unto us, and teach us what we shall do unto the child that shall be born.

9 And God hearkened to the voice of Ma-no'ah; and the angel of God came again unto the woman as she sat in the field: but Ma-no'ah her husband *was* not with her.

10 And the woman made haste, and ran, and shewed her husband, and said unto him, Behold, the man hath appeared unto me, that came unto me the *other* day.

11 And Ma-no'ah arose, and went after his wife, and came to the man, and said unto him, *Art* thou the man that spakest unto the woman? And he said, I *am.*

12 And Ma-no'ah said, Now let thy words come to pass. How shall we order the child, and *how* shall we do unto him?

13 And the angel of the LORD said unto Ma-no'ah, Of all that I said unto the woman let her beware.

14 She may not eat of any *thing* that cometh of the vine, neither let her drink wine or strong drink, nor eat any unclean *thing:* all that I commanded her let her observe.

15 And Ma-no'ah said unto the angel of the LORD, I pray thee, let us detain thee, until we shall have made ready a kid for thee.

16 And the angel of the LORD said unto Ma-no'ah, Though thou detain me, I will not eat of thy bread: and if thou wilt offer a burnt offering, thou

must offer it unto the Lord. For Ma-no'ah knew not that he *was* an angel of the Lord.

17 And Ma-no'ah said unto the angel of the Lord, What *is* thy name, that when thy sayings come to pass we may do thee honour?

18 And the angel of the Lord said unto him, Why askest thou thus after my name, seeing it *is* secret?

19 So Ma-no'ah took a kid with a meat offering, and offered *it* upon a rock unto the Lord: and *the angel* did wonderously; and Ma-no'ah and his wife looked on.

20 For it came to pass, when the flame went up toward heaven from off the altar, that the angel of the Lord ascended in the flame of the altar. And Ma-no'ah and his wife looked on *it,* and fell on their faces to the ground.

21 But the angel of the Lord did no more appear to Ma-no'ah and to his wife. Then Ma-no'ah knew that he *was* an angel of the Lord.

22 And Ma-no'ah said unto his wife, We shall surely die, because we have seen God.

23 But his wife said unto him, If the Lord were pleased to kill us, he would not have received a burnt offering and a meat offering at our hands, neither would he have shewed us all these *things,* nor would as at this time have told us *such things* as these.

24 And the woman bare a son, and called his name Sam'-son: and the child grew, and the Lord blessed him.

25 And the Spirit of the Lord began to move him at times in the camp of Dan between Zo'rah and Esh'ta-ol.

49

Human Weakness on Parade

_____

_____

_____

_____

_____

_____

_____

_____

_____

_____

_____

Samson Persists

_____

_____

_____

_____

_____

_____

_____

_____

_____

_____

_____

14 AND SAM'SON went down to Tim'nath, and saw a woman in Tim'nath of the daughters of the Phi-lis'tines.

2 And he came up, and told his father and his mother, and said, I have seen a woman in Tim'nath of the daughters of the Phi-lis'tines: now therefore get her for me to wife.

3 Then his father and his mother said unto him, *Is there* never a woman among the daughters of thy brethren, or among all my people, that thou goest to take a wife of the uncircumcised Phi-lis'tines? And Sam'son said unto his father, Get her for me; for she pleaseth me well.

4 But his father and his mother knew not that it *was* of the LORD, that he sought an occasion against the Phi-lis'tines: for at that time the Phi-lis'tines had dominion over Is'ra-el.

5 Then went Sam'son down, and his father and his mother, to Tim'nath, and came to the vineyards of Tim'nath: and, behold, a young lion roared against him.

6 And the Spirit of the LORD came mightily upon him, and he rent him as he would have rent a kid, and *he had* nothing in his hand: but he told not his father or his mother what he had done.

7 And he went down, and talked with the woman; and she pleased Sam'son well.

8 And after a time he returned to take her, and he turned aside to see the carcase of the lion: and, behold, *there was* a swarm of bees and honey in the carcase of the lion.

9 And he took thereof in his hands, and went on eating, and came to his father and mother, and he gave them, and they did eat: but he told not them that he had taken the honey out of the carcase of the lion.

50

10 So his father went down unto the woman: and Sam'son made there a feast; for so used the young men to do.

11 And it came to pass, when they saw him, that they brought thirty companions to be with him.

12 And Sam'son said unto them, I will now put forth a riddle unto you: if ye can certainly declare it me within the seven days of the feast, and find *it* out, then I will give you thirty sheets and thirty change of garments:

13 But if ye cannot declare *it* me, then shall ye give me thirty sheets and thirty change of garments. And they said unto him, Put forth thy riddle, that we may hear it.

14 And he said unto them, Out of the eater came forth meat, and out of the strong came forth sweetness. And they could not in three days expound the riddle.

15 And it came to pass on the seventh day, that they said unto Sam'son's wife, Entice thy husband, that he may declare unto us the riddle, lest we burn thee and thy father's house with fire: have ye called us to take that we have? *is it* not *so?*

16 And Sam'son's wife wept before him, and said, Thou dost but hate me, and lovest me not: thou hast put forth a riddle unto the children of my people, and hast not told *it* me. And he said unto her, Behold, I have not told *it* my father nor my mother, and shall I tell *it* thee?

17 And she wept before him the seven days, while their feast lasted: and it came to pass on the seventh day, that he told her, because she lay sore upon him: and she told the riddle to the children of her people.

18 And the men of the city said unto him on the seventh day before the sun went down, What *is*

The Wedding Celebration and the Riddle

51

sweeter than honey? and what *is* stronger than a lion? And he said unto them, If ye had not plowed with my heifer, ye had not found out my riddle.

19 And the Spirit of the LORD came upon him and he went down to Ash'ke-lon, and slew thirty men of them, and took their spoil, and gave change of garments unto them which expounded the riddle. And his anger was kindled, and he went up to his father's house.

20 But Sam'son's wife was *given* to his companion, whom he had used as his friend.

15 BUT IT came to pass within a while after, in the time of wheat harvest, that Sam'son visited his wife with a kid; and he said, I will go in to my wife into the chamber. But her father would not suffer him to go in.

2 And her father said, I verily thought that thou hadst utterly hated her; therefore I gave her to thy companion: *is* not her younger sister fairer than she? take her, I pray thee, instead of her.

3 And Sam'son said concerning them, Now shall I be more blameless than the Phi-lis'tines, though I do them a displeasure.

4 And Sam'son went and caught three hundred foxes, and took firebrands, and turned tail to tail, and put a firebrand in the midst between two tails.

5 And when he had set the brands on fire, he let *them* go into the standing corn of the Phi-lis'tines, and burnt up both the shocks, and also the standing corn, with the vineyards *and* olives.

6 Then the Phi-lis'tines said, Who hath done this? And they answered, Sam'son, the son in law oftheTim'nite, because he had taken his wife, and given her to his companion. And the Phi-lis'-

Samson Gets His Revenge

tines came up, and burnt her and her father with fire.

7 And Sam'son said unto them, Though ye have done this, yet will I be avenged of you, and after that I will cease.

8 And he smote them hip and thigh with a great slaughter: and he went down and dwelt in the top of the rock E'tam.

9 Then the Phi-lis'tines went up, and pitched in Ju'dah, and spread themselves in Le'hi.

10 And the men of Ju'dah said, Why are ye come up against us? And they answered, To bind Sam'-son are we come up, to do to him as he hath done to us.

11 Then three thousand men of Ju'dah went to the top of the rock E'tam, and said to Sam'son, Knowest thou not that the Phi-lis'tines *are* rulers over us? what *is* this *that* thou hast done unto us? And he said unto them, As they did unto me, so have I done unto them.

12 And they said unto him, We are come down to bind thee, that we may deliver thee into the hand of the Phi-lis'tines. And Sam'son said unto them, Swear unto me, that ye will not fall upon me yourselves.

13 And they spake unto him, saying, No; but we will bind thee fast, and deliver thee into their hand: but surely we will not kill thee. And they bound him with two new cords, and brought him up from the rock.

14 *And* when he came unto Le'hi, the Phi-lis'-tines shouted against him: and the Spirit of the LORD came mightily upon him, and the cords that *were* upon his arms became as flax that was burnt with fire, and his bands loosed from off his hands.

God's Victory

53

15 And he found a new jawbone of an ass, and put forth his hand, and took it, and slew a thousand men therewith.

16 And Sam'son said, With the jawbone of an ass, heaps upon heaps, with the jaw of an ass have I slain a thousand men.

17 And it came to pass, when he had made an end of speaking, that he cast away the jawbone out of his hand, and called that place Ra'math-le'hi.

18 And he was sore athirst, and called on the LORD, and said, Thou hast given this great deliverance into the hand of thy servant: and now shall I die for thirst, and fall into the hand of the uncircumcised?

19 But God clave an hollow place that *was* in the jaw, and there came water thereout; and when he had drunk, his spirit came again, and he revived: wherefore he called the name thereof En-hak'ko-re, which *is* in Le'hi unto this day.

20 And he judged Is'ra-el in the days of the Phi-lis'tines twenty years.

16 THEN WENT Sam'son to Ga'za, and saw there an harlot, and went in unto her.

2 *And it was told* the Ga'zites, saying, Sam'son is come hither. And they compassed *him* in, and laid wait for him all night in the gate of the city, and were quiet all the night, saying, In the morning, when it is day, we shall kill him.

3 And Sam'son lay till midnight, and arose at midnight, and took the doors of the gate of the city, and the two posts, and went away with them, bar and all, and put *them* upon his shoulders, and carried them up to the top of an hill that *is* before He'bron.

4 And it came to pass afterward, that he loved a woman in the valley of So'rek, whose name *was* De-li'lah.

5 And the lords of the Phi-lis'tines came up unto her, and said unto her, Entice him, and see wherein his great strength *lieth*, and by what *means* we may prevail against him, that we may bind him to afflict him: and we will give thee every one of us eleven hundred *pieces* of silver.

6 And De-li'lah said to Sam'son, Tell me, I pray thee, wherein thy great strength *lieth*, and wherewith thou mightest be bound to afflict thee.

7 And Sam'son said unto her, If they bind me with seven green withs that were never dried, then shall I be weak, and be as another man.

8 Then the lords of the Phi-lis'tines brought up to her seven green withs which had not been dried, and she bound him with them.

9 Now *there were* men lying in wait, abiding with her in the chamber. And she said unto him, The Phi-lis'tines *be* upon thee, Sam'son. And he brake the withs, as a thread of tow is broken when it toucheth the fire. So his strength was not known.

10 And De-li'lah said unto Sam'son, Behold, thou hast mocked me, and told me lies: now tell me, I pray thee, wherewith thou mightest be bound.

11 And he said unto her, If they bind me fast with new ropes that never were occupied, then shall I be weak, and be as another man.

12 De-li'lah therefore took new ropes, and bound him therewith, and said unto him, The Phi-lis'tines *be* upon thee, Sam'son. And *there were* liers in wait abiding in the chamber. And he brake them from off his arms like a thread.

Sin's Consequences

13 And De-li'lah said unto Sam'son, Hitherto thou hast mocked me, and told me lies: tell me wherewith thou mightest be bound. And he said unto her, If thou weavest the seven locks of my head with the web.

14 And she fastened *it* with the pin, and said unto him, The Phi-lis'tines *be* upon thee, Sam'son. And he awaked out of his sleep, and went away with the pin of the beam, and with the web.

15 And she said unto him, How canst thou say, I love thee, when thine heart *is* not with me? thou hast mocked me these three times, and hast not told me wherein thy great strength *lieth.*

16 And it came to pass, when she pressed him daily with her words, and urged him, *so* that his soul was vexed unto death;

17 That he told her all his heart, and said unto her, There hath not come a razor upon mine head; for I *have been* a Naz'a-rite unto God from my mother's womb: if I be shaven, then my strength will go from me, and I shall become weak, and be like any *other* man.

18 And when De-li'lah saw that he had told her all his heart, she sent and called for the lords of the Phi-lis'tines, saying, Come up this once, for he hath shewed me all his heart. Then the lords of the Phi-lis'tines came up unto her, and brought money in their hand.

19 And she made him sleep upon her knees; and she called for a man, and she caused him to shave off the seven locks of his head; and she began to afflict him, and his strength went from him.

20 And she said, The Phi-lis'tines *be* upon thee, Sam'son. And he awoke out of his sleep, and said, I will go out as at other times before, and shake

myself. And he wist not that the Lord was departed from him.

21 But the Phi-lis'tines took him, and put out his eyes, and brought him down to Ga'za, and bound him with fetters of brass; and he did grind in the prison house.

The Rest of the Story

22 Howbeit the hair of his head began to grow again after he was shaven.

23 Then the lords of the Phi-lis'tines gathered them together for to offer a great sacrifice unto Da'gon their god, and to rejoice: for they said, Our god hath delivered Sam'son our enemy into our hand.

24 And when the people saw him, they praised their god: for they said, Our god hath delivered into our hands our enemy, and the destroyer of our country, which slew many of us.

25 And it came to pass, when their hearts were merry, that they said, Call for Sam'son, that he may make us sport. And they called for Sam'son out of the prison house; and he made them sport: and they set him between the pillars.

26 And Sam'son said unto the lad that held him by the hand, Suffer me that I may feel the pillars whereupon the house standeth, that I may lean upon them.

27 Now the house was full of men and women; and all the lords of the Phi-lis'tines *were* there; and *there were* upon the roof about three thousand men and women, that beheld while Sam'son made sport.

28 And Sam'son called unto the Lord, and said, O Lord God, remember me, I pray thee, and strengthen me, I pray thee, only this once, O God,

that I may be at once avenged of the Phi-lis'tines for my two eyes.

29 And Sam'son took hold of the two middle pillars upon which the house stood, and on which it was borne up, of the one with his right hand, and of the other with his left.

30 And Sam'son said, Let me die with the Phi-lis'tines. And he bowed himself with *all his* might; and the house fell upon the lords, and upon all the people that *were* therein. So the dead which he slew at his death were more than *they* which he slew in his life.

31 Then his brethren and all the house of his father came down, and took him, and brought *him* up, and buried him between Zo'rah and Esh'ta-ol in the buryingplace of Ma-no'ah his father. And he judged Is'ra-el twenty years.

A Time of Anarchy
(17:1–21:25)

17 AND THERE was a man of mount E'phra-im, whose name *was* Mi'cah.

2 And he said unto his mother, The eleven hundred *shekels* of silver that were taken from thee, about which thou cursedst, and spakest of also in mine ears, behold, the silver *is* with me; I took it. And his mother said, Blessed *be thou* of the LORD, my son.

Micah and the Levite

3 And when he had restored the eleven hundred *shekels* of silver to his mother, his mother said, I had wholly dedicated the silver unto the LORD from my hand for my son, to make a graven image and a molten image: now therefore I will restore it unto thee.

4 Yet he restored the money unto his mother; and his mother took two hundred *shekels* of silver, and gave them to the founder, who made thereof

a graven image and a molten image: and they were in the house of Mi'cah.

5 And the man Mi'cah had an house of gods, and made an ephod, and teraphim, and consecrated one of his sons, who became his priest.

6 In those days *there was* no king in Is'ra-el, *but* every man did *that which was* right in his own eyes.

7 And there was a young man out of Beth'-le-hem-ju'dah of the family of Ju'dah, who *was* a Le'vite, and he sojourned there.

8 And the man departed out of the city from Beth'-le-hem-ju'dah to sojourn where he could find *a place:* and he came to mount E'phra-im to the house of Mi'cah, as he journeyed.

9 And Mi'cah said unto him, Whence comest thou? And he said unto him, I *am* a Le'vite of Beth'-le-hem-ju'dah, and I go to sojourn where I may find *a place.*

10 And Mi'cah said unto him, Dwell with me, and be unto me a father and a priest, and I will give thee ten *shekels* of silver by the year, and a suit of apparel, and thy victuals. So the Le'vite went in.

11 And the Le'vite was content to dwell with the man; and the young man was unto him as one of his sons.

12 And Mi'cah consecrated the Le'vite; and the young man became his priest, and was in the house of Mi'cah.

13 Then said Mi'cah, Now know I that the LORD will do me good, seeing I have a Le'vite to *my* priest.

18 IN THOSE days *there was* no king in Is'ra-el: and in those days the tribe of the Dan'ites sought them an inheritance to dwell in; for unto

The Migration of the Tribe of Dan

that day *all their* inheritance had not fallen unto them among the tribes of Is'ra-el.

2 And the children of Dan sent of their family five men from their coasts, men of valour, from Zo'rah, and from Esh'ta-ol, to spy out the land, and to search it; and they said unto them, Go, search the land: who when they came to mount E'phra-im to the house of Mi'cah, they lodged there.

3 When they *were* by the house of Mi'cah, they knew the voice of the young man the Le'vite: and they turned in thither, and said unto him, Who brought thee hither? and what makest thou in this *place?* and what hast thou here?

4 And he said unto them, Thus and thus dealeth Mi'cah with me, and hath hired me, and I am his priest.

5 And they said unto him, Ask counsel, we pray thee, of God, that we may know whether our way which we go shall be prosperous.

6 And the priest said unto them, Go in peace: before the LORD *is* your way wherein ye go.

7 Then the five men departed, and came to La'ish, and saw the people that *were* therein, how they dwelt careless, after the manner of the Zi-do'ni-ans, quiet and secure; and *there was* no magistrate in the land, that might put *them* to shame in *any* thing; and they *were* far from the Zi-do'ni-ans, and had no business with *any* man.

8 And they came unto their brethren to Zo'rah and Esh'ta-ol: and their brethren said unto them, What *say* ye?

9 And they said, Arise, that we may go up against them: for we have seen the land, and, behold, it *is* very good: and *are* ye still? be not slothful to go, *and* to enter to possess the land.

10 When ye go, ye shall come unto a people secure, and to a large land: for God hath given it into your hands; a place where *there is* no want of any thing that *is* in the earth.

11 And there went from thence of the family of the Dan'-ites, out of Zo'rah and out of Esh'ta-ol, six hundred men appointed with weapons of war.

12 And they went up, and pitched in Kir'jath-je'a-rim, in Ju'dah: wherefore they called that place Ma'ha-neh-dan unto this day: behold, *it is* behind Kir'jath-je'a-rim.

13 And they passed thence unto mount E'phra-im, and came unto the house of Mi'cah.

14 Then answered the five men that went to spy out the country of La'ish, and said unto their brethren, Do ye know that there is in these houses an ephod, and teraphim, and a graven image, and a molten image? now therefore consider what ye have to do.

15 And they turned thitherward, and came to the house of the young man the Le'vite, *even* unto the house of Mi'cah, and saluted him.

16 And the six hundred men appointed with their weapons of war, which *were* of the children of Dan, stood by the entering of the gate.

17 And the five men that went to spy out the land went up, *and* came in thither, *and* took the graven image, and the ephod, and the teraphim, and the molten image: and the priest stood in the entering of the gate with the six hundred men *that were* appointed with weapons of war.

18 And these went into Mi'-cah's house, and fetched the carved image, the ephod, and the teraphim, and the molten image. Then said the priest unto them, What do ye?

19 And they said unto him, Hold thy peace, lay thine hand upon thy mouth, and go with us, and be to us a father and a priest: *is it* better for thee to be a priest unto the house of one man, or that thou be a priest unto a tribe and a family in Is'ra-el?

20 And the priest's heart was glad, and he took the ephod, and the teraphim, and the graven image, and went in the midst of the people.

21 So they turned and departed, and put the little ones and the cattle and the carriage before them.

22 *And* when they were a good way from the house of Mi'cah, the men that *were* in the houses near to Mi'cah's house were gathered together, and overtook the children of Dan.

23 And they cried unto the children of Dan. And they turned their faces, and said unto Mi'cah, What aileth thee, that thou comest with such a company?

24 And he said, Ye have taken away my gods which I made, and the priest, and ye are gone away: and what have I more? and what *is* this *that* ye say unto me, What aileth thee?

25 And the children of Dan said unto him, Let not thy voice be heard among us, lest angry fellows run upon thee, and thou lose thy life, with the lives of thy household.

26 And the children of Dan went their way: and when Mi'cah saw that they *were* too strong for him, he turned and went back unto his house.

27 And they took *the things* which Mi'cah had made, and the priest which he had, and came unto La'ish, unto a people *that were* at quiet and secure: and they smote them with the edge of the sword, and burnt the city with fire.

28 And *there was* no deliverer, because it *was* far from Zi'don, and they had no business with *any* man; and it was in the valley that *lieth* by Beth-re'hob. And they built a city, and dwelt therein.

29 And they called the name of the city Dan, after the name of Dan their father, who was born unto Is'ra-el: howbeit the name of the city *was* La'ish at the first.

30 And the children of Dan set up the graven image: and Jon'a-than, the son of Ger'shom, the son of Ma-nas'seh, he and his sons were priests to the tribe of Dan until the day of the captivity of the land.

31 And they set them up Mi'cah's graven image, which he made, all the time that the house of God was in Shi'loh.

19 AND IT came to pass in those days, when *there was* no king in Is'ra-el, that there was a certain Le'vite sojourning on the side of mount E'phra-im, who took to him a concubine out of Beth'-le-hem-ju'dah.

2 And his concubine played the whore against him, and went away from him unto her father's house to Beth'-le-hem-ju'dah, and was there four whole months.

3 And her husband arose, and went after her, to speak friendly unto her, *and* to bring her again, having her servant with him, and a couple of asses: and she brought him into her father's house: and when the father of the damsel saw him, he rejoiced to meet him.

4 And his father in law, the damsel's father, retained him; and he abode with him three days: so they did eat and drink, and lodged there.

5 And it came to pass on the fourth day, when they arose early in the morning, that he rose up to depart: and the damsel's father said unto his son in law, Comfort thine heart with a morsel of bread, and afterward go your way.

6 And they sat down, and did eat and drink both of them together: for the damsel's father had said unto the man, Be content, I pray thee, and tarry all night, and let thine heart be merry.

7 And when the man rose up to depart, his father in law urged him: therefore he lodged there again.

8 And he arose early in the morning on the fifth day to depart: and the damsel's father said, Comfort thine heart, I pray thee. And they tarried until afternoon, and they did eat both of them.

9 And when the man rose up to depart, he, and his concubine, and his servant, his father in law, the damsel's father, said unto him, Behold, now the day draweth toward evening, I pray you tarry all night: behold, the day groweth to an end, lodge here, that thine heart may be merry; and to morrow get you early on your way, that thou mayest go home.

10 But the man would not tarry that night, but he rose up and departed, and came over against Je'bus, which is Je-ru'sa-lem; and there were with him two asses saddled, his concubine also was with him.

11 And when they were by Je'bus, the day was far spent; and the servant said unto his master, Come, I pray thee, and let us turn in into this city of the Jeb'u-sites, and lodge in it.

12 And his master said unto him, We will not turn aside hither into the city of a stranger, that is

not of the children of Is'ra-el; we will pass over to Gib'e-ah.

13 And he said unto his servant, Come, and let us draw near to one of these places to lodge all night, in Gib'e-ah, or in Ra'mah.

14 And they passed on and went their way; and the sun went down upon them *when they were* by Gib'e-ah, which *belongeth* to Ben'ja-min.

15 And they turned aside thither, to go in *and* to lodge in Gib'e-ah: and when he went in, he sat him down in a street of the city: for *there was* no man that took them into his house to lodging.

16 And, behold, there came an old man from his work out of the field at even, which *was* also of mount E'phra-im; and he sojourned in Gib'e-ah: but the men of the place *were* Ben'ja-mites.

17 And when he had lifted up his eyes, he saw a wayfaring man in the street of the city: and the old man said, Whither goest thou? and whence comest thou?

18 And he said unto him, We *are* passing from Beth'-le-hem-ju'dah toward the side of mount E'phra-im; from thence *am* I: and I went to Beth'-le-hem-ju'dah, but I *am now* going to the house of the LORD; and there *is* no man that receiveth me to house.

19 Yet there is both straw and provender for our asses; and there is bread and wine also for me, and for thy handmaid, and for the young man *which is* with thy servants: *there is* no want of any thing.

20 And the old man said, Peace *be* with thee; howsoever *let* all thy wants *lie* upon me; only lodge not in the street.

21 So he brought him into his house, and gave provender unto the asses: and they washed their feet, and did eat and drink.

22 *Now* as they were making their hearts merry, behold, the men of the city, certain sons of Be'li-al, beset the house round about, *and* beat at the door, and spake to the master of the house, the old man, saying, Bring forth the man that came into thine house, that we may know him.

23 And the man, the master of the house, went out unto them, and said unto them, Nay, my brethren, *nay,* I pray you, do not *so* wickedly; seeing that this man is come into mine house, do not this folly.

24 Behold, *here is* my daughter a maiden, and his concubine; them I will bring out now, and humble ye them, and do with them what seemeth good unto you: but unto this man do not so vile a thing.

25 But the men would not hearken to him: so the man took his concubine, and brought her forth unto them; and they knew her, and abused her all the night until the morning: and when the day began to spring, they let her go.

26 Then came the woman in the dawning of the day, and fell down at the door of the man's house where her lord *was,* till it was light.

27 And her lord rose up in the morning, and opened the doors of the house, and went out to go his way: and, behold, the woman his concubine was fallen down *at* the door of the house, and her hands *were* upon the threshold.

28 And he said unto her, Up, and let us be going. But none answered. Then the man took her *up* upon an ass, and the man rose up, and gat him unto his place.

29 And when he was come into his house, he took a knife, and laid hold on his concubine, and divided her, *together* with her bones, into twelve pieces, and sent her into all the coasts of Is'ra-el.

30 And it was so, that all that saw it said, There was no such deed done nor seen from the day that the children of Is'ra-el came up out of the land of E'gypt unto this day: consider of it, take advice, and speak *your minds.*

20 THEN ALL the children of Is'ra-el went out, and the congregation was gathered together as one man, from Dan even to Be'er-she'ba, with the land of Gil'e-ad, unto the LORD in Miz'peh.

2 And the chief of all the people, *even* of all the tribes of Is'ra-el, presented themselves in the assembly of the people of God, four hundred thousand footmen that drew sword.

3 (Now the children of Ben'ja-min heard that the children of Is'ra-el were gone up to Miz'peh.) Then said the children of Is'ra-el, Tell *us*, how was this wickedness?

4 And the Le'vite, the husband of the woman that was slain, answered and said, I came into Gib'e-ah that *belongeth* to Ben'ja-min, I and my concubine, to lodge.

5 And the men of Gib'e-ah rose against me, and beset the house round about upon me by night, *and* thought to have slain me: and my concubine have they forced, that she is dead.

6 And I took my concubine, and cut her in pieces, and sent her throughout all the country of the inheritance of Is'ra-el: for they have committed lewdness and folly in Is'ra-el.

7 Behold, ye *are* all children of Is'ra-el; give here your advice and counsel.

8 And all the people arose as one man, saying, We will not any *of us* go to his tent, neither will we any *of us* turn into his house.

9 But now this *shall be* the thing which we will do to Gib'e-ah; *we will go up* by lot against it;

10 And we will take ten men of an hundred throughout all the tribes of Is'ra-el, and an hundred of a thousand, and a thousand out of ten thousand, to fetch victual for the people, that they may do, when they come to Gib'e-ah of Ben'ja-min, according to all the folly that they have wrought in Is'ra-el.

11 So all the men of Is'ra-el were gathered against the city, knit together as one man.

12 And the tribes of Is'ra-el sent men through all the tribe of Ben'ja-min, saying, What wickedness *is* this that is done among you?

13 Now therefore, deliver *us* the men, the children of Be'li-al, which *are* in Gib'e-ah, that we may put them to death, and put away evil from Is'ra-el. But the children of Ben'ja-min would not hearken to the voice of their brethren the children of Is'ra-el:

14 But the children of Ben'ja-min gathered themselves together out of the cities unto Gib'e-ah, to go out to battle against the children of Is'ra-el.

15 And the children of Ben'ja-min were numbered at that time out of the cities twenty and six thousand men that drew sword, beside the inhabitants of Gib'e-ah, which were numbered seven hundred chosen men.

16 Among all this people *there were* seven hundred chosen men lefthanded; every one could sling stones at an hair *breadth,* and not miss.

17 And the men of Is'ra-el, beside Ben'ja-min, were numbered four hundred thousand men that drew sword: all these *were* men of war.

18 And the children of Is'ra-el arose, and went up to the house of God, and asked counsel of God, and said, Which of us shall go up first to the battle against the children of Ben'ja-min? And the LORD said, Ju'dah *shall go up* first.

19 And the children of Is'ra-el rose up in the morning, and encamped against Gib'e-ah.

20 And the men of Is'ra-el went out to battle against Ben'ja-min; and the men of Is'ra-el put themselves in array to fight against them at Gib'e-ah.

21 And the children of Ben'ja-min came forth out of Gib'e-ah, and destroyed down to the ground of the Is'ra-el-ites that day twenty and two thousand men.

22 And the people the men of Is'ra-el encouraged themselves, and set their battle again in array in the place where they put themselves in array the first day.

23 (And the children of Is'ra-el went up and wept before the LORD until even, and asked counsel of the LORD, saying, Shall I go up again to battle against the children of Ben'ja-min my brother? And the LORD said, Go up against him.)

24 And the children of Is'ra-el came near against the children of Ben'ja-min the second day.

25 And Ben'ja-min went forth against them out of Gib'e-ah the second day, and destroyed down to the ground of the children of Is'ra-el again eighteen thousand men; all these drew the sword.

26 Then all the children of Is'ra-el, and all the people, went up, and came unto the house of God,

and wept, and sat there before the LORD, and fasted that day until even, and offered burnt offerings and peace offerings before the LORD.

27 And the children of Is'ra-el enquired of the LORD, (for the ark of the covenant of God *was* there in those days,

28 And Phin'e-has, the son of E-le-a'zar, the son of Aar'on, stood before it in those days,) saying, Shall I yet again go out to battle against the children of Ben'ja-min my brother, or shall I cease? And the LORD said, Go up; for to-morrow I will deliver them into thine hand.

29 And Is'ra-el set liers in wait round about Gib'e-ah.

30 And the children of Is'ra-el went up against the children of Ben'ja-min on the third day, and put themselves in array against Gib'e-ah, as at other times.

31 And the children of Ben'ja-min went out against the people, *and* were drawn away from the city; and they began to smite of the people, *and* kill, as at other times, in the highways, of which one goeth up to the house of God, and the other to Gib'e-ah in the field, about thirty men of Is'ra-el.

32 And the children of Ben'ja-min said, They *are* smitten down before us, as at the first. But the children of Is'ra-el said, Let us flee, and draw them from the city unto the highways.

33 And all the men of Is'ra-el rose up out of their place, and put themselves in array at Ba'al-ta'mar: and the liers in wait of Is'ra-el came forth out of their places, *even* out of the meadows of Gib'e-ah.

34 And there came against Gib'e-ah ten thousand chosen men out of all Is'ra-el, and the battle was sore: but they knew not that evil *was* near them.

35 And the LORD smote Ben'ja-min before Is'ra-el: and the children of Is'ra-el destroyed of the Ben'ja-mites that day twenty and five thousand and an hundred men: all these drew the sword.

36 So the children of Ben'ja-min saw that they were smitten: for the men of Is'ra-el gave place to the Ben'ja-mites, because they trusted unto the liers in wait which they had set beside Gib'e-ah.

37 And the liers in wait hasted, and rushed upon Gib'e-ah; and the liers in wait drew *themselves* along, and smote all the city with the edge of the sword.

38 Now there was an appointed sign between the men of Is'ra-el and the liers in wait, that they should make a great flame with smoke rise up out of the city.

39 And when the men of Is'ra-el retired in the battle, Ben'ja-min began to smite *and* kill of the men of Is'ra-el about thirty persons: for they said, Surely they are smitten down before us, as *in* the first battle.

40 But when the flame began to arise up out of the city with a pillar of smoke, the Ben'ja-mites looked behind them, and, behold, the flame of the city ascended up to heaven.

41 And when the men of Is'ra-el turned again, the men of Ben'ja-min were amazed: for they saw that evil was come upon them.

42 Therefore they turned *their backs* before the men of Is'ra-el unto the way of the wilderness; but the battle overtook them; and them which *came* out of the cities they destroyed in the midst of them.

43 *Thus* they inclosed the Ben'ja-mites round about, *and* chased them, *and* trode them down with ease over against Gib'e-ah toward the sunrising.

44 And there fell of Ben'ja-min eighteen thousand men; all these *were* men of valour.

45 And they turned and fled toward the wilderness unto the rock of Rim'mon: and they gleaned of them in the highways five thousand men; and pursued hard after them unto Gi'dom, and slew two thousand men of them.

46 So that all which fell that day of Ben'ja-min were twenty and five thousand men that drew the sword; all these *were* men of valour.

47 But six hundred men turned and fled to the wilderness unto the rock Rim'mon, and abode in the rock Rim'mon four months.

48 And the men of Is'ra-el turned again upon the children of Ben'ja-min, and smote them with the edge of the sword, as well the men of *every* city, as the beast, and all that came to hand: also they set on fire all the cities that they came to.

21 NOW THE men of Is'ra-el had sworn in Miz'peh, saying, There shall not any of us give his daughter unto Ben'ja-min to wife.

2 And the people came to the house of God, and abode there till even before God, and lifted up their voices, and wept sore;

3 And said, O LORD God of Is'ra-el, why is this come to pass in Is'ra-el, that there should be to day one tribe lacking in Is'ra-el?

4 And it came to pass on the morrow, that the people rose early, and built there an altar, and offered burnt offerings and peace offerings.

5 And the children of Is'ra-el said, Who *is there* among all the tribes of Is'ra-el that came not up with the congregation unto the LORD? For they had made a great oath concerning him that came not up to the LORD to Miz'peh, saying, He shall surely be put to death.

6 And the children of Is'ra-el repented them for Ben'ja-min their brother, and said, There is one tribe cut off from Is'ra-el this day.

7 How shall we do for wives for them that remain, seeing we have sworn by the LORD that we will not give them of our daughters to wives?

8 And they said, What one *is there* of the tribes of Is'ra-el that came not up to Miz'peh to the LORD? And, behold, there came none to the camp from Ja'besh-gil'e-ad to the assembly.

9 For the people were numbered, and, behold, *there were* none of the inhabitants of Ja'besh-gil'e-ad there.

10 And the congregation sent thither twelve thousand men of the valiantest, and commanded them, saying, Go and smite the inhabitants of Ja'-besh-gil'e-ad with the edge of the sword, with the women and the children.

11 And this *is* the thing that ye shall do, Ye shall utterly destroy every male, and every woman that hath lain by man.

12 And they found among the inhabitants of Ja'besh-gil'e-ad four hundred young virgins, that had known no man by lying with any male: and they brought them unto the camp to Shi'loh, which *is* in the land of Ca'naan.

13 And the whole congregation sent *some* to speak to the children of Ben'ja-min that *were* in the rock Rim'mon, and to call peaceably unto them.

14 And Ben'ja-min came again at that time; and they gave them wives which they had saved alive of the women of Ja'besh-gil'e-ad: and yet so they sufficed them not.

15 And the people repented them for Ben'ja-min, because that the LORD had made a breach in the tribes of Is'ra-el.

16 Then the elders of the congregation said, How shall we do for wives for them that remain, seeing the women are destroyed out of Ben'ja-min?

17 And they said, *There must be* an inheritance for them that be escaped of Ben'ja-min, that a tribe be not destroyed out of Is'ra-el.

18 Howbeit we may not give them wives of our daughters: for the children of Is'ra-el have sworn, saying, Cursed *be* he that giveth a wife to Ben'ja-min.

19 Then they said, Behold, *there is* a feast of the Lord in Shi'loh yearly *in a place* which *is* on the north side of Beth'-el, on the east side of the highway that goeth up from Beth'-el to She'-chem, and on the south of Le'bo-nah.

20 Therefore they commanded the children of Ben'ja-min, saying, Go and lie in wait in the vineyards;

21 And see, and, behold, if the daughters of Shi'loh come out to dance in dances, then come ye out of the vineyards, and catch you every man his wife of the daughters of Shi'loh, and go to the land of Ben'ja-min.

22 And it shall be, when their fathers or their brethren come unto us to complain, that we will say unto them, Be favourable unto them for our sakes: because we reserved not to each man his wife in the war: for ye did not give unto them at this time, *that* ye should be guilty.

23 And the children of Ben'ja-min did so, and took *them* wives, according to their number, of them that danced, whom they caught: and they went and returned unto their inheritance, and repaired the cities, and dwelt in them.

24 And the children of Is'ra-el departed thence at that time, every man to his tribe and to his family, and they went out from thence every man to his inheritance.

25 In those days *there was* no king in Is'ra-el: every man did *that which was* right in his own eyes.

Sin's High Cost

LESSON 3
RUTH 1:1–4:8
Love Which Leads to Loyalty

Human Love with Divine Consequences (1:1)

_____

_____

The Nature of the Book

_____

_____

Naomi's Family Tragedies

The Message of Ruth

_____

_____

Living Through Calamity (1:1–7)

_____

A Time of Famine

_____

_____

The Sad Journey Home

_____

_____

1 NOW IT came to pass in the days when the judges ruled, that there was a famine in the land. And a certain man of Beth'-le-hem-ju'dah went to sojourn in the country of Mo'ab, he, and his wife, and his two sons.

2 And the name of the man *was* E-lim'e-lech, and the name of his wife Na-o'mi, and the name of his two sons Mah'lon and Chil'i-on, Eph'rathites of Beth'-le-hem-ju'dah. And they came into the country of Mo'ab, and continued there.

3 And E-lim'e-lech Na-o'mi's husband died; and she was left, and her two sons.

4 And they took them wives of the women of Mo'ab; the name of the one *was* Or'pah, and the name of the other Ruth: and they dwelled there about ten years.

5 And Mah'lon and Chil'i-on died also both of them; and the woman was left of her two sons and her husband.

6 Then she arose with her daughters in law, that she might return from the country of Mo'ab: for she had heard in the country of Mo'ab how that the LORD had visited his people in giving them bread.

7 Wherefore she went forth out of the place where she was, and her two daughters in law with

her; and they went on the way to return unto the land of Ju'dah.

8 And Na-o'mi said unto her two daughters in law, Go, return each to her mother's house: the LORD deal kindly with you, as ye have dealt with the dead, and with me.

9 The LORD grant you that ye may find rest, each *of you* in the house of her husband. Then she kissed them; and they lifted up their voice, and wept.

10 And they said unto her, Surely we will return with thee unto thy people.

11 And Na-o'mi said, Turn again, my daughters: why will ye go with me? *are* there yet *any more* sons in my womb, that they may be your husbands?

12 Turn again, my daughters, go *your way;* for I am too old to have an husband. If I should say, I have hope, *if* I should have an husband also to night, and should also bear sons;

13 Would ye tarry for them till they were grown? would ye stay for them from having husbands? nay, my daughters; for it grieveth me much for your sakes that the hand of the LORD is gone out against me.

14 And they lifted up their voice, and wept again: and Or'-pah kissed her mother in law; but Ruth clave unto her.

15 And she said, Behold, thy sister in law is gone back unto her people, and unto her gods: return thou after thy sister in law.

16 And Ruth said, Intreat me not to leave thee, *or* to return from following after thee: for whither thou goest, I will go; and where thou lodgest, I will lodge: thy people *shall be* my people, and thy God my God:

The Commitment of Love (1:8–22)

Urging the Daughters-in-Law to Return

Ruth's Bold Declaration

Naomi's Bitter Return

An Important Hint

Devoted Service (2:1–7)

Boaz Introduced

Ruth's Gleaning

17 Where thou diest, will I die, and there will I be buried: the LORD do so to me, and more also, *if ought* but death part thee and me.

18 When she saw that she was stedfastly minded to go with her, then she left speaking unto her.

19 So they two went until they came to Beth'-le-hem. And it came to pass, when they were come to Beth'-le-hem, that all the city was moved about them, and they said, *Is* this Na-o'mi?

20 And she said unto them, Call me not Na-o'mi, call me Ma'ra: for the Almighty hath dealt very bitterly with me.

21 I went out full, and the LORD hath brought me home again empty: why *then* call ye me Na-o'mi, seeing the LORD hath testified against me, and the Almighty hath afflicted me?

22 So Na-o'mi returned, and Ruth the Mo'ab-it-ess, her daughter in law, with her, which returned out of the country of Mo'ab: and they came to Beth'-le-hem in the beginning of barley harvest.

2 AND NA-O'MI had a kinsman of her husband's, a mighty man of wealth, of the family of E-lim'e-lech; and his name *was* Bo'az.

2 And Ruth the Mo'ab-it-ess said unto Na-o'mi, Let me now go to the field, and glean ears of corn after *him* in whose sight I shall find grace. And she said unto her, Go, my daughter.

3 And she went, and came, and gleaned in the field after the reapers: and her hap was to light on a part of the field *belonging* unto Bo'az, who *was* of the kindred of E-lim'e-lech.

4 And, behold, Bo'az came from Beth'-le-hem, and said unto the reapers, The LORD be with you. And they answered him, The LORD bless thee.

5 Then said Bo'az unto his servant that was set over the reapers, Whose damsel is this?

6 And the servant that was set over the reapers answered and said, It is the Mo'ab-it-ish damsel that came back with Na-o'mi out of the country of Mo'ab:

7 And she said, I pray you, let me glean and gather after the reapers among the sheaves: so she came, and hath continued even from the morning until now, that she tarried a little in the house.

8 Then said Bo'az unto Ruth, Hearest thou not, my daughter? Go not to glean in another field, neither go from hence, but abide here fast by my maidens:

9 Let thine eyes be on the field that they do reap, and go thou after them: have I not charged the young men that they shall not touch thee? and when thou art athirst, go unto the vessels, and drink of that which the young men have drawn.

10 Then she fell on her face, and bowed herself to the ground, and said unto him, Why have I found grace in thine eyes, that thou shouldest take knowledge of me, seeing I am a stranger?

11 And Bo'az answered and said unto her, It hath fully been shewed me, all that thou hast done unto thy mother in law since the death of thine husband: and how thou hast left thy father and thy mother, and the land of thy nativity, and art come unto a people which thou knewest not heretofore.

12 The LORD recompense thy work, and a full reward be given thee of the LORD God of Is'ra-el, under whose wings thou art come to trust.

Provision for the Poor
_____

Boaz's Watchful Concern

_____
_____
_____
_____
_____

Compassionate Concern (2:8–18)

_____
_____
_____
_____
_____

Ruth's Responsible Response

_____
_____

Caring for the Helpless

_____
_____
_____
_____
_____

13 Then she said, Let me find favour in thy sight, my lord; for that thou hast comforted me, and for that thou hast spoken friendly unto thine handmaid, though I be not like unto one of thine handmaidens.

14 And Bo'az said unto her, At mealtime come thou hither, and eat of the bread, and dip thy morsel in the vinegar. And she sat beside the reapers: and he reached her parched *corn,* and she did eat, and was sufficed, and left.

15 And when she was risen up to glean, Bo'az commanded his young men, saying, Let her glean even among the sheaves, and reproach her not:

16 And let fall also *some* of the handfuls of purpose for her, and leave *them,* that she may glean *them,* and rebuke her not.

17 So she gleaned in the field until even, and beat out that she had gleaned: and it was about an ephah of barley.

18 And she took *it* up, and went into the city: and her mother in law saw what she had gleaned: and she brought forth, and gave to her that she had reserved after she was sufficed.

Coincidence? Or Faith at Work? (2:19–3:18)

19 And her mother in law said unto her, Where hast thou gleaned to day? and where wroughtest thou? blessed be he that did take knowledge of thee. And she shewed her mother in law with whom she had wrought, and said, The man's name with whom I wrought to day *is* Bo'az.

20 And Na-o'mi said unto her daughter in law, Blessed *be* he of the LORD, who hath not left off his kindness to the living and to the dead. And Na-o'mi said unto her, The man *is* near of kin unto us, one of our next kinsmen.

21 And Ruth the Mo'ab-it-ess said, He said unto me also, Thou shalt keep fast by my young men, until they have ended all my harvest.

22 And Na-o'mi said unto Ruth her daughter in law, *It is* good, my daughter, that thou go out with his maidens, that they meet thee not in any other field.

23 So she kept fast by the maidens of Bo'az to glean unto the end of barley harvest and of wheat harvest; and dwelt with her mother in law.

3 THEN NA-O'MI her mother in law said unto her, My daughter, shall I not seek rest for thee, that it may be well with thee?

2 And now *is* not Bo'az of our kindred, with whose maidens thou wast? Behold, he winnoweth barley to night in the threshing-floor.

3 Wash thyself therefore, and anoint thee, and put thy raiment upon thee, and get thee down to the floor: *but* make not thyself known unto the man, until he shall have done eating and drinking.

4 And it shall be, when he lieth down, that thou shalt mark the place where he shall lie, and thou shalt go in, and uncover his feet, and lay thee down; and he will tell thee what thou shalt do.

5 And she said unto her, All that thou sayest unto me I will do.

6 And she went down unto the floor, and did according to all that her mother in law bade her.

7 And when Bo'az had eaten and drunk, and his heart was merry, he went to lie down at the end of the heap of corn: and she came softly, and uncovered his feet, and laid her down.

The Patriarchal Faith

The Nature of Ruth's "Luck"

Ruth Takes Advantage of the Opportunity

8 And it came to pass at midnight, that the man was afraid, and turned himself: and, behold, a woman lay at his feet.

9 And he said, Who *art* thou? And she answered, I *am* Ruth thine handmaid: spread therefore thy skirt over thine handmaid; for thou *art* a near kinsman.

10 And he said, Blessed *be* thou of the LORD, my daughter: *for* thou hast shewed more kindness in the latter end than at the beginning, inasmuch as thou followedst not young men, whether poor or rich.

11 And now, my daughter, fear not; I will do to thee all that thou requirest: for all the city of my people doth know that thou *art* a virtuous woman.

12 And now it is true that I *am thy* near kinsman: howbeit there is a kinsman nearer than I.

13 Tarry this night, and it shall be in the morning, *that* if he will perform unto thee the part of a kinsman, well; let him do the kinsman's part: but if he will not do the part of a kinsman to thee, then will I do the part of a kinsman to thee, *as* the LORD liveth: lie down until the morning.

14 And she lay at his feet until the morning: and she rose up before one could know another. And he said, Let it not be known that a woman came into the floor.

15 Also he said, Bring the veil that *thou hast* upon thee, and hold it. And when she held it, he measured six *measures* of barley, and laid *it* on her: and she went into the city.

16 And when she came to her mother in law, she said, Who *art* thou, my daughter? And she told her all that the man had done to her.

Waiting with Patience

82

17 And she said, These six *measures* of barley gave he me; for he said to me, Go not empty unto thy mother in law.

18 Then said she, Sit still, my daughter, until thou know how the matter will fall: for the man will not be in rest, until he have finished the thing this day.

4 THEN WENT Bo'az up to the gate, and sat him down there: and, behold, the kinsman of whom Bo'az spake came by; unto whom he said, Ho, such a one! turn aside, sit down here. And he turned aside, and sat down.

2 And he took ten men of the elders of the city, and said, Sit ye down here. And they sat down.

3 And he said unto the kinsman, Na-o'mi, that is come again out of the country of Mo'ab, selleth a parcel of land, which *was* our brother E-lim'e-lech's:

4 And I thought to advertise thee, saying, Buy *it* before the inhabitants, and before the elders of my people. If thou wilt redeem *it,* redeem *it:* but if thou wilt not redeem *it, then* tell me, that I may know: for *there is* none to redeem *it* beside thee; and I *am* after thee. And he said, I will redeem *it.*

5 Then said Bo'az, What day thou buyest the field of the hand of Na-o'mi, thou must buy *it* also of Ruth the Mo'ab-it-ess, the wife of the dead, to raise up the name of the dead upon his inheritance.

6 And the kinsman said, I cannot redeem *it* for myself, lest I mar mine own inheritance: redeem thou my right to thyself; for I cannot redeem *it.*

7 Now this *was the manner* in former time in Is'ra-el concerning redeeming and concerning changing,

The Necessity and Freedom of Choosing (4:1–12)

An Opportunity Offered by Boaz

The Opportunity Rejected

for to confirm all things; a man plucked off his shoe, and gave *it* to his neighbour: and this *was* a testimony in Is'ra-el.

8 Therefore the kinsman said unto Bo'az, Buy *it* for thee. So he drew off his shoe.

An Opportunity Seized

9 And Bo'az said unto the elders, and *unto* all the people, Ye *are* witnesses this day, that I have bought all that *was* E-lim'e-lech's, and all that *was* Chil'i-on's and Mah'lon's, of the hand of Na-o'mi.

10 Moreover Ruth the Mo'ab-it-ess, the wife of Mah'lon, have I purchased to be my wife, to raise up the name of the dead upon his inheritance, that the name of the dead be not cut off from among his brethren, and from the gate of his place: ye *are* witnesses this day.

11 And all the people that *were* in the gate, and the elders, said, *We are* witnesses. The LORD make the woman that is come into thine house like Ra'-chel and like Le'ah, which two did build the house of Is'ra-el: and do thou worthily in Eph'ra-tah, and be famous in Beth'-le-hem:

12 And let thy house be like the house of Pha'rez, whom Ta'-mar bare unto Ju'dah, of the seed which the LORD shall give thee of this young woman.

The Fruits of Love (4:13–22)

13 So Bo'az took Ruth, and she was his wife: and when he went in unto her, the LORD gave her conception, and she bare a son.

Personal Blessings

14 And the women said unto Na-o'mi, Blessed *be* the LORD, which hath not left thee this day without a kinsman, that his name may be famous in Is'ra-el.

15 And he shall be unto thee a restorer of *thy* life, and a nourisher of thine old age: for thy daughter in law, which loveth thee, which is better to thee than seven sons, hath born him.

16 And Na-o'mi took the child, and laid it in her bosom, and became nurse unto it.

17 And the women her neighbours gave it a name, saying, There is a son born to Na-o'mi; and they called his name O'bed: he *is* the father of Jes'se, the father of Da'vid.

18 Now these *are* the generations of Pha'rez: Pha'rez begat Hez'ron,

19 And Hez'ron begat Ram, and Ram begat Am-min'a-dab,

20 And Am-min'a-dab begat Nah'shon, and Nah'shon begat Sal'mon,

21 And Sal'mon begat Bo'az, and Bo'az begat O'bed,

22 And O'bed begat Jes'se, and Jes'se begat Da'vid.

The Rest of the Story

LESSON 4

1 SAMUEL 1:1–10:27
Listening Leads to Service

Prayer's Surprising Answers (1:1–2:11)

_____

_____

Hannah's Plight

_____

_____

_____

_____

_____

_____

_____

_____

_____

_____

_____

1 NOW THERE was a certain man of Ra-math-a'im-zo'phim, of mount E'phra-im, and his name *was* El'ka-nah, the son of Jer'o-ham, the son of E-li'hu, the son of To'hu, the son of Zuph, an Eph'rath-ite:

2 And he had two wives; the name of the one *was* Han'nah, and the name of the other Pe-nin'-nah: and Pe-nin'nah had children, but Han'nah had no children.

3 And this man went up out of his city yearly to worship and to sacrifice unto the LORD of hosts in Shi'loh: And the two sons of E'li, Hoph'ni and Phin'e-has, the priests of the LORD, *were* there.

4 And when the time was that El'ka-nah offered, he gave to Pe-nin'nah his wife, and to all her sons and her daughters, portions:

5 But unto Han'nah he gave a worthy portion; for he loved Han'nah: but the LORD had shut up her womb.

6 And her adversary also provoked her sore, for to make her fret, because the LORD had shut up her womb.

7 And *as* he did so year by year, when she went up to the house of the LORD, so she provoked her; therefore she wept, and did not eat.

8 Then said El'ka-nah her husband to her, Han'-nah, why weepest thou? and why eatest thou not? and why is thy heart grieved? *am* not I better to thee than ten sons?

9 So Han'nah rose up after they had eaten in Shi'loh, and after they had drunk. Now E'li the priest sat upon a seat by a post of the temple of the LORD.

10 And she *was* in bitterness of soul, and prayed unto the LORD, and wept sore.

Turning to God for Help

11 And she vowed a vow, and said, O LORD of hosts, if thou wilt indeed look on the affliction of thine handmaid, and remember me, and not forget thine handmaid, but wilt give unto thine handmaid a man child, then I will give him unto the LORD all the days of his life, and there shall no razor come upon his head.

12 And it came to pass, as she continued praying before the LORD, that E'li marked her mouth.

13 Now Han'nah, she spake in her heart; only her lips moved, but her voice was not heard: therefore E'li thought she had been drunken.

14 And E'li said unto her, How long wilt thou be drunken? put away thy wine from thee.

15 And Han'nah answered and said, No, my lord, I *am* a woman of a sorrowful spirit: I have drunk neither wine nor strong drink, but have poured out my soul before the LORD.

16 Count not thine handmaid for a daughter of Be'li-al: for out of the abundance of my complaint and grief have I spoken hitherto.

17 Then E'li answered and said, Go in peace: and the God of Is'ra-el grant *thee* thy petition that thou hast asked of him.

18 And she said, Let thine handmaid find grace in thy sight. So the woman went her way, and did eat, and her countenance was no more *sad.*

19 And they rose up in the morning early, and worshipped before the Lord, and returned, and came to their house to Ra'-mah: and El'ka-nah knew Han'-nah his wife; and the Lord remembered her.

20 Wherefore it came to pass, when the time was come about after Han'nah had conceived, that she bare a son, and called his name Sam'u-el, *saying,* Because I have asked him of the Lord.

21 And the man El'ka-nah, and all his house, went up to offer unto the Lord the yearly sacrifice, and his vow.

22 But Han'nah went not up; for she said unto her husband, *I will not go up* until the child be weaned, and *then* I will bring him, that he may appear before the Lord, and there abide for ever.

23 And El'ka-nah her husband said unto her, Do what seemeth thee good; tarry until thou have weaned him; only the Lord establish his word. So the woman abode, and gave her son suck until she weaned him.

The Dedication of Samuel

24 And when she had weaned him, she took him up with her, with three bullocks, and one ephah of flour, and a bottle of wine, and brought him unto the house of the Lord in Shi'loh: and the child *was* young.

25 And they slew a bullock, and brought the child to E'li.

26 And she said, Oh my lord, *as* thy soul liveth, my lord, I *am* the woman that stood by thee here, praying unto the Lord.

27 For this child I prayed; and the Lord hath given me my petition which I asked of him:

28 Therefore also I have lent him to the LORD; as long as he liveth he shall be lent to the LORD. And he worshipped the LORD there.

2 AND HAN'NAH prayed, and said, My heart rejoiceth in the LORD, mine horn is exalted in the LORD: my mouth is enlarged over mine enemies; because I rejoice in thy salvation.

Hannah's Prayer Song of Dedication

2 *There is* none holy as the LORD: for *there is* none beside thee: neither *is there* any rock like our God.

3 Talk no more so exceeding proudly; let *not* arrogancy come out of your mouth: for the LORD *is* a God of knowledge, and by him actions are weighed.

4 The bows of the mighty men *are* broken, and they that stumbled are girded with strength.

5 *They that were* full have hired out themselves for bread; and *they that were* hungry ceased: so that the barren hath born seven; and she that hath many children is waxed feeble.

6 The LORD killeth, and maketh alive: he bringeth down to the grave, and bringeth up.

7 The LORD maketh poor, and maketh rich: he bringeth low, and lifteth up.

8 He raiseth up the poor out of the dust, *and* lifteth up the beggar from the dunghill, to set *them* among princes, and to make them inherit the throne of glory: for the pillars of the earth *are* the LORD's, and he hath set the world upon them.

9 He will keep the feet of his saints, and the wicked shall be silent in darkness; for by strength shall no man prevail.

10 The adversaries of the LORD shall be broken to pieces; out of heaven shall he thunder upon

them: the LORD shall judge the ends of the earth; and he shall give strength unto his king, and exalt the horn of his anointed.

11 And El'ka-nah went to Ra'mah to his house. And the child did minister unto the LORD before E'li the priest.

12 Now the sons of E'li *were* sons of Be'li-al; they knew not the LORD.

13 And the priest's custom with the people *was, that,* when any man offered sacrifice, the priest's servant came, while the flesh was in seething, with a fleshhook of three teeth in his hand;

14 And he struck *it* into the pan, or kettle, or caldron, or pot; all that the fleshhook brought up the priest took for himself. So they did in Shi'loh unto all the Is'ra-el-ites that came thither.

15 Also before they burnt the fat, the priest's servant came, and said to the man that sacrificed, Give flesh to roast for the priest; for he will not have sodden flesh of thee, but raw.

16 And *if* any man said unto him, Let them not fail to burn the fat presently, and *then* take *as much* as thy soul desireth; then he would answer him, *Nay;* but thou shalt give *it me* now: and if not, I will take *it* by force.

17 Wherefore the sin of the young men was very great before the LORD: for men abhorred the offering of the LORD.

18 But Sam'u-el ministered before the LORD, *being* a child, girded with a linen ephod.

19 Moreover his mother made him a little coat, and brought *it* to him from year to year, when she came up with her husband to offer the yearly sacrifice.

20 And E'li blessed El'ka-nah and his wife, and said, The Lord give thee seed of this woman for the loan which is lent to the Lord. And they went unto their own home.

21 And the Lord visited Han'nah, so that she conceived, and bare three sons and two daughters. And the child Sam'u-el grew before the Lord.

God's Faithfulness to Samuel's Family

22 Now E'li was very old, and heard all that his sons did unto all Is'ra-el; and how they lay with the women that assembled at the door of the tabernacle of the congregation.

23 And he said unto them, Why do ye such things? for I hear of your evil dealings by all this people.

The High Cost of Sin

24 Nay, my sons; for it is no good report that I hear: ye make the Lord's people to transgress.

25 If one man sin against another, the judge shall judge him: but if a man sin against the Lord, who shall intreat for him? Notwithstanding they hearkened not unto the voice of their father, because the Lord would slay them.

26 And the child Sam'u-el grew on, and was in favour both with the Lord, and also with men.

The Promise of a New Priest

27 And there came a man of God unto E'li, and said unto him, Thus saith the Lord, Did I plainly appear unto the house of thy father, when they were in E'gypt in Pha'raoh's house?

28 And did I choose him out of all the tribes of Is'ra-el to be my priest, to offer upon mine altar, to burn incense, to wear an ephod before me? and did I give unto the house of thy father all the offerings made by fire of the children of Is'ra-el?

29 Wherefore kick ye at my sacrifice and at mine offering, which I have commanded in my habita-

tion; and honourest thy sons above me, to make yourselves fat with the chiefest of all the offerings of Is'ra-el my people?

30 Wherefore the LORD God of Is'ra-el saith, I said indeed *that* thy house, and the house of thy father, should walk before me for ever: but now the LORD saith, Be it far from me; for them that honour me I will honour, and they that despise me shall be lightly esteemed.

31 Behold, the days come, that I will cut off thine arm, and the arm of thy father's house, that there shall not be an old man in thine house.

32 And thou shalt see an enemy *in my* habitation, in all *the wealth* which *God* shall give Is'ra-el: and there shall not be an old man in thine house for ever.

33 And the man of thine, *whom* I shall not cut off from mine altar, *shall be* to consume thine eyes, and to grieve thine heart: and all the increase of thine house shall die in the flower of their age.

34 And this *shall be* a sign unto thee, that shall come upon thy sons, on Hoph'ni and Phin'e-has; in one day they shall die both of them.

35 And I will raise me up a faithful priest, *that* shall do according to *that* which *is* in mine heart and in my mind: and I will build him a sure house; and he shall walk before mine anointed for ever.

36 And it shall come to pass, *that* every one that is left in thine house shall come *and* crouch to him for a piece of silver and a morsel of bread, and shall say, Put me, I pray thee, into one of the priests' offices, that I may eat a piece of bread.

God's Listening Servant
(3:1–4:1a)

3 AND THE child Sam'u-el ministered unto the LORD before E'li. And the word of the LORD

was precious in those days; *there was* no open vision.

2 And it came to pass at that time, when E'li *was* laid down in his place, and his eyes began to wax dim, *that* he could not see;

The Fading Vision

3 And ere the lamp of God went out in the temple of the LORD, where the ark of God *was,* and Sam'u-el was laid down *to sleep;*

A Listening Ear

4 That the LORD called Sam'u-el: and he answered, Here *am* I.

5 And he ran unto E'li, and said, Here *am* I; for thou calledst me. And he said, I called not; lie down again. And he went and lay down.

6 And the LORD called yet again, Sam'u-el. And Sam'u-el arose and went to E'li, and said, Here *am* I; for thou didst call me. And he answered, I called not, my son; lie down again.

7 Now Sam'u-el did not yet know the LORD, neither was the word of the LORD yet revealed unto him.

8 And the LORD called Sam'u-el again the third time. And he arose and went to E'li, and said, Here *am* I; for thou didst call me. And E'li perceived that the LORD had called the child.

9 Therefore E'li said unto Sam'u-el, Go, lie down: and it shall be, if he call thee, that thou shalt say, Speak, LORD; for thy servant heareth. So Sam'u-el went and lay down in his place.

10 And the LORD came, and stood, and called as at other times, Sam'u-el, Sam'u-el. Then Sam'u-el answered, Speak; for thy servant heareth.

Samuel's Heavy Burden

11 And the LORD said to Sam'u-el, Behold, I will do a thing in Is'ra-el, at which both the ears of every one that heareth it shall tingle.

12 In that day I will perform against E'li all *things* which I have spoken concerning his house: when I begin, I will also make an end.

13 For I have told him that I will judge his house for ever for the iniquity which he knoweth; because his sons made themselves vile, and he restrained them not.

14 And therefore I have sworn unto the house of E'li, that the iniquity of E'li's house shall not be purged with sacrifice nor offering for ever.

15 And Sam'u-el lay until the morning, and opened the doors of the house of the LORD. And Sam'u-el feared to shew E'li the vision.

16 Then E'li called Sam'u-el, and said, Sam'u-el, my son. And he answered, Here *am* I.

17 And he said, What *is* the thing that *the Lord* hath said unto thee? I pray thee hide *it* not from me: God do so to thee, and more also, if thou hide *any* thing from me of all the things that he said unto thee.

18 And Sam'u-el told him every whit, and hid nothing from him. And he said, It *is* the LORD: let him do what seemeth him good.

19 And Sam'u-el grew, and the LORD was with him, and did let none of his words fall to the ground.

The Ongoing Ministry of Samuel

20 And all Is'ra-el from Dan even to Be'er-she'ba knew that Sam'u-el *was* established *to be* a prophet of the LORD.

21 And the LORD appeared again in Shi'loh: for the LORD revealed himself to Sam'u-el in Shi'loh by the word of the LORD.

When Defeat Is Victory (4:1b–7:1)

4 AND THE word of Sam'u-el came to all Is'ra-el. Now Is'ra-el went out against the Phi-

lis'tines to battle, and pitched beside Eb'en-e'zer: and the Phi-lis'tines pitched in A'phek.

2 And the Phi-lis'tines put themselves in array against Is'ra-el: and when they joined battle, Is'ra-el was smitten before the Phi-lis'tines: and they slew of the army in the field about four thousand men.

3 And when the people were come into the camp, the elders of Is'ra-el said, Wherefore hath the LORD smitten us to day before the Phi-lis'tines? Let us fetch the ark of the covenant of the LORD out of Shi'loh unto us, that, when it cometh among us, it may save us out of the hand of our enemies.

4 So the people sent to Shi'loh, that they might bring from thence the ark of the covenant of the LORD of hosts, which dwelleth *between* the cherubims: and the two sons of E'li, Hoph'ni and Phin'e-has, *were* there with the ark of the covenant of God.

5 And when the ark of the covenant of the LORD came into the camp, all Is'ra-el shouted with a great shout, so that the earth rang again.

6 And when the Phi-lis'tines heard the noise of the shout, they said, What *meaneth* the noise of this great shout in the camp of the He'brews? And they understood that the ark of the LORD was come into the camp.

7 And the Phi-lis'tines were afraid, for they said, God is come into the camp. And they said, Woe unto us! for there hath not been such a thing heretofore.

8 Woe unto us! who shall deliver us out of the hand of these mighty Gods? these *are* the Gods that smote the E-gyp'tians with all the plagues in the wilderness.

9 Be strong, and quit yourselves like men, O ye Phi-lis'tines, that ye be not servants unto the He'-

Conflict with the Philistines

brews, as they have been to you: quit yourselves like men, and fight.

10 And the Phi-lis'tines fought, and Is'ra-el was smitten, and they fled every man into his tent: and there was a very great slaughter; for there fell of Is'ra-el thirty thousand footmen.

11 And the ark of God was taken; and the two sons of E'li, Hoph'ni and Phin'e-has, were slain.

12 And there ran a man of Ben'ja-min out of the army, and came to Shi'loh the same day with his clothes rent, and with earth upon his head.

13 And when he came, lo, E'li sat upon a seat by the wayside watching: for his heart trembled for the ark of God. And when the man came into the city, and told *it,* all the city cried out.

14 And when E'li heard the noise of the crying, he said, What *meaneth* the noise of this tumult? And the man came in hastily, and told E'li.

15 Now E'li was ninety and eight years old; and his eyes were dim, that he could not see.

16 And the man said unto E'li, I *am* he that came out of the army, and I fled to day out of the army. And he said, What is there done, my son?

17 And the messenger answered and said, Is'ra-el is fled before the Phi-lis'tines, and there hath been also a great slaughter among the people, and thy two sons also, Hoph'ni and Phin'e-has, are dead, and the ark of God is taken.

18 And it came to pass, when he made mention of the ark of God, that he fell from off the seat backward by the side of the gate, and his neck brake, and he died: for he was an old man, and heavy. And he had judged Is'ra-el forty years.

19 And his daughter in law, Phin'e-has' wife, was with child, *near* to be delivered: and when she

heard the tidings that the ark of God was taken, and that her father in law and her husband were dead, she bowed herself and travailed; for her pains came upon her.

20 And about the time of her death the women that stood by her said unto her, Fear not; for thou hast born a son. But she answered not, neither did she regard *it*.

21 And she named the child I'-cha-bod, saying, The glory is departed from Is'ra-el: because the ark of God was taken, and because of her father in law and her husband.

22 And she said, The glory is departed from Is'ra-el: for the ark of God is taken.

5 AND THE Phi-lis'tines took the ark of God, and brought it from Eb'en-e'zer unto Ash'dod.

2 When the Phi-lis'tines took the ark of God, they brought it into the house of Da'gon, and set it by Da'gon.

3 And when they of Ash'-dod arose early on the morrow, behold, Da'gon *was* fallen upon his face to the earth before the ark of the Lord. And they took Da'gon, and set him in his place again.

4 And when they arose early on the morrow morning, behold, Da'gon *was* fallen upon his face to the ground before the ark of the Lord; and the head of Da'gon and both the palms of his hands *were* cut off upon the threshold; only *the stump of* Da'gon was left to him.

5 Therefore neither the priests of Da'gon, nor any that come into Da'gon's house, tread on the threshold of Da'gon in Ash'dod unto this day.

6 But the hand of the Lord was heavy upon them of Ash'dod, and he destroyed them, and

The Bitter Fruits of Victory

smote them with emerods, *even* Ash'dod and the coasts thereof.

7 And when the men of Ash'dod saw that *it was* so, they said, The ark of the God of Is'ra-el shall not abide with us: for his hand is sore upon us, and upon Da'gon our god.

8 They sent therefore and gathered all the lords of the Phi-lis'tines unto them, and said, What shall we do with the ark of the God of Is'ra-el? And they answered, Let the ark of the God of Is'ra-el be carried about unto Gath. And they carried the ark of the God of Is'ra-el about *thither.*

9 And it was *so,* that, after they had carried it about, the hand of the LORD was against the city with a very great destruction: and he smote the men of the city, both small and great, and they had emerods in their secret parts.

10 Therefore they sent the ark of God to Ek'ron. And it came to pass, as the ark of God came to Ek'ron, that the Ek'ron-ites cried out, saying, They have brought about the ark of the God of Is'ra-el to us, to slay us and our people.

11 So they sent and gathered together all the lords of the Phi-lis'tines, and said, Send away the ark of the God of Is'ra-el, and let it go again to his own place, that it slay us not, and our people: for there was a deadly destruction throughout all the city; the hand of God was very heavy there.

12 And the men that died not were smitten with the emerods: and the cry of the city went up to heaven.

The Return of the Ark to Israel

6 AND THE ark of the LORD was in the country of the Phi-lis'tines seven months.

2 And the Phi-lis'tines called for the priests and the diviners, saying, What shall we do to the ark of the LORD? tell us wherewith we shall send it to his place.

3 And they said, If ye send away the ark of the God of Is'ra-el, send it not empty; but in any wise return him a trespass offering: then ye shall be healed, and it shall be known to you why his hand is not removed from you.

4 Then said they, What *shall be* the trespass offering which we shall return to him? They answered, Five golden emerods, and five golden mice, *according to* the number of the lords of the Phi-lis'-tines: for one plague *was* on you all, and on your lords.

5 Wherefore ye shall make images of your emerods, and images of your mice that mar the land; and ye shall give glory unto the God of Is'ra-el: peradventure he will lighten his hand from off you, and from off your gods, and from off your land.

6 Wherefore then do ye harden your hearts, as the E-gyp'tians and Pha'raoh hardened their hearts? when he had wrought wonderfully among them, did they not let the people go, and they departed?

7 Now therefore make a new cart, and take two milch kine, on which there hath come no yoke, and tie the kine to the cart, and bring their calves home from them:

8 And take the ark of the LORD, and lay it upon the cart; and put the jewels of gold, which ye return him *for* a trespass offering, in a coffer by the side thereof; and send it away, that it may go.

9 And see, if it goeth up by the way of his own coast to Beth-she'mesh, *then* he hath done us this

great evil: but if not, then we shall know that *it is* not his hand *that* smote us; it *was* a chance *that* happened to us.

10 And the men did so; and took two milch kine, and tied them to the cart, and shut up their calves at home:

11 And they laid the ark of the LORD upon the cart, and the coffer with the mice of gold and the images of their emerods.

12 And the kine took the straight way to the way of Beth-she'mesh, *and* went along the highway, lowing as they went, and turned not aside *to* the right hand or *to* the left; and the lords of the Phi-lis'tines went after them unto the border of Beth-she'mesh.

13 And *they of* Beth-she'mesh *were* reaping their wheat harvest in the valley: and they lifted up their eyes, and saw the ark, and rejoiced to see *it.*

14 And the cart came into the field of Josh'u-a, a Beth-she'mite, and stood there, where *there was* a great stone: and they clave the wood of the cart, and offered the kine a burnt offering unto the LORD.

15 And the Le'vites took down the ark of the LORD, and the coffer that *was* with it, wherein the jewels of gold *were,* and put *them* on the great stone: and the men of Beth-she'mesh offered burnt offerings and sacrificed sacrifices the same day unto the LORD.

16 And when the five lords of the Phi-lis'tines had seen *it,* they returned to Ek'ron the same day.

17 And these *are* the golden emerods which the Phi-lis'tines returned *for* a trespass offering unto the LORD; for Ash'dod one, for Ga'za one, for As'ke-lon one, for Gath one, for Ek'ron one;

18 And the golden mice, *according to* the number of all the cities of the Phi-lis'tines *belonging* to the

five lords, *both* of fenced cities, and of country villages, even unto the great *stone of* A'bel, whereon they set down the ark of the LORD: *which stone remaineth* unto this day in the field of Josh'u-a, the Beth-she'mite.

19 And he smote the men of Beth-she'mesh, because they had looked into the ark of the LORD, even he smote of the people fifty thousand and threescore and ten men: and the people lamented, because the LORD had smitten *many* of the people with a great slaughter.

20 And the men of Beth-she'mesh said, Who is able to stand before this holy LORD God? and to whom shall he go up from us?

21 And they sent messengers to the inhabitants of Kir'jath-je'a-rim, saying, The Phi-lis'tines have brought again the ark of the LORD; come ye down, *and* fetch it up to you.

7 AND THE men of Kir'jath-je'a-rim came, and fetched up the ark of the LORD, and brought it into the house of A-bin'a-dab in the hill, and sanctified E-le-a'zar his son to keep the ark of the LORD.

2 And it came to pass, while the ark abode in Kir'jath-je'a-rim, that the time was long; for it was twenty years: and all the house of Is'ra-el lamented after the LORD.

The Help of God (7:2–17)

3 And Sam'u-el spake unto all the house of Is'ra-el, saying, If ye do return unto the LORD with all your hearts, *then* put away the strange gods and Ash'ta-roth from among you, and prepare your hearts unto the LORD, and serve him only: and he will deliver you out of the hand of the Phi-lis'tines.

Guilty of Idolatry

4 Then the children of Is'ra-el did put away Ba'al-im and Ash'ta-roth, and served the LORD only.

5 And Sam'u-el said, Gather all Is'ra-el to Miz'-peh, and I will pray for you unto the LORD.

6 And they gathered together to Miz'peh, and drew water, and poured *it* out before the LORD, and fasted on that day, and said there, We have sinned against the LORD. And Sam'u-el judged the children of Is'ra-el in Miz'peh.

7 And when the Phi-lis'tines heard that the children of Is'ra-el were gathered together to Miz'peh, the lords of the Phi-lis'tines went up against Is'ra-el. And when the children of Is'ra-el heard *it,* they were afraid of the Phi-lis'tines.

8 And the children of Is'ra-el said to Sam'u-el, Cease not to cry unto the LORD our God for us, that he will save us out of the hand of the Phi-lis'tines.

Victory for a Time

9 And Sam'u-el took a sucking lamb, and offered *it for* a burnt offering wholly unto the LORD: and Sam'u-el cried unto the LORD for Is'ra-el; and the LORD heard him.

10 And as Sam'u-el was offering up the burnt offering, the Phi-lis'tines drew near to battle against Is'ra-el: but the LORD thundered with a great thunder on that day upon the Phi-lis'tines, and discomfited them; and they were smitten before Is'ra-el.

11 And the men of Is'ra-el went out of Miz'peh, and pursued the Phi-lis'tines, and smote them, until *they came* under Beth'-car.

12 Then Sam'u-el took a stone, and set *it* between Miz'peh and Shen, and called the name of it Eb'en-e'zer, saying, Hitherto hath the LORD helped us.

13 So the Phi-lis'tines were subdued, and they came no more into the coast of Is'ra-el: and the hand of the LORD was against the Phi-lis'tines all the days of Sam'u-el.

14 And the cities which the Phi-lis'tines had taken from Is'ra-el were restored to Is'ra-el, from Ek'ron even unto Gath; and the coasts thereof did Is'ra-el deliver out of the hands of the Phi-lis'tines. And there was peace between Is'ra-el and the Am'or-ites.

15 And Sam'u-el judged Is'ra-el all the days of his life.

16 And he went from year to year in circuit to Beth'-el, and Gil'gal, and Miz'peh, and judged Is'ra-el in all those places.

17 And his return *was* to Ra'-mah; for there *was* his house; and there he judged Is'ra-el; and there he built an altar unto the Lord.

8 AND IT came to pass, when Sam'u-el was old, that he made his sons judges over Is'ra-el.

The Desire to Be Like Others (8:1–22)

2 Now the name of his first-born was Jo'el; and the name of his second, A-bi'ah: *they were* judges in Be'er-she'ba.

3 And his sons walked not in his ways, but turned aside after lucre, and took bribes, and per-verted judgment.

Samuel's Problem Sons

4 Then all the elders of Is'ra-el gathered them-selves together, and came to Sam'u-el unto Ra'-mah,

5 And said unto him, Behold, thou art old, and thy sons walk not in thy ways: now make us a king to judge us like all the nations.

6 But the thing displeased Sam'u-el, when they said, Give us a king to judge us. And Sam'u-el prayed unto the Lord.

Samuel Is Displeased over the Request for a King

7 And the Lord said unto Sam'u-el, Hearken unto the voice of the people in all that they say

unto thee: for they have not rejected thee, but they have rejected me, that I should not reign over them.

8 According to all the works which they have done since the day that I brought them up out of E'gypt even unto this day, wherewith they have forsaken me, and served other gods, so do they also unto thee.

9 Now therefore hearken unto their voice: howbeit yet protest solemnly unto them, and shew them the manner of the king that shall reign over them.

10 And Sam'u-el told all the words of the LORD unto the people that asked of him a king.

The Cost of Having a King

11 And he said, This will be the manner of the king that shall reign over you: He will take your sons, and appoint *them* for himself, for his chariots, and *to be* his horsemen; and *some* shall run before his chariots.

12 And he will appoint him captains over thousands, and captains over fifties; and *will set them* to ear his ground, and to reap his harvest, and to make his instruments of war, and instruments of his chariots.

13 And he will take your daughters *to be* confectionaries, and *to be* cooks, and *to be* bakers.

14 And he will take your fields, and your vineyards, and your oliveyards, *even* the best *of them,* and give *them* to his servants.

15 And he will take the tenth of your seed, and of your vineyards, and give to his officers, and to his servants.

16 And he will take your menservants, and your maidservants, and your goodliest young men, and your asses, and put *them* to his work.

17 He will take the tenth of your sheep: and ye shall be his servants.

18 And ye shall cry out in that day because of your king which ye shall have chosen you; and the LORD will not hear you in that day.

19 Nevertheless the people refused to obey the voice of Sam'u-el; and they said, Nay; but we will have a king over us;

20 That we also may be like all the nations; and that our king may judge us, and go out before us, and fight our battles.

21 And Sam'u-el heard all the words of the people, and he rehearsed them in the ears of the LORD.

22 And the LORD said to Sam'u-el, Hearken unto their voice, and make them a king. And Sam'u-el said unto the men of Is'ra-el, Go ye every man unto his city.

9 NOW THERE was a man of Ben'ja-min, whose name *was* Kish, the son of A-bi'el, the son of Ze'ror, the son of Be-cho'rath, the son of A-phi'ah, a Ben'ja-mite, a mighty man of power.

2 And he had a son, whose name *was* Saul, a choice young man, and a goodly: and *there was* not among the children of Is'ra-el a goodlier person than he: from his shoulders and upward *he was* higher than any of the people.

3 And the asses of Kish Saul's father were lost. And Kish said to Saul his son, Take now one of the servants with thee, and arise, go seek the asses.

4 And he passed through mount E'phra-im, and passed through the land of Shal'i-sha, but they found *them* not: then they passed through the land

Israel's Stubborn Insistence

Serendipity (9:1–10:8)

The Search for the Lost Donkeys

of Sha'lim, and *there they were* not: and he passed through the land of the Ben'ja-mites, but they found *them* not.

5 *And* when they were come to the land of Zuph, Saul said to his servant that *was* with him, Come, and let us return; lest my father leave *caring* for the asses, and take thought for us.

6 And he said unto him, Behold now, *there is* in this city a man of God, and *he is* an honourable man; all that he saith cometh surely to pass: now let us go thither; peradventure he can shew us our way that we should go.

7 Then said Saul to his servant, But, behold, *if* we go, what shall we bring the man? for the bread is spent in our vessels, and *there is* not a present to bring to the man of God: what have we?

8 And the servant answered Saul again, and said, Behold, I have here at hand the fourth part of a shekel of silver: *that* will I give to the man of God, to tell us our way.

9 (Beforetime in Is'ra-el, when a man went to enquire of God, thus he spake, Come, and let us go to the seer: for *he that is* now *called* a Prophet was before-time called a Seer.)

10 Then said Saul to his servant, Well said; come, let us go. So they went unto the city where the man of God *was.*

11 *And* as they went up the hill to the city, they found young maidens going out to draw water, and said unto them, Is the seer here?

12 And they answered them, and said, He is; behold, *he is* before you: make haste now, for he came to day to the city; for *there is* a sacrifice of the people to day in the high place:

13 As soon as ye be come into the city, ye shall straightway find him, before he go up to the high

place to eat: for the people will not eat until he come, because he doth bless the sacrifice; *and* afterwards they eat that be bidden. Now therefore get you up; for about this time ye shall find him.

14 And they went up into the city: *and* when they were come into the city, behold, Sam'u-el came out against them, for to go up to the high place.

15 Now the Lord had told Sam'u-el in his ear a day before Saul came, saying,

16 To morrow about this time I will send thee a man out of the land of Ben'ja-min, and thou shalt anoint him *to be* captain over my people Is'ra-el, that he may save my people out of the hand of the Phi-lis'tines: for I have looked upon my people, because their cry is come unto me.

17 And when Sam'u-el saw Saul, the Lord said unto him, Behold the man whom I spake to thee of! this same shall reign over my people.

18 Then Saul drew near to Sam'u-el in the gate, and said, Tell me, I pray thee, where the seer's house *is.*

19 And Sam'u-el answered Saul, and said, I *am* the seer: go up before me unto the high place; for ye shall eat with me to day, and to morrow I will let thee go, and will tell thee all that *is* in thine heart.

20 And as for thine asses that were lost three days ago, set not thy mind on them; for they are found. And on whom *is* all the desire of Is'ra-el? *Is it* not on thee, and on all thy father's house?

21 And Saul answered and said, *Am* not I a Ben'ja-mite, of the smallest of the tribes of Is'ra-el? and my family the least of all the families of the tribe of Ben'ja-min? wherefore then speakest thou so to me?

God Alerts Samuel to Saul's Coming

Saul Is Crowned King

107

22 And Sam'u-el took Saul and his servant, and brought them into the parlour, and made them sit in the chiefest place among them that were bidden, which *were* about thirty persons.

23 And Sam'u-el said unto the cook, Bring the portion which I gave thee, of which I said unto thee, Set it by thee.

24 And the cook took up the shoulder, and *that* which *was* upon it, and set *it* before Saul. And *Sam'u-el* said, Behold that which is left! set *it* before thee, *and* eat: for unto this time hath it been kept for thee since I said, I have invited the people. So Saul did eat with Sam'u-el that day.

25 And when they were come down from the high place into the city, *Sam'u-el* communed with Saul upon the top of the house.

26 And they arose early: and it came to pass about the spring of the day, that Sam'u-el called Saul to the top of the house, saying, Up, that I may send thee away. And Saul arose, and they went out both of them, he and Sam'u-el, abroad.

27 *And* as they were going down to the end of the city, Sam'u-el said to Saul, Bid the servant pass on before us, (and he passed on,) but stand thou still a while, that I may shew thee the word of God.

10 THEN SAM'U-EL took a vial of oil, and poured *it* upon his head, and kissed him, and said, *Is it* not because the LORD hath anointed thee *to be* captain over his inheritance?

2 When thou art departed from me to day, then thou shalt find two men by Ra'chel's sepulchre in the border of Ben'ja-min at Zel'zah; and they will say unto thee, The asses which thou wentest to seek are found: and, lo, thy father hath left the care

of the asses, and sorroweth for you, saying, What shall I do for my son?

3 Then shalt thou go on forward from thence, and thou shalt come to the plain of Ta'bor, and there shall meet thee three men going up to God to Beth'-el, one carrying three kids, and another carrying three loaves of bread, and another carrying a bottle of wine:

4 And they will salute thee, and give thee two *loaves* of bread; which thou shalt receive of their hands.

5 After that thou shalt come to the hill of God, where *is* the garrison of the Phi-lis'tines: and it shall come to pass, when thou art come thither to the city, that thou shalt meet a company of prophets coming down from the high place with a psaltery, and a tabret, and a pipe, and a harp, before them; and they shall prophesy:

6 And the Spirit of the LORD will come upon thee, and thou shalt prophesy with them, and shalt be turned into another man.

7 And let it be, when these signs are come unto thee, *that* thou do as occasion serve thee; for God *is* with thee.

8 And thou shalt go down before me to Gil'gal; and, behold, I will come down unto thee, to offer burnt offerings, *and* to sacrifice sacrifices of peace offerings: seven days shalt thou tarry, till I come to thee, and shew thee what thou shalt do.

9 And it was *so,* that when he had turned his back to go from Sam'u-el, God gave him another heart: and all those signs came to pass that day.

10 And when they came thither to the hill, behold, a company of prophets met him; and the Spirit of God came upon him, and he prophesied among them.

Who Is Our King? (10:9–27)

A Time of Preparation

11 And it came to pass, when all that knew him beforetime saw that, behold, he prophesied among the prophets, then the people said one to another, What *is* this *that* is come unto the son of Kish? *Is* Saul also among the prophets?

12 And one of the same place answered and said, But who *is* their father? Therefore it became a proverb, *Is* Saul also among the prophets?

13 And when he had made an end of prophesying, he came to the high place.

14 And Saul's uncle said unto him and to his servant, Whither went ye? And he said, To seek the asses: and when we saw that *they were* no where, we came to Sam'u-el.

15 And Saul's uncle said, Tell me, I pray thee, what Sam'u-el said unto you.

16 And Saul said unto his uncle, He told us plainly that the asses were found. But of the matter of the kingdom, whereof Sam'u-el spake, he told him not.

Saul Is Crowned King

17 And Sam'u-el called the people together unto the LORD to Miz'peh;

18 And said unto the children of Is'ra-el, Thus saith the LORD God of Is'ra-el, I brought up Is'ra-el out of E'gypt, and delivered you out of the hand of the E-gyp'tians, and out of the hand of all kingdoms, *and* of them that oppressed you:

19 And ye have this day rejected your God, who himself saved you out of all your adversities and your tribulations; and ye have said unto him, *Nay,* but set a king over us. Now therefore present yourselves before the LORD by your tribes, and by your thousands.

20 And when Sam'u-el had caused all the tribes of Is'ra-el to come near, the tribe of Ben'ja-min was taken.

21 When he had caused the tribe of Ben'ja-min to come near by their families, the family of Ma'tri was taken, and Saul the son of Kish was taken: and when they sought him, he could not be found.

22 Therefore they enquired of the Lord further, if the man should yet come thither. And the Lord answered, Behold, he hath hid himself among the stuff.

23 And they ran and fetched him thence: and when he stood among the people, he was higher than any of the people from his shoulders and upward.

24 And Sam'u-el said to all the people, See ye him whom the Lord hath chosen, that *there is* none like him among all the people? And all the people shouted, and said, God save the king.

25 Then Sam'u-el told the people the manner of the kingdom, and wrote *it* in a book, and laid *it* up before the Lord. And Sam'u-el sent all the people away, every man to his house.

26 And Saul also went home to Gib'e-ah; and there went with him a band of men, whose hearts God had touched.

27 But the children of Be'li-al said, How shall this man save us? And they despised him, and brought him no presents. But he held his peace.

The Reception of Their King

A New Day for Israel

111

LESSON 5

1 SAMUEL 11:1–20:42
Disobedience That Leads to Rejection

Decisiveness in Rescue

_____

_____

The Ammonite Crisis

_____

_____

_____

_____

Saul's Quick Rescue

_____

_____

_____

_____

_____

_____

_____

11 THEN NA'HASH the Am'mon-ite came up, and encamped against Ja'besh-gil'e-ad: and all the men of Ja'besh said unto Na'hash, Make a covenant with us, and we will serve thee.

2 And Na'hash the Am'mon-ite answered them, On this *condition* will I make *a covenant* with you, that I may thrust out all your right eyes, and lay it *for* a reproach upon all Is'ra-el.

3 And the elders of Ja'besh said unto him, Give us seven days' respite, that we may send messengers unto all the coasts of Is'ra-el: and then, if *there be* no man to save us, we will come out to thee.

4 Then came the messengers to Gib'e-ah of Saul, and told the tidings in the ears of the people: and all the people lifted up their voices, and wept.

5 And, behold, Saul came after the herd out of the field; and Saul said, What *aileth* the people that they weep? And they told him the tidings of the men of Ja'besh.

6 And the Spirit of God came upon Saul when he heard those tidings, and his anger was kindled greatly.

7 And he took a yoke of oxen, and hewed them in pieces, and sent *them* throughout all the coasts of Is'ra-el by the hands of messengers, saying, Who-

soever cometh not forth after Saul and after Sam'u-el, so shall it be done unto his oxen. And the fear of the Lord fell on the people, and they came out with one consent.

8 And when he numbered them in Be'zek, the children of Is'ra-el were three hundred thousand, and the men of Ju'dah thirty thousand.

9 And they said unto the messengers that came, Thus shall ye say unto the men of Ja'besh-gil'e-ad, To morrow, by *that time* the sun be hot, ye shall have help. And the messengers came and shewed *it* to the men of Ja'besh; and they were glad.

10 Therefore the men of Ja'-besh said, To morrow we will come out unto you, and ye shall do with us all that seemeth good unto you.

11 And it was *so* on the morrow, that Saul put the people in three companies; and they came into the midst of the host in the morning watch, and slew the Am'mon-ites until the heat of the day: and it came to pass, that they which remained were scattered, so that two of them were not left together.

12 And the people said unto Sam'u-el, Who *is* he that said, Shall Saul reign over us? bring the men, that we may put them to death.

13 And Saul said, There shall not a man be put to death this day: for to day the Lord hath wrought salvation in Is'ra-el.

14 Then said Sam'u-el to the people, Come, and let us go to Gil'gal, and renew the kingdom there.

15 And all the people went to Gil'gal; and there they made Saul king before the Lord in Gil'gal; and there they sacrificed sacrifices of peace offerings before the Lord; and there Saul and all the men of Is'ra-el rejoiced greatly.

The Divine Source of Victory

————————————

————————————

————————————

————————————

Samuel's Faithfulness

————————————

————————————

————————————

————————————

————————————

————————————

See What You Have Done

————————————

————————————

————————————

————————————

————————————

————————————

————————————

————————————

12 AND SAM'U-EL said unto all Is'ra-el, Behold, I have hearkened unto your voice in all that ye said unto me, and have made a king over you.

2 And now, behold, the king walketh before you: and I am old and grayheaded; and, behold, my sons *are* with you: and I have walked before you from my childhood unto this day.

3 Behold, here I *am:* witness against me before the LORD, and before his anointed: whose ox have I taken? or whose ass have I taken? or whom have I defrauded? whom have I oppressed? or of whose hand have I received *any* bribe to blind mine eyes therewith? and I will restore it you.

4 And they said, Thou hast not defrauded us, nor oppressed us, neither hast thou taken ought of any man's hand.

5 And he said unto them, The LORD *is* witness against you, and his anointed *is* witness this day, that ye have not found ought in my hand. And they answered, *He is* witness.

6 And Sam'u-el said unto the people, *It is* the LORD that advanced Mo'ses and Aar'on, and that brought your fathers up out of the land of E'gypt.

7 Now therefore stand still, that I may reason with you before the LORD of all the righteous acts of the LORD, which he did to you and to your fathers.

8 When Ja'cob was come into E'gypt, and your fathers cried unto the LORD, then the LORD sent Mo'ses and Aar'on, which brought forth your fathers out of E'gypt, and made them dwell in this place.

9 And when they forgat the LORD their God, he sold them into the hand of Sis'e-ra, captain of the

host of Ha'zor, and into the hand of the Phi-lis'-tines, and into the hand of the king of Mo'ab, and they fought against them.

10 And they cried unto the LORD, and said, We have sinned, because we have forsaken the LORD, and have served Ba'al-im and Ash'ta-roth: but now deliver us out of the hand of our enemies, and we will serve thee.

11 And the LORD sent Je-rub'ba-al, and Be'dan, and Jeph'-thah, and Sam'u-el, and delivered you out of the hand of your enemies on every side, and ye dwelled safe.

12 And when ye saw that Na'-hash the king of the children of Am'mon came against you, ye said unto me, Nay; but a king shall reign over us: when the LORD your God *was* your king.

13 Now therefore behold the king whom ye have chosen, *and* whom ye have desired! and, behold, the LORD hath set a king over you.

14 If ye will fear the LORD, and serve him, and obey his voice, and not rebel against the commandment of the LORD, then shall both ye and also the king that reigneth over you continue following the LORD your God:

15 But if ye will not obey the voice of the LORD, but rebel against the commandment of the LORD, then shall the hand of the LORD be against you, as *it was* against your fathers.

16 Now therefore stand and see this great thing, which the LORD will do before your eyes.

17 *Is it* not wheat harvest today? I will call unto the LORD, and he shall send thunder and rain; that ye may perceive and see that your wickedness *is* great, which ye have done in the sight of the LORD, in asking you a king.

The Sign of Samuel's Power

115

18 So Sam'u-el called unto the LORD; and the LORD sent thunder and rain that day: and all the people greatly feared the LORD and Sam'u-el.

19 And all the people said unto Sam'u-el, Pray for thy servants unto the LORD thy God, that we die not: for we have added unto all our sins *this* evil, to ask us a king.

20 And Sam'u-el said unto the people, Fear not: ye have done all this wickedness: yet turn not aside from following the LORD, but serve the LORD with all your heart;

21 And turn ye not aside: for *then should ye go* after vain *things,* which cannot profit nor deliver; for they *are* vain.

22 For the LORD will not forsake his people for his great name's sake: because it hath pleased the LORD to make you his people.

Samuel's Promise of Support

23 Moreover as for me, God forbid that I should sin against the LORD in ceasing to pray for you: but I will teach you the good and the right way:

24 Only fear the LORD, and serve him in truth with all your heart: for consider how great *things* he hath done for you.

25 But if ye shall still do wickedly, ye shall be consumed, both ye and your king.

The Costs of Disobedience

13 SAUL REIGNED one year; and when he had reigned two years over Is'ra-el,

2 Saul chose him three thousand *men* of Is'ra-el; *whereof* two thousand were with Saul in Mich'mash and in mount Beth'-el, and a thousand were with Jon'a-than in Gib'e-ah of Ben'ja-min: and the rest of the people he sent every man to his tent.

3 And Jon'a-than smote the garrison of the Phi-lis'tines that *was* in Ge'ba, and the Phi-lis'-tines heard *of it.* And Saul blew the trumpet throughout all the land, saying, Let the He'brews hear.

4 And all Is'ra-el heard say *that* Saul had smitten a garrison of the Phi-lis'tines, and *that* Is'ra-el also was had in abomination with the Phi-lis'tines. And the people were called together after Saul to Gil'-gal.

5 And the Phi-lis'tines gathered themselves together to fight with Is'ra-el, thirty thousand chariots, and six thousand horsemen, and people as the sand which *is* on the sea shore in multitude: and they came up, and pitched in Mich'mash, eastward from Beth-a'ven.

6 When the men of Is'ra-el saw that they were in a strait, (for the people were distressed,) then the people did hide themselves in caves, and in thickets, and in rocks, and in high places, and in pits.

7 And *some of* the He'brews went over Jor'dan to the land of Gad and Gil'e-ad. As for Saul, he *was* yet in Gil'gal, and all the people followed him trembling.

8 And he tarried seven days, according to the set time that Sam'u-el *had appointed:* but Sam'u-el came not to Gil'gal; and the people were scattered from him.

9 And Saul said, Bring hither a burnt offering to me, and peace offerings. And he offered the burnt offering.

10 And it came to pass, that as soon as he had made an end of offering the burnt offering, behold, Sam'u-el came; and Saul went out to meet him, that he might salute him.

Conflict with the Philistines

Saul's Kingdom Is Beginning to Crumble

117

11 And Sam'u-el said, What hast thou done? And Saul said, Because I saw that the people were scattered from me, and *that* thou camest not within the days appointed, and *that* the Phi-lis'tines gathered themselves together at Mich'mash;

12 Therefore said I, The Phi-lis'tines will come down now upon me to Gil'gal, and I have not made supplication unto the LORD: I forced myself therefore, and offered a burnt offering.

13 And Sam'u-el said to Saul, Thou hast done foolishly: thou hast not kept the commandment of the LORD thy God, which he commanded thee: for now would the LORD have established thy kingdom upon Is'ra-el for ever.

14 But now thy kingdom shall not continue: the LORD hath sought him a man after his own heart, and the LORD hath commanded him *to be* captain over his people, because thou hast not kept *that* which the LORD commanded thee.

15 And Sam'u-el arose, and gat him up from Gil'gal unto Gib'e-ah of Ben'ja-min. And Saul numbered the people *that were* present with him, about six hundred men.

16 And Saul, and Jon'a-than his son, and the people *that were* present with them, abode in Gib'e-ah of Ben'ja-min: but the Phi-lis'tines encamped in Mich'-mash.

17 And the spoilers came out of the camp of the Phi-lis'tines in three companies: one company turned unto the way *that leadeth to* Oph'rah, unto the land of Shu'al:

18 And another company turned the way *to* Beth-ho'ron: and another company turned *to* the way of the border that looketh to the valley of Ze-bo'im toward the wilderness.

19 Now there was no smith found throughout all the land of Is'ra-el: for the Phi-lis'tines said, Lest the He'brews make *them* swords or spears:

20 But all the Is'ra-el-ites went down to the Phi-lis'tines, to sharpen every man his share, and his coulter, and his ax, and his mattock.

21 Yet they had a file for the mattocks, and for the coulters, and for the forks, and for the axes, and to sharpen the goads.

22 So it came to pass in the day of battle, that there was neither sword nor spear found in the hand of any of the people that *were* with Saul and Jon'a-than: but with Saul and with Jon'a-than his son was there found.

23 And the garrison of the Phi-lis'tines went out to the passage of Mich'mash.

Victory in the Arms Race

14 NOW IT came to pass upon a day, that Jon'a-than the son of Saul said unto the young man that bare his armour, Come, and let us go over to the Phi-lis'tines' garrison, that *is* on the other side. But he told not his father.

2 And Saul tarried in the uttermost part of Gib'e-ah under a pomegranate tree which *is* in Mig'ron: and the people that *were* with him *were* about six hundred men;

3 And A-hi'ah, the son of A-hi'tub, I-cha-bod's brother, the son of Phin'e-has, the son of E'li, the LORD's priest in Shi'loh, wearing an ephod. And the people knew not that Jon'a-than was gone.

4 And between the passages, by which Jon'a-than sought to go over unto the Phi-lis'tines' garrison, *there was* a sharp rock on the one side, and a sharp rock on the other side: and the name of one *was* Bo'zez, and the name of the other Se'neh.

Israel's Unexpected Victory

119

5 The forefront of the one *was* situate northward over against Mich'mash, and the other southward over against Gib'e-ah.

6 And Jon'a-than said to the young man that bare his armour, Come, and let us go over unto the garrison of these uncircumcised: it may be that the Lord will work for us: for *there is* no restraint to the Lord to save by many or by few.

7 And his armourbearer said unto him, Do all that *is* in thine heart: turn thee; behold, I *am* with thee according to thy heart.

8 Then said Jon'a-than, Behold, we will pass over unto *these* men, and we will discover ourselves unto them.

9 If they say thus unto us, Tarry until we come to you; then we will stand still in our place, and will not go up unto them.

10 But if they say thus, Come up unto us; then we will go up: for the Lord hath delivered them into our hand: and this *shall be* a sign unto us.

11 And both of them discovered themselves unto the garrison of the Phi-lis'tines: and the Phi-lis'tines said, Behold, the He'-brews come forth out of the holes where they had hid themselves.

12 And the men of the garrison answered Jon'a-than and his armourbearer, and said, Come up to us, and we will shew you a thing. And Jon'a-than said unto his armourbearer, Come up after me: for the Lord hath delivered them into the hand of Is'ra-el.

13 And Jon'a-than climbed up upon his hands and upon his feet, and his armourbearer after him: and they fell before Jon'a-than; and his armourbearer slew after him.

14 And that first slaughter, which Jon'a-than and his armourbearer made, was about twenty

men, within as it were an half acre of land, *which a yoke of oxen might plow.*

15 And there was trembling in the host, in the field, and among all the people: the garrison, and the spoilers, they also trembled, and the earth quaked: so it was a very great trembling.

16 And the watchmen of Saul in Gib'e-ah of Ben'ja-min looked; and, behold, the multitude melted away, and they went on beating down *one another.*

17 Then said Saul unto the people that *were* with him, Number now, and see who is gone from us. And when they had numbered, behold, Jon'a-than and his armourbearer *were* not *there.*

18 And Saul said unto A-hi'ah, Bring hither the ark of God. For the ark of God was at that time with the children of Is'ra-el.

19 And it came to pass, while Saul talked unto the priest, that the noise that *was* in the host of the Phi-lis'tines went on and increased: and Saul said unto the priest, Withdraw thine hand.

20 And Saul and all the people that *were* with him assembled themselves, and they came to the battle: and, behold, every man's sword was against his fellow, *and there was* a very great discomfiture.

21 Moreover the He'brews *that* were with the Phi-lis'tines before that time, which went up with them into the camp *from the country* round about, even they also *turned* to be with the Is'ra-el-ites that *were* with Saul and Jon'a-than.

22 Likewise all the men of Is'ra-el which had hid themselves in mount E'phra-im, *when* they heard that the Phi-lis'tines fled, even they also followed hard after them in the battle.

23 So the LORD saved Is'ra-el that day: and the battle passed over unto Beth-a'ven.

24 And the men of Is'ra-el were distressed that day: for Saul had adjured the people, saying, Cursed *be* the man that eateth *any* food until evening, that I may be avenged on mine enemies. So none of the people tasted *any* food.

25 And all *they of* the land came to a wood; and there was honey upon the ground.

26 And when the people were come into the wood, behold, the honey dropped; but no man put his hand to his mouth: for the people feared the oath.

27 But Jon'a-than heard not when his father charged the people with the oath: wherefore he put forth the end of the rod that *was* in his hand, and dipped it in an honeycomb, and put his hand to his mouth; and his eyes were enlightened.

28 Then answered one of the people, and said, Thy father straitly charged the people with an oath, saying, Cursed *be* the man that eateth *any* food this day. And the people were faint.

29 Then said Jon'a-than, My father hath troubled the land: see, I pray you, how mine eyes have been enlightened, because I tasted a little of this honey.

30 How much more, if haply the people had eaten freely to day of the spoil of their enemies which they found? for had there not been now a much greater slaughter among the Phi-lis'-tines?

31 And they smote the Phi-lis'tines that day from Mich'-mash to Aij'a-lon: and the people were very faint.

32 And the people flew upon the spoil, and took sheep, and oxen, and calves, and slew *them* on the ground: and the people did eat *them* with the blood.

33 Then they told Saul, saying, Behold, the people sin against the LORD, in that they eat with the

blood. And he said, Ye have transgressed: roll a great stone unto me this day.

34 And Saul said, Disperse yourselves among the people, and say unto them, Bring me hither every man his ox, and every man his sheep, and slay *them* here, and eat; and sin not against the LORD in eating with the blood. And all the people brought every man his ox with him that night, and slew *them* there.

35 And Saul built an altar unto the LORD: the same was the first altar that he built unto the LORD.

36 And Saul said, Let us go down after the Phi-lis'tines by night, and spoil them until the morning light, and let us not leave a man of them. And they said, Do whatsoever seemeth good unto thee. Then said the priest, Let us draw near hither unto God.

37 And Saul asked counsel of God, Shall I go down after the Phi-lis'tines? wilt thou deliver them into the hand of Is'ra-el? But he answered him not that day.

38 And Saul said, Draw ye near hither, all the chief of the people: and know and see wherein this sin hath been this day.

39 For, *as* the LORD liveth, which saveth Is'ra-el, though it be in Jon'a-than my son, he shall surely die. But *there was* not a man among all the people *that* answered him.

40 Then said he unto all Is'ra-el, Be ye on one side, and I and Jon'a-than my son will be on the other side. And the people said unto Saul, Do what seemeth good unto thee.

41 Therefore Saul said unto the LORD God of Is'ra-el, Give a perfect *lot.* And Saul and Jon'a-than were taken: but the people escaped.

42 And Saul said, Cast *lots* between me and Jon'a-than my son. And Jon'a-than was taken.

123

The Mood Changes

A Summary of the King's Business

43 Then Saul said to Jon'a-than, Tell me what thou hast done. And Jon'a-than told him, and said, I did but taste a little honey with the end of the rod that *was* in mine hand, *and,* lo, I must die.

44 And Saul answered, God do so and more also: for thou shalt surely die, Jon'a-than.

45 And the people said unto Saul, Shall Jon'a-than die, who hath wrought this great salvation in Is'ra-el? God forbid: *as* the Lord liveth, there shall not one hair of his head fall to the ground; for he hath wrought with God this day. So the people rescued Jon'a-than, that he died not.

46 Then Saul went up from following the Phi-lis'tines: and the Phi-lis'tines went to their own place.

47 So Saul took the kingdom over Is'ra-el, and fought against all his enemies on every side, against Mo'ab, and against the children of Am'mon, and against E'dom, and against the kings of Zo'bah, and against the Phi-lis'tines: and whithersoever he turned himself, he vexed *them.*

48 And he gathered an host, and smote the Am'a-lek-ites, and delivered Is'ra-el out of the hands of them that spoiled them.

49 Now the sons of Saul were Jon'a-than, and Ish'u-i, and Mel'chi-shu'a: and the names of his two daughters *were these;* the name of the firstborn Me'rab, and the name of the younger Mi'chal:

50 And the name of Saul's wife *was* A-hin'o-am, the daughter of A-him'a-az: and the name of the captain of his host *was* Ab'ner, the son of Ner, Saul's uncle.

51 And Kish *was* the father of Saul; and Ner the father of Ab'-ner *was* the son of A-bi'el.

52 And there was sore war against the Phi-lis'-tines all the days of Saul: and when Saul saw any

strong man, or any valiant man, he took him unto him.

15 SAM'U-EL ALSO said unto Saul, The Lord sent me to anoint thee *to be* king over his people, over Is'ra-el: now therefore hearken thou unto the voice of the words of the Lord.

2 Thus saith the Lord of hosts, I remember *that* which Am'a-lek did to Is'ra-el, how he laid *wait* for him in the way, when he came up from E'gypt.

3 Now go and smite Am'a-lek, and utterly destroy all that they have, and spare them not; but slay both man and woman, infant and suckling, ox and sheep, camel and ass.

4 And Saul gathered the people together, and numbered them in Tel'a-im, two hundred thousand footmen, and ten thousand men of Ju'dah.

5 And Saul came to a city of Am'a-lek, and laid wait in the valley.

6 And Saul said unto the Ken'ites, Go, depart, get you down from among the Am'a-lek-ites, lest I destroy you with them: for ye shewed kindness to all the children of Is'ra-el, when they came up out of E'gypt. So the Ken'ites departed from among the Am'a-lek-ites.

7 And Saul smote the Am'a-lek-ites from Hav'i-lah *until* thou comest to Shur, that *is* over against E'gypt.

8 And he took A'gag the king of the Am'a-lek-ites alive, and utterly destroyed all the people with the edge of the sword.

9 But Saul and the people spared A'gag, and the best of the sheep, and of the oxen, and of the fatlings, and the lambs, and all *that was* good, and

125

would not utterly destroy them: but every thing *that was* vile and refuse, that they destroyed utterly.

10 Then came the word of the LORD unto Sam'u-el, saying,

11 It repenteth me that I have set up Saul *to be* king: for he is turned back from following me, and hath not performed my commandments. And it grieved Sam'u-el; and he cried unto the LORD all night.

12 And when Sam'u-el rose early to meet Saul in the morning, it was told Sam'u-el, saying, Saul came to Car'mel, and, behold, he set him up a place, and is gone about, and passed on, and gone down to Gil'gal.

13 And Sam'u-el came to Saul: and Saul said unto him, Blessed *be* thou of the LORD: I have performed the commandment of the LORD.

14 And Sam'u-el said, What *meaneth* then this bleating of the sheep in mine ears, and the lowing of the oxen which I hear?

15 And Saul said, They have brought them from the Am'a-lek-ites: for the people spared the best of the sheep and of the oxen, to sacrifice unto the LORD thy God; and the rest we have utterly destroyed.

16 Then Sam'u-el said unto Saul, Stay, and I will tell thee what the LORD hath said to me this night. And he said unto him, Say on.

17 And Sam'u-el said, When thou *wast* little in thine own sight, *wast* thou not *made* the head of the tribes of Is'ra-el, and the LORD anointed thee king over Is'ra-el?

18 And the LORD sent thee on a journey, and said, Go and utterly destroy the sinners the Am'a-lek-ites, and fight against them until they be consumed.

19 Wherefore then didst thou not obey the voice of the LORD, but didst fly upon the spoil, and didst evil in the sight of the LORD?

20 And Saul said unto Sam'u-el, Yea, I have obeyed the voice of the LORD, and have gone the way which the LORD sent me, and have brought A'gag the king of Am'a-lek, and have utterly destroyed the Am'a-lek-ites.

21 But the people took of the spoil, sheep and oxen, the chief of the things which should have been utterly destroyed, to sacrifice unto the LORD thy God in Gil'gal.

22 And Sam'u-el said, Hath the LORD *as great* delight in burnt offerings and sacrifices, as in obeying the voice of the LORD? Behold, to obey *is* better than sacrifice, *and* to hearken than the fat of rams.

Obedience Is Better than Sacrifice

23 For rebellion *is as* the sin of witchcraft, and stubbornness *is as* iniquity and idolatry. Because thou hast rejected the word of the LORD, he hath also rejected thee from *being* king.

24 And Saul said unto Sam'u-el, I have sinned: for I have transgressed the commandment of the LORD, and thy words: because I feared the people, and obeyed their voice.

25 Now therefore, I pray thee, pardon my sin, and turn again with me, that I may worship the LORD.

26 And Sam'u-el said unto Saul, I will not return with thee: for thou hast rejected the word of the LORD, and the LORD hath rejected thee from being king over Is'ra-el.

27 And as Sam'u-el turned about to go away, he laid hold upon the skirt of his mantle, and it rent.

28 And Sam'u-el said unto him, The LORD hath rent the kingdom of Is'ra-el from thee this day, and

hath given it to a neighbour of thine, *that is* better than thou.

29 And also the Strength of Is'ra-el will not lie nor repent: for he *is* not a man, that he should repent.

30 Then he said, I have sinned: *yet* honour me now, I pray thee, before the elders of my people, and before Is'ra-el, and turn again with me, that I may worship the LORD thy God.

31 So Sam'u-el turned again after Saul; and Saul worshipped the LORD.

32 Then said Sam'u-el, Bring ye hither to me A'gag the king of the Am'a-lek-ites. And A'gag came unto him delicately. And A'gag said, Surely the bitterness of death is past.

33 And Sam'u-el said, As thy sword hath made women childless, so shall thy mother be childless among women. And Sam'u-el hewed A'gag in pieces before the LORD in Gil'gal.

34 Then Sam'u-el went to Ra'mah; and Saul went up to his house to Gib'e-ah of Saul.

35 And Sam'u-el came no more to see Saul until the day of his death: nevertheless Sam'u-el mourned for Saul: and the LORD repented that he had made Saul king over Is'ra-el.

Dedicated Devotion

16 AND THE LORD said unto Sam'u-el, How long wilt thou mourn for Saul, seeing I have rejected him from reigning over Is'ra-el? fill thine horn with oil, and go, I will send thee to Jes'se the Beth'-le-hem-ite: for I have provided me a king among his sons.

Finding a New King

2 And Sam'u-el said, How can I go? if Saul hear *it,* he will kill me. And the LORD said, Take an heifer

with thee, and say, I am come to sacrifice to the Lord.

3 And call Jes'se to the sacrifice, and I will shew thee what thou shalt do: and thou shalt anoint unto me *him* whom I name unto thee.

4 And Sam'u-el did that which the Lord spake, and came to Beth'-le-hem. And the elders of the town trembled at his coming, and said, Comest thou peaceably?

5 And he said, Peaceably: I am come to sacrifice unto the Lord: sanctify yourselves, and come with me to the sacrifice. And he sanctified Jes'se and his sons, and called them to the sacrifice.

6 And it came to pass, when they were come, that he looked on E-li'ab, and said, Surely the Lord's anointed *is* before him.

7 But the Lord said unto Sam'u-el, Look not on his countenance, or on the height of his stature; because I have refused him: for *the Lord seeth* not as man seeth; for man looketh on the outward appearance, but the Lord looketh on the heart.

8 Then Jes'se called A-bin'a-dab, and made him pass before Sam'u-el. And he said, Neither hath the Lord chosen this.

9 Then Jes'se made Sham'-mah to pass by. And he said, Neither hath the Lord chosen this.

10 Again, Jes'se made seven of his sons to pass before Sam'u-el. And Sam'u-el said unto Jes'se, The Lord hath not chosen these.

11 And Sam'u-el said unto Jes'se, Are here all *thy* children? And he said, There remaineth yet the youngest, and, behold, he keepeth the sheep. And Sam'u-el said unto Jes'se, Send and fetch him: for we will not sit down till he come hither.

12 And he sent, and brought him in. Now he *was* ruddy, *and* withal of a beautiful countenance, and goodly to look to. And the LORD said, Arise, anoint him: for this *is* he.

13 Then Sam'u-el took the horn of oil, and anointed him in the midst of his brethren: and the Spirit of the LORD came upon Da'vid from that day forward. So Sam'u-el rose up, and went to Ra'mah.

14 But the Spirit of the LORD departed from Saul, and an evil spirit from the LORD troubled him.

15 And Saul's servants said unto him, Behold now, an evil spirit from God troubleth thee.

16 Let our lord now command thy servants, *which are* before thee, to seek out a man, *who is* a cunning player on an harp: and it shall come to pass, when the evil spirit from God is upon thee, that he shall play with his hand, and thou shalt be well.

17 And Saul said unto his servants, Provide me now a man that can play well, and bring *him* to me.

18 Then answered one of the servants, and said, Behold, I have seen a son of Jes'se the Beth'-le-hem-ite, *that is* cunning in playing, and a mighty valiant man, and a man of war, and prudent in matters, and a comely person, and the LORD *is* with him.

Saul and David Meet

19 Wherefore Saul sent messengers unto Jes'se, and said, Send me Da'vid thy son, which *is* with the sheep.

20 And Jes'se took an ass *laden* with bread, and a bottle of wine, and a kid, and sent *them* by Da'vid his son unto Saul.

21 And Da'vid came to Saul, and stood before him: and he loved him greatly; and he became his armourbearer.

22 And Saul sent to Jes'se, saying, Let Da'vid, I pray thee, stand before me; for he hath found favour in my sight.

23 And it came to pass, when the *evil* spirit from God was upon Saul, that Da'vid took an harp, and played with his hand: so Saul was refreshed, and was well, and the evil spirit departed from him.

17 NOW THE Phi-lis'tines gathered together their armies to battle, and were gathered together at Sho'choh, which *belongeth* to Ju'dah, and pitched between Sho'choh and A-ze'kah, in E'phes-dam'mim.

Snatching Victory From the Jaws of Defeat

2 And Saul and the men of Is'ra-el were gathered together, and pitched by the valley of E'lah, and set the battle in array against the Phi-lis'tines.

3 And the Phi-lis'tines stood on a mountain on the one side, and Is'ra-el stood on a mountain on the other side: and *there was* a valley between them.

4 And there went out a champion out of the camp of the Phi-lis'tines, named Go-li'ath, of Gath, whose height *was* six cubits and a span.

5 And *he had* an helmet of brass upon his head, and he *was* armed with a coat of mail; and the weight of the coat *was* five thousand shekels of brass.

6 And *he had* greaves of brass upon his legs, and a target of brass between his shoulders.

7 And the staff of his spear *was* like a weaver's beam; and his spear's head *weighed* six hundred shekels of iron: and one bearing a shield went before him.

8 And he stood and cried unto the armies of Is'ra-el, and said unto them, Why are ye come out

to set *your* battle in array? *am* not I a Phi-lis'tine, and ye servants to Saul? choose you a man for you, and let him come down to me.

9 If he be able to fight with me, and to kill me, then will we be your servants: but if I prevail against him, and kill him, then shall ye be our servants, and serve us.

10 And the Phi-lis'tine said, I defy the armies of Is'ra-el this day; give me a man, that we may fight together.

11 When Saul and all Is'ra-el heard those words of the Phi-lis'tine, they were dismayed, and greatly afraid.

12 Now Da'vid *was* the son of that Eph'rath-ite of Beth'-le-hem-ju'dah, whose name *was* Jes'se; and he had eight sons: and the man went among men *for* an old man in the days of Saul.

13 And the three eldest sons of Jes'se went *and* followed Saul to the battle: and the names of his three sons that went to the battle *were* E-li'ab the firstborn, and next unto him A-bin'a-dab, and the third Sham'mah.

14 And Da'vid *was* the youngest: and the three eldest followed Saul.

15 But Da'vid went and returned from Saul to feed his father's sheep at Beth'-le-hem.

16 And the Phi-lis'tine drew near morning and evening, and presented himself forty days.

17 And Jes'se said unto Da'-vid his son, Take now for thy brethren an ephah of this parched *corn,* and these ten loaves, and run to the camp to thy brethren;

18 And carry these ten cheeses unto the captain of *their* thousand, and look how thy brethren fare, and take their pledge.

19 Now Saul, and they, and all the men of Is'ra-el, *were* in the valley of E'lah, fighting with the Phi-lis'tines.

20 And Da'vid rose up early in the morning, and left the sheep with a keeper, and took, and went, as Jes'se had commanded him; and he came to the trench, as the host was going forth to the fight, and shouted for the battle.

21 For Is'ra-el and the Phi-lis'tines had put the battle in array, army against army.

22 And Da'vid left his carriage in the hand of the keeper of the carriage, and ran into the army, and came and saluted his brethren.

23 And as he talked with them, behold, there came up the champion, the Phi-lis'tine of Gath, Go-li'ath by name, out of the armies of the Phi-lis'tines, and spake according to the same words: and Da'vid heard *them.*

24 And all the men of Is'ra-el, when they saw the man, fled from him, and were sore afraid.

25 And the men of Is'ra-el said, Have ye seen this man that is come up? surely to defy Is'ra-el is he come up: and it shall be, *that* the man who killeth him, the king will enrich him with great riches, and will give him his daughter, and make his father's house free in Is'ra-el.

26 And Da'vid spake to the men that stood by him, saying, What shall be done to the man that killeth this Phi-lis'tine, and taketh away the reproach from Is'ra-el? for who *is* this uncircumcised Phi-lis'tine, that he should defy the armies of the living God?

27 And the people answered him after this manner, saying, So shall it be done to the man that killeth him.

133

28 And E-li′ab his eldest brother heard when he spake unto the men; and E-li′ab's anger was kindled against Da′vid, and he said, Why camest thou down hither? and with whom hast thou left those few sheep in the wilderness? I know thy pride, and the naughtiness of thine heart; for thou art come down that thou mightest see the battle.

29 And Da′vid said, What have I now done? *Is there* not a cause?

30 And he turned from him toward another, and spake after the same manner: and the people answered him again after the former manner.

31 And when the words were heard which Da′vid spake, they rehearsed *them* before Saul: and he sent for him.

32 And Da′vid said to Saul, Let no man's heart fail because of him; thy servant will go and fight with this Phi-lis′tine.

33 And Saul said to Da′vid, Thou art not able to go against this Phi-lis′tine to fight with him: for thou *art but* a youth, and he a man of war from his youth.

34 And Da′vid said unto Saul, Thy servant kept his father's sheep, and there came a lion, and a bear, and took a lamb out of the flock:

35 And I went out after him, and smote him, and delivered *it* out of his mouth: and when he arose against me, I caught *him* by his beard, and smote him, and slew him.

36 Thy servant slew both the lion and the bear: and this uncircumcised Phi-lis′tine shall be as one of them, seeing he hath defied the armies of the living God.

37 Da′vid said moreover, The LORD that delivered me out of the paw of the lion, and out of the

paw of the bear, he will deliver me out of the hand of this Phi-lis'tine. And Saul said unto Da'vid, Go, and the LORD be with thee.

38 And Saul armed Da'vid with his armour, and he put an helmet of brass upon his head; also he armed him with a coat of mail.

39 And Da'vid girded his sword upon his armour, and he assayed to go; for he had not proved *it.* And Da'vid said unto Saul, I cannot go with these; for I have not proved *them.* And Da'vid put them off him.

40 And he took his staff in his hand, and chose him five smooth stones out of the brook, and put them in a shepherd's bag which he had, even in a scrip; and his sling *was* in his hand: and he drew near to the Phi-lis'tine.

41 And the Phi-lis'tine came on and drew near unto Da'vid; and the man that bare the shield *went* before him.

42 And when the Phi-lis'tine looked about, and saw Da'vid, he disdained him: for he was *but* a youth, and ruddy, and of a fair countenance.

43 And the Phi-lis'tine said unto Da'vid, *Am* I a dog, that thou comest to me with staves? And the Phi-lis'tine cursed Da'vid by his gods.

44 And the Phi-lis'tine said to Da'vid, Come to me, and I will give thy flesh unto the fowls of the air, and to the beasts of the field.

45 Then said Da'vid to the Phi-lis'tine, Thou comest to me with a sword, and with a spear, and with a shield: but I come to thee in the name of the LORD of hosts, the God of the armies of Is'ra-el, whom thou hast defied.

46 This day will the LORD deliver thee into mine hand; and I will smite thee, and take thine head

from thee; and I will give the carcases of the host of the Phi-lis'tines this day unto the fowls of the air, and to the wild beasts of the earth; that all the earth may know that there is a God in Is'ra-el.

47 And all this assembly shall know that the LORD saveth not with sword and spear: for the battle *is* the LORD's, and he will give you into our hands.

48 And it came to pass, when the Phi-lis'tine arose, and came and drew nigh to meet Da'vid, that Da'vid hasted, and ran toward the army to meet the Phi-lis'tine.

49 And Da'vid put his hand in his bag, and took thence a stone, and slang *it,* and smote the Phi-lis'tine in his forehead, that the stone sunk into his forehead; and he fell upon his face to the earth.

50 So Da'vid prevailed over the Phi-lis'tine with a sling and with a stone, and smote the Phi-lis'tine, and slew him; but *there was* no sword in the hand of Da'vid.

51 Therefore Da'vid ran, and stood upon the Phi-lis'tine, and took his sword, and drew it out of the sheath thereof, and slew him, and cut off his head therewith. And when the Phi-lis'tines saw their champion was dead, they fled.

52 And the men of Is'ra-el and of Ju'dah arose, and shouted, and pursued the Phi-lis'tines, until thou come to the valley, and to the gates of Ek'ron. And the wounded of the Phi-lis'tines fell down by the way to Sha-a-ra'im, even unto Gath, and unto Ek'ron.

53 And the children of Is'ra-el returned from chasing after the Phi-lis'tines, and they spoiled their tents.

54 And Da'vid took the head of the Phi-lis'tine, and brought it to Je-ru'sa-lem; but he put his armour in his tent.

55 And when Saul saw Da'vid go forth against the Phi-lis'tine, he said unto Ab'ner, the captain of the host, Ab'ner, whose son *is* this youth? And Ab'ner said, *As* thy soul liveth, O king, I cannot tell.

56 And the king said, Enquire thou whose son the stripling *is.*

57 And as Da'vid returned from the slaughter of the Phi-lis'tine, Ab'ner took him, and brought him before Saul with the head of the Phi-lis'tine in his hand.

58 And Saul said to him, Whose son *art* thou, *thou* young man? And Da'vid answered, *I am* the son of thy servant Jes'se the Beth'-le-hem-ite.

18 AND IT came to pass, when he had made an end of speaking unto Saul, that the soul of Jon'a-than was knit with the soul of Da'vid, and Jon'a-than loved him as his own soul.

2 And Saul took him that day, and would let him go no more home to his father's house.

3 Then Jon'a-than and Da'vid made a covenant, because he loved him as his own soul.

4 And Jon'a-than stripped himself of the robe that *was* upon him, and gave it to Da'vid, and his garments, even to his sword, and to his bow, and to his girdle.

5 And Da'vid went out whithersoever Saul sent him, *and* behaved himself wisely: and Saul set him over the men of war, and he was accepted in the

Jealousy's Destructiveness

The Relationship Between David and Jonathan

sight of all the people, and also in the sight of Saul's servants.

6 And it came to pass as they came, when Da'vid was returned from the slaughter of the Phi-lis'tine, that the women came out of all cities of Is'ra-el, singing and dancing, to meet king Saul, with tabrets, with joy, and with instruments of musick.

7 And the women answered *one another* as they played, and said, Saul hath slain his thousands, and Da'vid his ten thousands.

Jealousy's Burning Passion

8 And Saul was very wroth, and the saying displeased him; and he said, They have ascribed unto Da'vid ten thousands, and to me they have ascribed *but* thousands: and *what* can he have more but the kingdom?

9 And Saul eyed Da'vid from that day and forward.

Attempted Murder

10 And it came to pass on the morrow, that the evil spirit from God came upon Saul, and he prophesied in the midst of the house: and Da'vid played with his hand, as at other times: and *there was* a javelin in Saul's hand.

11 And Saul cast the javelin; for he said, I will smite Da'vid even to the wall *with it.* And Da'vid avoided out of his presence twice.

12 And Saul was afraid of Da'vid, because the LORD was with him, and was departed from Saul.

13 Therefore Saul removed him from him, and made him his captain over a thousand; and he went out and came in before the people.

14 And Da'vid behaved himself wisely in all his ways; and the LORD *was* with him.

15 Wherefore when Saul saw that he behaved himself very wisely, he was afraid of him.

16 But all Is'ra-el and Ju'dah loved Da'vid, because he went out and came in before them.

17 And Saul said to Da'vid, Behold my elder daughter Me'rab, her will I give thee to wife: only be thou valiant for me, and fight the LORD's battles. For Saul said, Let not mine hand be upon him, but let the hand of the Phi-lis'tines be upon him.

18 And Da'vid said unto Saul, Who *am* I? and what *is* my life, *or* my father's family in Is'ra-el, that I should be son in law to the king?

19 But it came to pass at the time when Me'rab Saul's daughter should have been given to Da'vid, that she was given unto A'dri-el the Me-hol'ath-ite to wife.

20 And Mi'chal Saul's daughter loved Da'vid: and they told Saul, and the thing pleased him.

21 And Saul said, I will give him her, that she may be a snare to him, and that the hand of the Phi-lis'tines may be against him. Wherefore Saul said to Da'vid, Thou shalt this day be my son in law in *the one of* the twain.

22 And Saul commanded his servants, *saying,* Commune with Da'vid secretly, and say, Behold, the king hath delight in thee, and all his servants love thee: now therefore be the king's son in law.

23 And Saul's servants spake those words in the ears of Da'vid. And Da'vid said, Seemeth it to you *a* light *thing* to be a king's son in law, seeing that I *am* a poor man, and lightly esteemed?

24 And the servants of Saul told him, saying, On this manner spake Da'vid.

25 And Saul said, Thus shall ye say to Da'vid, The king desireth not any dowry, but an hundred foreskins of the Phi-lis'tines, to be avenged of the king's enemies. But Saul thought to make Da'vid fall by the hand of the Phi-lis'tines.

26 And when his servants told Da'vid these words, it pleased Da'vid well to be the king's son in law: and the days were not expired.

27 Wherefore Da'vid arose and went, he and his men, and slew of the Phi-lis'tines two hundred men; and Da'vid brought their foreskins, and they gave them in full tale to the king, that he might be the king's son in law. And Saul gave him Mi'chal his daughter to wife.

28 And Saul saw and knew that the LORD *was* with Da'vid, and *that* Mi'chal Saul's daughter loved him.

Saul's Jealousy Intensified

29 And Saul was yet the more afraid of Da'vid; and Saul became Da'vid's enemy continually.

30 Then the princes of the Phi-lis'tines went forth: and it came to pass, after they went forth, *that* Da'vid behaved himself more wisely than all the servants of Saul; so that his name was much set by.

Love and Hate Contrasted

19 AND SAUL spake to Jon'a-than his son, and to all his servants, that they should kill Da'vid.

Love Tries to Find a Way

2 But Jon'a-than Saul's son delighted much in Da'vid: and Jon'a-than told Da'vid, saying, Saul my father seeketh to kill thee: now therefore, I pray thee, take heed to thyself until the morning, and abide in a secret *place*, and hide thyself:

3 And I will go out and stand beside my father in the field where thou *art*, and I will commune with my father of thee; and what I see, that I will tell thee.

4 And Jon'a-than spake good of Da'vid unto Saul his father, and said unto him, Let not the king sin against his servant, against Da'vid; because he

hath not sinned against thee, and because his works *have been* to thee-ward very good:

5 For he did put his life in his hand, and slew the Phi-lis'tine, and the Lord wrought a great salvation for all Is'ra-el: thou sawest *it,* and didst rejoice: wherefore then wilt thou sin against innocent blood, to slay Da'vid without a cause?

6 And Saul hearkened unto the voice of Jon'a-than: and Saul sware, *As* the Lord liveth, he shall not be slain.

7 And Jon'a-than called Da'vid, and Jon'a-than shewed him all those things. And Jon'a-than brought Da'vid to Saul, and he was in his presence, as in times past.

8 And there was war again: and Da'vid went out, and fought with the Phi-lis'tines, and slew them with a great slaughter; and they fled from him.

9 And the evil spirit from the Lord was upon Saul, as he sat in his house with his javelin in his hand: and Da'vid played with *his* hand.

10 And Saul sought to smite Da'vid even to the wall with the javelin; but he slipped away out of Saul's presence, and he smote the javelin into the wall: and Da'vid fled, and escaped that night.

11 Saul also sent messengers unto Da'vid's house, to watch him, and to slay him in the morning: and Mi'chal Da'vid's wife told him, saying, If thou save not thy life to night, to morrow thou shalt be slain.

12 So Mi'chal let Da'vid down through a window: and he went, and fled, and escaped.

13 And Mi'chal took an image, and laid *it* in the bed, and put a pillow of goats' *hair* for his bolster, and covered *it* with a cloth.

Love Makes a Choice

141

14 And when Saul sent messengers to take Da'vid, she said, He *is* sick.

15 And Saul sent the messengers *again* to see Da'vid, saying, Bring him up to me in the bed, that I may slay him.

16 And when the messengers were come in, behold, *there was* an image in the bed, with a pillow of goats' *hair* for his bolster.

17 And Saul said unto Mi'chal, Why hast thou deceived me so, and sent away mine enemy, that he is escaped? And Mi'chal answered Saul, He said unto me, Let me go; why should I kill thee?

18 So Da'vid fled, and escaped, and came to Sam'u-el to Ra'mah, and told him all that Saul had done to him. And he and Sam'u-el went and dwelt in Na'ioth.

19 And it was told Saul, saying, Behold, Da'vid *is* at Na'ioth in Ra'mah.

20 And Saul sent messengers to take Da'vid: and when they saw the company of the prophets prophesying, and Sam'u-el standing *as* appointed over them, the Spirit of God was upon the messengers of Saul, and they also prophesied.

21 And when it was told Saul, he sent other messengers, and they prophesied likewise. And Saul sent messengers again the third time, and they prophesied also.

22 Then went he also to Ra'mah, and came to a great well that *is* in Se'chu: and he asked and said, Where *are* Sam'u-el and Da'vid? And *one* said, Behold, *they be* at Na'ioth in Ra'mah.

23 And he went thither to Na'ioth in Ra'mah: and the Spirit of God was upon him also, and he went on, and prophesied, until he came to Na'ioth in Ra'mah.

24 And he stripped off his clothes also, and prophesied before Sam'u-el in like manner, and lay down naked all that day and all that night. Wherefore they say, *Is* Saul also among the prophets?

20 AND DA'VID fled from Na'ioth in Ra'mah, and came and said before Jon'a-than, What have I done? what *is* mine iniquity? and what *is* my sin before thy father, that he seeketh my life?

2 And he said unto him, God forbid; thou shalt not die: behold, my father will do nothing either great or small, but that he will shew it me: and why should my father hide this thing from me? it *is* not *so.*

3 And Da'vid sware moreover, and said, Thy father certainly knoweth that I have found grace in thine eyes; and he saith, Let not Jon'a-than know this, lest he be grieved: but truly *as* the LORD liveth, and *as* thy soul liveth, *there is* but a step between me and death.

4 Then said Jon'a-than unto Da'vid, Whatsoever thy soul desireth, I will even do *it* for thee.

5 And Da'vid said unto Jon'a-than, Behold, to morrow *is* the new moon, and I should not fail to sit with the king at meat: but let me go, that I may hide myself in the field unto the third *day* at even.

6 If thy father at all miss me, then say, Da'vid earnestly asked *leave* of me that he might run to Beth'-le-hem his city: for *there is* a yearly sacrifice there for all the family.

7 If he say thus, *It is* well; thy servant shall have peace: but if he be very wroth, *then* be sure that evil is determined by him.

143

8 Therefore thou shalt deal kindly with thy servant; for thou hast brought thy servant into a covenant of the LORD with thee: notwithstanding, if there be in me iniquity, slay me thyself; for why shouldest thou bring me to thy father?

9 And Jon'a-than said, Far be it from thee: for if I knew certainly that evil were determined by my father to come upon thee, then would not I tell it thee?

10 Then said Da'vid to Jon'a-than, Who shall tell me? or what *if* thy father answer thee roughly?

11 And Jon'a-than said unto Da'vid, Come, and let us go out into the field. And they went out both of them into the field.

12 And Jon'a-than said unto Da'vid, O LORD God of Is'ra-el, when I have sounded my father about to morrow any time, *or* the third *day,* and, behold, *if there be* good toward Da'vid, and I then send not unto thee, and shew it thee;

13 The LORD do so and much more to Jon'a-than: but if it please my father *to do* thee evil, then I will shew it thee, and send thee away, that thou mayest go in peace: and the LORD be with thee, as he hath been with my father.

14 And thou shalt not only while yet I live shew me the kindness of the LORD, that I die not:

15 But *also* thou shalt not cut off thy kindness from my house for ever: no, not when the LORD hath cut off the enemies of Da'vid every one from the face of the earth.

16 So Jon'a-than made *a covenant* with the house of Da'vid, *saying,* Let the LORD even require *it* at the hand of Da'vid's enemies.

17 And Jon'a-than caused Da'vid to swear again, because he loved him: for he loved him as he loved his own soul.

144

18 Then Jon'a-than said to Da'vid, To morrow *is* the new moon: and thou shalt be missed, because thy seat will be empty.

19 And *when* thou hast stayed three days, *then* thou shalt go down quickly, and come to the place where thou didst hide thyself when the business was *in hand,* and shalt remain by the stone E'zel.

20 And I will shoot three arrows on the side *thereof,* as though I shot at a mark.

21 And, behold, I will send a lad, *saying,* Go, find out the arrows. If I expressly say unto the lad, Behold, the arrows *are* on this side of thee, take them; then come thou: for *there is* peace to thee, and no hurt; *as* the LORD liveth.

22 But if I say thus unto the young man, Behold, the arrows *are* beyond thee; go thy way: for the LORD hath sent thee away.

23 And *as touching* the matter which thou and I have spoken of, behold, the LORD *be* between thee and me for ever.

24 So Da'vid hid himself in the field: and when the new moon was come, the king sat him down to eat meat.

25 And the king sat upon his seat, as at other times, *even* upon a seat by the wall: and Jon'a-than arose, and Ab'ner sat by Saul's side, and Da'vid's place was empty.

26 Nevertheless Saul spake not any thing that day: for he thought, Something hath befallen him, he *is* not clean; surely he *is* not clean.

27 And it came to pass on the morrow, *which was* the second *day* of the month, that Da'vid's place was empty: and Saul said unto Jon'a-than his son, Wherefore cometh not the son of Jes'se to meat, neither yesterday, nor to day?

28 And Jon'a-than answered Saul, Da'vid earnestly asked *leave* of me *to go* to Beth'-le-hem:

29 And he said, Let me go, I pray thee; for our family hath a sacrifice in the city; and my brother, he hath commanded me *to be there:* and now, if I have found favour in thine eyes, let me get away, I pray thee, and see my brethren. Therefore he cometh not unto the king's table.

30 Then Saul's anger was kindled against Jon'a-than, and he said unto him, Thou son of the perverse rebellious *woman,* do not I know that thou hast chosen the son of Jes'se to thine own confusion, and unto the confusion of thy mother's nakedness?

31 For as long as the son of Jes'se liveth upon the ground, thou shalt not be established, nor thy kingdom. Wherefore now send and fetch him unto me, for he shall surely die.

32 And Jon'a-than answered Saul his father, and said unto him, Wherefore shall he be slain? what hath he done?

33 And Saul cast a javelin at him to smite him: whereby Jon'a-than knew that it was determined of his father to slay Da'vid.

34 So Jon'a-than arose from the table in fierce anger, and did eat no meat the second day of the month: for he was grieved for Da'vid, because his father had done him shame.

35 And it came to pass in the morning, that Jon'a-than went out into the field at the time appointed with Da'vid, and a little lad with him.

36 And he said unto his lad, Run, find out now the arrows which I shoot. *And* as the lad ran, he shot an arrow beyond him.

37 And when the lad was come to the place of the arrow which Jon'a-than had shot, Jon'a-than

cried after the lad, and said, *Is* not the arrow beyond thee?

38 And Jon'a-than cried after the lad, Make speed, haste, stay not. And Jon'a-than's lad gathered up the arrows, and came to his master.

39 But the lad knew not any thing: only Jon'a-than and Da'vid knew the matter.

40 And Jon'a-than gave his artillery unto his lad, and said unto him, Go, carry *them* to the city.

41 *And* as soon as the lad was gone, Da'vid arose out of *a place* toward the south, and fell on his face to the ground, and bowed himself three times: and they kissed one another, and wept one with another, until Da'vid exceeded.

42 And Jon'a-than said to Da'vid, Go in peace, forasmuch as we have sworn both of us in the name of the LORD, saying, The LORD be between me and thee, and between my seed and thy seed for ever. And he arose and departed: and Jon'a-than went into the city.

When Love Lets Go

LESSON 6

1 SAMUEL 21:1–31:13
Faith Which Leads to Patience

Patiently Waiting in Danger

_____

_____

David's Flight to Nob

_____

_____

_____

_____

_____

_____

_____

_____

_____

_____

_____

21 THEN CAME Da'vid to Nob to A-him'e-lech the priest: and A-him'e-lech was afraid at the meeting of Da'vid, and said unto him, Why *art* thou alone, and no man with thee?

2 And Da'vid said unto A-him'e-lech the priest, The king hath commanded me a business, and hath said unto me, Let no man know any thing of the business whereabout I send thee, and what I have commanded thee: and I have appointed *my* servants to such and such a place.

3 Now therefore what is under thine hand? give *me* five *loaves of* bread in mine hand, or what there is present.

4 And the priest answered Da'vid, and said, *There is* no common bread under mine hand, but there is hallowed bread; if the young men have kept themselves at least from women.

5 And Da'vid answered the priest, and said unto him, Of a truth women *have been* kept from us about these three days, since I came out, and the vessels of the young men are holy, and *the bread is* in a manner common, yea, though it were sanctified this day in the vessel.

6 So the priest gave him hallowed *bread:* for there was no bread there but the shewbread, that was

taken from before the LORD, to put hot bread in the day when it was taken away.

7 Now a certain man of the servants of Saul *was* there that day, detained before the LORD; and his name *was* Do'eg, an E'dom-ite, the chiefest of the herdmen that *belonged* to Saul.

8 And Da'vid said unto A-him'e-lech, And is there not here under thine hand spear or sword? for I have neither brought my sword nor my weapons with me, because the king's business required haste.

9 And the priest said, The sword of Go-li'ath the Phi-lis'-tine, whom thou slewest in the valley of E'lah, behold, it *is here* wrapped in a cloth behind the ephod: if thou wilt take that, take *it:* for *there is* no other save that here. And Da'vid said, *There is* none like that; give it me.

10 And Da'vid arose, and fled that day for fear of Saul, and went to A'chish the king of Gath.

David's Flight to a Foreign Refuge

11 And the servants of A'chish said unto him, *Is* not this Da'vid the king of the land? did they not sing one to another of him in dances, saying, Saul hath slain his thousands, and Da'vid his ten thousands?

12 And Da'vid laid up these words in his heart, and was sore afraid of A'chish the king of Gath.

13 And he changed his behaviour before them, and feigned himself mad in their hands, and scrabbled on the doors of the gate, and let his spittle fall down upon his beard.

14 Then said A'chish unto his servants, Lo, ye see the man is mad: wherefore *then* have ye brought him to me?

15 Have I need of mad men, that ye have brought this *fellow* to play the mad man in my presence? shall this *fellow* come into my house?

On to the Southern Wilderness

22 DA'VID THEREFORE departed thence, and escaped to the cave A-dul'lam: and when his brethren and all his father's house heard *it,* they went down thither to him.

2 And every one *that was* in distress, and every one that *was* in debt, and every one *that was* discontented, gathered themselves unto him; and he became a captain over them: and there were with him about four hundred men.

3 And Da'vid went thence to Miz'peh of Mo'ab: and he said unto the king of Mo'ab, Let my father and my mother, I pray thee, come forth, *and be* with you, till I know what God will do for me.

4 And he brought them before the king of Mo'ab: and they dwelt with him all the while that Da'vid was in the hold.

5 And the prophet Gad said unto Da'vid, Abide not in the hold; depart, and get thee into the land of Ju'dah. Then Da'vid departed, and came into the forest of Ha'reth.

6 When Saul heard that Da'vid was discovered, and the men that *were* with him, (now Saul abode in Gib'e-ah under a tree in Ra'mah, having his spear in his hand, and all his servants *were* standing about him;)

7 Then Saul said unto his servants that stood about him, Hear now, ye Ben'ja-mites; will the son of Jes'se give every one of you fields and vineyards, *and* make you all captains of thousands, and captains of hundreds;

8 That all of you have conspired against me, and *there is* none that sheweth me that my son hath made a league with the son of Jes'se, and *there is* none of you that is sorry for me, or sheweth unto me that my son hath stirred up my servant against me, to lie in wait, as at this day?

9 Then answered Do'eg the E'dom-ite, which was set over the servants of Saul, and said, I saw the son of Jes'se coming to Nob, to A-him'e-lech the son of A-hi'tub.

10 And he enquired of the LORD for him, and gave him victuals, and gave him the sword of Go-li'ath the Phi-lis'tine.

11 Then the king sent to call A-him'e-lech the priest, the son of A-hi'tub, and all his father's house, the priests that *were* in Nob: and they came all of them to the king.

12 And Saul said, Hear now, thou son of A-hi'tub. And he answered, Here I *am,* my lord.

13 And Saul said unto him, Why have ye conspired against me, thou and the son of Jes'se, in that thou hast given him bread, and a sword, and hast enquired of God for him, that he should rise against me, to lie in wait, as at this day?

14 Then A-him'e-lech answered the king, and said, And who *is so* faithful among all thy servants as Da'vid, which is the king's son in law, and goeth at thy bidding, and is honourable in thine house?

15 Did I then begin to enquire of God for him? be it far from me: let not the king impute *any* thing unto his servant, *nor* to all the house of my father: for thy servant knew nothing of all this, less or more.

16 And the king said, Thou shalt surely die, A-him'e-lech, thou, and all thy father's house.

Betrayal and Slaughter

17 And the king said unto the footmen that stood about him, Turn, and slay the priests of the Lord; because their hand also *is* with Da'vid, and because they knew when he fled, and did not shew it to me. But the servants of the king would not put forth their hand to fall upon the priests of the Lord.

18 And the king said to Do'eg, Turn thou, and fall upon the priests. And Do'eg the E'dom-ite turned, and he fell upon the priests, and slew on that day fourscore and five persons that did wear a linen ephod.

19 And Nob, the city of the priests, smote he with the edge of the sword, both men and women, children and sucklings, and oxen, and asses, and sheep, with the edge of the sword.

20 And one of the sons of A-him'e-lech the son of A-hi'tub, named A-bi'a-thar, escaped, and fled after Da'vid.

21 And A-bi'a-thar shewed Da'vid that Saul had slain the Lord's priests.

22 And Da'vid said unto A-bi'a-thar, I knew *it* that day, when Do'eg the E'dom-ite *was* there, that he would surely tell Saul: I have occasioned *the death* of all the persons of thy father's house.

23 Abide thou with me, fear not: for he that seeketh my life seeketh thy life: but with me thou *shalt be* in safeguard.

Mercy as a Way of Life

An Interlude for Mercy

23 THEN THEY told Da'vid, saying, Behold, the Phi-lis'tines fight against Kei'lah, and they rob the threshingfloors.

2 Therefore Da'vid enquired of the Lord, saying, Shall I go and smite these Phi-lis'tines? And the Lord said unto Da'vid, Go, and smite the Phi-lis'-tines, and save Kei'lah.

3 And Da'vid's men said unto him, Behold, we be afraid here in Ju'dah: how much more then if we come to Kei'lah against the armies of the Phi-lis'-tines?

4 Then Da'vid enquired of the LORD yet again. And the LORD answered him and said, Arise, go down to Kei'lah; for I will deliver the Phi-lis'tines into thine hand.

5 So Da'vid and his men went to Kei'lah, and fought with the Phi-lis'tines, and brought away their cattle, and smote them with a great slaughter. So Da'vid saved the inhabitants of Kei'lah.

6 And it came to pass, when A-bi'a-thar the son of A-him'e-lech fled to Da'vid to Kei'lah, *that* he came down *with* an ephod in his hand.

7 And it was told Saul that Da'vid was come to Kei'lah. And Saul said, God hath delivered him into mine hand; for he is shut in, by entering into a town that hath gates and bars.

8 And Saul called all the people together to war, to go down to Kei'lah, to besiege Da'vid and his men.

9 And Da'vid knew that Saul secretly practised mischief against him; and he said to A-bi'a-thar the priest, Bring hither the ephod.

10 Then said Da'vid, O LORD God of Is'ra-el, thy servant hath certainly heard that Saul seeketh to come to Kei'lah, to destroy the city for my sake.

11 Will the men of Kei'lah deliver me up into his hand? will Saul come down, as thy servant hath heard? O LORD God of Is'ra-el, I beseech thee, tell thy servant. And the LORD said, He will come down.

12 Then said Da'vid, Will the men of Kei'lah deliver me and my men into the hand of Saul? And the LORD said, They will deliver *thee* up.

On the Run Again

153

13 Then Da'vid and his men, *which were* about six hundred, arose and departed out of Kei'lah, and went whithersoever they could go. And it was told Saul that Da'vid was escaped from Kei'lah; and he forbare to go forth.

14 And Da'vid abode in the wilderness in strong holds, and remained in a mountain in the wilderness of Ziph. And Saul sought him every day, but God delivered him not into his hand.

15 And Da'vid saw that Saul was come out to seek his life: and Da'vid *was* in the wilderness of Ziph in a wood.

16 And Jon'a-than Saul's son arose, and went to Da'vid into the wood, and strengthened his hand in God.

17 And he said unto him, Fear not: for the hand of Saul my father shall not find thee; and thou shalt be king over Is'ra-el, and I shall be next unto thee; and that also Saul my father knoweth.

18 And they two made a covenant before the LORD: and Da'vid abode in the wood, and Jon'a-than went to his house.

19 Then came up the Ziph'-ites to Saul to Gib'e-ah, saying, Doth not Da'vid hide himself with us in strong holds in the wood, in the hill of Hach'i-lah, which *is* on the south of Jesh'i-mon?

20 Now therefore, O king, come down according to all the desire of thy soul to come down; and our part *shall be* to deliver him into the king's hand.

21 And Saul said, Blessed *be* ye of the LORD; for ye have compassion on me.

22 Go, I pray you, prepare yet, and know and see his place where his haunt is, *and* who hath seen him there: for it is told me *that* he dealeth very subtilly.

23 See therefore, and take knowledge of all the lurking places where he hideth himself, and come ye again to me with the certainty, and I will go with you: and it shall come to pass, if he be in the land, that I will search him out throughout all the thousands of Ju'dah.

24 And they arose, and went to Ziph before Saul: but Da'vid and his men *were* in the wilderness of Ma'on, in the plain on the south of Jesh'i-mon.

25 Saul also and his men went to seek *him.* And they told Da'vid: wherefore he came down into a rock, and abode in the wilderness of Ma'on. And when Saul heard *that,* he pursued after Da'vid in the wilderness of Ma'on.

26 And Saul went on this side of the mountain, and Da'vid and his men on that side of the mountain: and Da'vid made haste to get away for fear of Saul; for Saul and his men compassed Da'vid and his men round about to take them.

27 But there came a messenger unto Saul, saying, Haste thee, and come; for the Phi-lis'tines have invaded the land.

28 Wherefore Saul returned from pursuing after Da'vid, and went against the Phi-lis'tines: therefore they called that place Se'la-ham-mah-le'koth.

29 And Da'vid went up from thence, and dwelt in strong holds at En-ge'di.

24 AND IT came to pass, when Saul was returned from following the Phi-lis'tines, that it was told him, saying, Behold, Da'vid *is* in the wilderness of En-ge'di.

2 Then Saul took three thousand chosen men

David Shows Mercy to King Saul

out of all Is'ra-el, and went to seek Da'vid and his men upon the rocks of the wild goats.

3 And he came to the sheepcotes by the way, where *was* a cave; and Saul went in to cover his feet: and Da'vid and his men remained in the sides of the cave.

4 And the men of Da'vid said unto him, Behold the day of which the LORD said unto thee, Behold, I will deliver thine enemy into thine hand, that thou mayest do to him as it shall seem good unto thee. Then Da'vid arose, and cut off the skirt of Saul's robe privily.

5 And it came to pass afterward, that Da'vid's heart smote him, because he had cut off Saul's skirt.

6 And he said unto his men, The LORD forbid that I should do this thing unto my master, the LORD's anointed, to stretch forth mine hand against him, seeing he *is* the anointed of the LORD.

7 So Da'vid stayed his servants with these words, and suffered them not to rise against Saul. But Saul rose up out of the cave, and went on *his* way.

8 Da'vid also arose afterward, and went out of the cave, and cried after Saul, saying, My lord the king. And when Saul looked behind him, Da'vid stooped with his face to the earth, and bowed himself.

9 And Da'vid said to Saul, Wherefore hearest thou men's words, saying, Behold, Da'vid seeketh thy hurt?

10 Behold, this day thine eyes have seen how that the LORD had delivered thee to day into mine hand in the cave: and *some* bade *me* kill thee: but *mine eye* spared thee; and I said, I will not put forth

156

mine hand against my lord; for he *is* the LORD's anointed.

11 Moreover, my father, see, yea, see the skirt of thy robe in my hand: for in that I cut off the skirt of thy robe, and killed thee not, know thou and see that *there is* neither evil nor transgression in mine hand, and I have not sinned against thee; yet thou huntest my soul to take it.

12 The LORD judge between me and thee, and the LORD avenge me of thee: but mine hand shall not be upon thee.

13 As saith the proverb of the ancients, Wickedness proceedeth from the wicked: but mine hand shall not be upon thee.

14 After whom is the king of Is'ra-el come out? after whom dost thou pursue? after a dead dog, after a flea.

15 The LORD therefore be judge, and judge between me and thee, and see, and plead my cause, and deliver me out of thine hand.

16 And it came to pass, when Da'vid had made an end of speaking these words unto Saul, that Saul said, *Is* this thy voice, my son Da'vid? And Saul lifted up his voice, and wept.

17 And he said to Da'vid, Thou *art* more righteous than I: for thou hast rewarded me good, whereas I have rewarded thee evil.

18 And thou hast shewed this day how that thou hast dealt well with me: forasmuch as when the LORD had delivered me into thine hand, thou killedst me not.

19 For if a man find his enemy, will he let him go well away? wherefore the LORD reward thee good for that thou hast done unto me this day.

20 And now, behold, I know well that thou shalt

surely be king, and that the kingdom of Is'ra-el shall be established in thine hand.

21 Swear now therefore unto me by the LORD, that thou wilt not cut off my seed after me, and that thou wilt not destroy my name out of my father's house.

22 And Da'vid sware unto Saul. And Saul went home; but Da'vid and his men gat them up unto the hold.

A Foreshadow of Weaknesses (25:1–43)
Samuel's Death

25 AND SAM'U-EL died; and all the Is'ra-el-ites were gathered together, and lamented him, and buried him in his house at Ra-'mah. And Da'vid arose, and went down to the wilderness of Pa'ran.

The Saga of Abigail and Nabal

2 And *there was* a man in Ma'on, whose possessions *were* in Car'mel; and the man *was* very great, and he had three thousand sheep, and a thousand goats: and he was shearing his sheep in Car'mel.

3 Now the name of the man *was* Na'bal; and the name of his wife Ab'i-gail: and *she was* a woman of good understanding, and of a beautiful countenance: but the man *was* churlish and evil in his doings; and he *was* of the house of Ca'leb.

4 And Da'vid heard in the wilderness that Na'bal did shear his sheep.

5 And Da'vid sent out ten young men, and Da'vid said unto the young men, Get you up to Car'mel, and go to Na'bal, and greet him in my name:

6 And thus shall ye say to him that liveth *in prosperity*, Peace *be* both to thee, and peace *be* to thine house, and peace *be* unto all that thou hast.

7 And now I have heard that thou hast shearers: now thy shepherds which were with us, we hurt

them not, neither was there ought missing unto them, all the while they were in Car'mel.

8 Ask thy young men, and they will shew thee. Wherefore let the young men find favour in thine eyes: for we come in a good day: give, I pray thee, whatsoever cometh to thine hand unto thy servants, and to thy son Da'vid.

9 And when Da'vid's young men came, they spake to Na'bal according to all those words in the name of Da'vid, and ceased.

10 And Na'bal answered Da'vid's servants, and said, Who *is* Da'vid? and who *is* the son of Jes'se? there be many servants now a days that break away every man from his master.

11 Shall I then take my bread, and my water, and my flesh that I have killed for my shearers, and give *it* unto men, whom I know not whence they *be?*

12 So Da'vid's young men turned their way, and went again, and came and told him all those sayings.

13 And Da'vid said unto his men, Gird ye on every man his sword. And they girded on every man his sword; and Da'vid also girded on his sword: and there went up after Da'vid about four hundred men; and two hundred abode by the stuff.

14 But one of the young men told Ab'i-gail, Na'bal's wife, saying, Behold, Da'vid sent messengers out of the wilderness to salute our master; and he railed on them.

15 But the men *were* very good unto us, and we were not hurt, neither missed we any thing, as long as we were conversant with them, when we were in the fields:

16 They were a wall unto us both by night and

day, all the while we were with them keeping the sheep.

17 Now therefore know and consider what thou wilt do; for evil is determined against our master, and against all his household: for he *is such* a son of Be'li-al, that *a man* cannot speak to him.

18 Then Ab'i-gail made haste, and took two hundred loaves, and two bottles of wine, and five sheep ready dressed, and five measures of parched *corn,* and an hundred clusters of raisins, and two hundred cakes of figs, and laid *them* on asses.

19 And she said unto her servants, Go on before me; behold, I come after you. But she told not her husband Na'bal.

20 And it was *so, as* she rode on the ass, that she came down by the covert of the hill, and, behold, Da'vid and his men came down against her; and she met them.

21 Now Da'vid had said, Surely in vain have I kept all that this *fellow* hath in the wilderness, so that nothing was missed of all that *pertained* unto him: and he hath requited me evil for good.

22 So and more also do God unto the enemies of Da'vid, if I leave of all that *pertain* to him by the morning light any that pisseth against the wall.

23 And when Ab'i-gail saw Da'vid, she hasted, and lighted off the ass, and fell before Da'vid on her face, and bowed herself to the ground.

24 And fell at his feet, and said, Upon me, my lord, *upon* me *let this* iniquity *be:* and let thine handmaid, I pray thee, speak in thine audience, and hear the words of thine handmaid.

25 Let not my lord, I pray thee, regard this man of Be'li-al, *even* Na'bal: for as his name *is,* so *is* he; Na'bal *is* his name, and folly *is* with him: but I

thine handmaid saw not the young men of my lord, whom thou didst send.

26 Now therefore, my lord, *as* the LORD liveth, and *as* thy soul liveth, seeing the LORD hath withholden thee from coming to *shed* blood, and from avenging thyself with thine own hand, now let thine enemies, and they that seek evil to my lord, be as Na'bal.

27 And now this blessing which thine handmaid hath brought unto my lord, let it even be given unto the young men that follow my lord.

28 I pray thee, forgive the trespass of thine handmaid: for the LORD will certainly make my lord a sure house; because my lord fighteth the battles of the LORD, and evil hath not been found in thee *all* thy days.

29 Yet a man is risen to pursue thee, and to seek thy soul: but the soul of my lord shall be bound in the bundle of life with the LORD thy God; and the souls of thine enemies, them shall he sling out, *as out* of the middle of a sling.

30 And it shall come to pass, when the LORD shall have done to my lord according to all the good that he hath spoken concerning thee, and shall have appointed thee ruler over Is'ra-el;

31 That this shall be no grief unto thee, nor offence of heart unto my lord, either that thou hast shed blood causeless, or that my lord hath avenged himself: but when the LORD shall have dealt well with my lord, then remember thine handmaid.

32 And Da'vid said to Ab'i-gail, Blessed *be* the LORD God of Is'ra-el, which sent thee this day to meet me:

33 And blessed *be* thy advice, and blessed *be* thou, which hast kept me this day from coming to

shed blood, and from avenging myself with mine own hand.

34 For in very deed, *as* the LORD God of Is'ra-el liveth, which hath kept me back from hurting thee, except thou hadst hasted and come to meet me, surely there had not been left unto Na'bal by the morning light any that pisseth against the wall.

35 So Da'vid received of her hand *that* which she had brought him, and said unto her, Go up in peace to thine house; see, I have hearkened to thy voice, and have accepted thy person.

36 And Ab'i-gail came to Na'bal; and, behold, he held a feast in his house, like the feast of a king; and Na'bal's heart *was* merry within him, for he *was* very drunken: wherefore she told him nothing, less or more, until the morning light.

37 But it came to pass in the morning, when the wine was gone out of Na'bal, and his wife had told him these things, that his heart died within him, and he became *as* a stone.

38 And it came to pass about ten days *after,* that the LORD smote Na'bal, that he died.

39 And when Da'vid heard that Na'bal was dead, he said, Blessed *be* the LORD, that hath pleaded the cause of my reproach from the hand of Na'bal, and hath kept his servant from evil: for the LORD hath returned the wickedness of Na'bal upon his own head. And Da'vid sent and communed with Ab'i-gail, to take her to him to wife.

40 And when the servants of Da'vid were come to Ab'i-gail to Car'mel, they spake unto her, saying, Da'vid sent us unto thee, to take thee to him to wife.

41 And she arose, and bowed herself on *her* face to the earth, and said, Behold, *let* thine handmaid

be a servant to wash the feet of the servants of my lord.

42 And Ab'i-gail hasted, and arose, and rode upon an ass, with five damsels of hers that went after her; and she went after the messengers of Da'vid, and became his wife.

43 Da'vid also took A-hin'o-am of Jez're-el; and they were also both of them his wives.

44 But Saul had given Mi'chal his daughter, Da'vid's wife, to Phal'ti the son of La'ish, which *was* of Gal'lim.

26 AND THE Ziph'ites came unto Saul to Gib'e-ah, saying, Doth not Da'vid hide himself in the hill of Hach'i-lah, *which is* before Jesh'i-mon?

2 Then Saul arose, and went down to the wilderness of Ziph, having three thousand chosen men of Is'ra-el with him, to seek Da'vid in the wilderness of Ziph.

3 And Saul pitched in the hill of Hach'i-lah, which *is* before Jesh'i-mon, by the way. But Da'vid abode in the wilderness, and he saw that Saul came after him into the wilderness.

4 Da'vid therefore sent out spies, and understood that Saul was come in very deed.

5 And Da'vid arose, and came to the place where Saul had pitched: and Da'vid beheld the place where Saul lay, and Ab'ner the son of Ner, the captain of his host: and Saul lay in the trench, and the people pitched round about him.

6 Then answered Da'vid and said to A-him'e-lech the Hit'tite, and to A-bish'a-i the son of Zer-u-i'ah, brother to Jo'ab, saying, Who will go down

*A Renewal of Mercy
(26:1–25)*

David Betrayed Again

The Quality of Mercy

163

with me to Saul to the camp? And A-bish'a-i said, I will go down with thee.

7 So Da'vid and A-bish'a-i came to the people by night: and, behold, Saul lay sleeping within the trench, and his spear stuck in the ground at his bolster: but Ab'ner and the people lay round about him.

8 Then said A-bish'a-i to Da'vid, God hath delivered thine enemy into thine hand this day: now therefore let me smite him, I pray thee, with the spear even to the earth at once, and I will not *smite* him the second time.

9 And Da'vid said to A-bish'a-i, Destroy him not: for who can stretch forth his hand against the Lord's anointed, and be guiltless?

10 Da'vid said furthermore, *As* the Lord liveth, the Lord shall smite him; or his day shall come to die; or he shall descend into battle, and perish.

11 The Lord forbid that I should stretch forth mine hand against the Lord's anointed: but, I pray thee, take thou now the spear that *is* at his bolster, and the cruse of water, and let us go.

12 So Da'vid took the spear and the cruse of water from Saul's bolster; and they gat them away, and no man saw *it,* nor knew *it,* neither awaked: for they *were* all asleep; because a deep sleep from the Lord was fallen upon them.

Confrontation from a Safe Distance

13 Then Da'vid went over to the other side, and stood on the top of an hill afar off; a great space *being* between them:

14 And Da'vid cried to the people, and to Ab'ner the son of Ner, saying, Answerest thou not, Ab'ner? Then Ab'ner answered and said, Who *art* thou *that* criest to the king?

15 And Da'vid said to Ab'ner, *Art* not thou a *valiant* man? and who *is* like to thee in Is'ra-el?

wherefore then hast thou not kept thy lord the king? for there came one of the people in to destroy the king thy lord.

16 This thing *is* not good that thou hast done. *As* the LORD liveth, ye *are* worthy to die, because ye have not kept your master, the LORD's anointed. And now see where the king's spear *is,* and the cruse of water that *was* at his bolster.

17 And Saul knew Da'vid's voice, and said, *Is* this thy voice, my son Da'vid? And Da'vid said, *It is* my voice, my lord, O king.

18 And he said, Wherefore doth my lord thus pursue after his servant? for what have I done? or what evil *is* in mine hand?

19 Now therefore, I pray thee, let my lord the king hear the words of his servant. If the LORD have stirred thee up against me, let him accept an offering; but if *they be* the children of men, cursed *be* they before the LORD; for they have driven me out this day from abiding in the inheritance of the LORD, saying, Go, serve other gods.

20 Now therefore, let not my blood fall to the earth before the face of the LORD: for the king of Is'ra-el is come out to seek a flea, as when one doth hunt a partridge in the mountains.

21 Then said Saul, I have sinned: return, my son Da'vid: for I will no more do thee harm, because my soul was precious in thine eyes this day: behold, I have played the fool, and have erred exceedingly.

22 And Da'vid answered and said, Behold the king's spear! and let one of the young men come over and fetch it.

23 The LORD render to every man his righteousness and his faithfulness: for the LORD delivered

thee into *my* hand to day, but I would not stretch forth mine hand against the LORD's anointed.

24 And, behold, as thy life was much set by this day in mine eyes, so let my life be much set by in the eyes of the LORD, and let him deliver me out of all tribulation.

25 Then Saul said to Da'vid, Blessed *be* thou, my son Da'vid: thou shalt both do great *things,* and also shalt still prevail. So Da'vid went on his way, and Saul returned to his place.

Living On the Edge of Danger (27:1–28:25)

Finding Security in an Insecure Place

27 AND DA'VID said in his heart, I shall now perish one day by the hand of Saul: *there is* nothing better for me than that I should speedily escape into the land of the Phi-lis'tines; and Saul shall despair of me, to see me any more in any coast of Is'ra-el: so shall I escape out of his hand.

2 And Da'vid arose, and he passed over with the six hundred men that *were* with him unto A'chish, the son of Ma'och, king of Gath.

3 And Da'vid dwelt with A'chish at Gath, he and his men, every man with his household, *even* Da'vid with his two wives, A-hin'o-am the Jez're-el-it-ess, and Ab'i-gail the Car'mel-it-ess, Na'bal's wife.

4 And it was told Saul that Da'vid was fled to Gath: and he sought no more again for him.

5 And Da'vid said unto A'chish, If I have now found grace in thine eyes, let them give me a place in some town in the country, that I may dwell there: for why should thy servant dwell in the royal city with thee?

6 Then A'chish gave him Zik'lag that day: wherefore Zik'lag pertaineth unto the kings of Ju'dah unto this day.

166

7 And the time that Da'vid dwelt in the country of the Phi-lis'tines was a full year and four months.

8 And Da'vid and his men went up, and invaded the Gesh'u-rites, and the Gez'rites, and the Am'a-lek-ites: for those *nations were* of old the inhabitants of the land, as thou goest to Shur, even unto the land of E'gypt.

9 And Da'vid smote the land, and left neither man nor woman alive, and took away the sheep, and the oxen, and the asses, and the camels, and the apparel, and returned, and came to A'chish.

10 And A'chish said, Whither have ye made a road to day? And Da'vid said, Against the south of Ju'dah, and against the south of the Je-rah'me-el-ites, and against the south of the Ken'ites.

11 And Da'vid saved neither man nor woman alive, to bring *tidings* to Gath, saying, Lest they should tell on us, saying, So did Da'vid, and so *will be* his manner all the while he dwelleth in the country of the Phi-lis'tines.

12 And A'chish believed Da'vid, saying, He hath made his people Is'ra-el utterly to abhor him; therefore he shall be my servant for ever.

28 AND IT came to pass in those days, that the Phi-lis'tines gathered their armies together for warfare, to fight with Is'ra-el. And A'chish said unto Da'vid, Know thou assuredly, that thou shalt go out with me to battle, thou and thy men.

2 And Da'vid said to A'chish, Surely thou shalt know what thy servant can do. And A'chish said to Da'vid, Therefore will I make thee keeper of mine head for ever.

When Everything Nailed Down Comes Loose

167

————————————
————————————
————————————
————————————
————————————
————————————
————————————
————————————
————————————
————————————
————————————
————————————
————————————
————————————
————————————
————————————
————————————
————————————
————————————
————————————
————————————
————————————
————————————

3 Now Sam'u-el was dead, and all Is'ra-el had lamented him, and buried him in Ra'mah, even in his own city. And Saul had put away those that had familiar spirits, and the wizards, out of the land.

4 And the Phi-lis'tines gathered themselves together, and came and pitched in Shu'nem: and Saul gathered all Is'ra-el together, and they pitched in Gil-bo'a.

5 And when Saul saw the host of the Phi-lis'-tines, he was afraid, and his heart greatly trembled.

6 And when Saul enquired of the LORD, the LORD answered him not, neither by dreams, nor by U'rim, nor by prophets.

7 Then said Saul unto his servants, Seek me a woman that hath a familiar spirit, that I may go to her, and enquire of her. And his servants said to him, Behold, *there is* a woman that hath a familiar spirit at En'-dor.

8 And Saul disguised himself, and put on other raiment, and he went, and two men with him, and they came to the woman by night: and he said, I pray thee, divine unto me by the familiar spirit, and bring me *him* up, whom I shall name unto thee.

9 And the woman said unto him, Behold, thou knowest what Saul hath done, how he hath cut off those that have familiar spirits, and the wizards, out of the land: wherefore then layest thou a snare for my life, to cause me to die?

10 And Saul sware to her by the LORD, saying, *As* the LORD liveth, there shall no punishment happen to thee for this thing.

11 Then said the woman, Whom shall I bring up unto thee? And he said, Bring me up Sam'u-el.

12 And when the woman saw Sam'u-el, she cried with a loud voice: and the woman spake to

Saul, saying, Why hast thou deceived me? for thou *art* Saul.

13 And the king said unto her, Be not afraid: for what sawest thou? And the woman said unto Saul, I saw gods ascending out of the earth.

14 And he said unto her, What form *is* he of? And she said, An old man cometh up; and he *is* covered with a mantle. And Saul perceived that it *was* Sam'u-el, and he stooped with *his* face to the ground, and bowed himself.

15 And Sam'u-el said to Saul, Why hast thou disquieted me, to bring me up? And Saul answered, I am sore distressed; for the Phi-lis'tines make war against me, and God is departed from me, and answereth me no more, neither by prophets, nor by dreams: therefore I have called thee, that thou mayest make known unto me what I shall do.

16 Then said Sam'u-el, Wherefore then dost thou ask of me, seeing the LORD is departed from thee, and is become thine enemy?

17 And the LORD hath done to him, as he spake by me: for the LORD hath rent the kingdom out of thine hand, and given it to thy neighbour, *even* to Da'vid:

18 Because thou obeyedst not the voice of the LORD, nor executedst his fierce wrath upon Am'a-lek, therefore hath the LORD done this thing unto thee this day.

19 Moreover the LORD will also deliver Is'ra-el with thee into the hand of the Phi-lis'tines: and to morrow *shalt* thou and thy sons *be* with me: the LORD also shall deliver the host of Is'ra-el into the hand of the Phi-lis'tines.

20 Then Saul fell straightway all along on the earth, and was sore afraid, because of the words of

Sam'u-el: and there was no strength in him; for he had eaten no bread all the day, nor all the night.

21 And the woman came unto Saul, and saw that he was sore troubled, and said unto him, Behold, thine handmaid hath obeyed thy voice, and I have put my life in my hand, and have hearkened unto thy words which thou spakest unto me.

22 Now therefore, I pray thee, hearken thou also unto the voice of thine handmaid, and let me set a morsel of bread before thee; and eat, that thou mayest have strength, when thou goest on thy way.

23 But he refused, and said, I will not eat. But his servants, together with the woman, compelled him; and he hearkened unto their voice. So he arose from the earth, and sat upon the bed.

24 And the woman had a fat calf in the house; and she hasted, and killed it, and took flour, and kneaded *it,* and did bake unleavened bread thereof:

25 And she brought *it* before Saul, and before his servants; and they did eat. Then they rose up, and went away that night.

The Unseen Hand of God
(29:1–30:31)

29 NOW THE Phi-lis'tines gathered together all their armies to A'phek: and the Is'ra-el-ites pitched by a fountain which *is* in Jez're-el.

2 And the lords of the Phi-lis'tines passed on by hundreds, and by thousands: but Da'vid and his men passed on in the rereward with A'chish.

3 Then said the princes of the Phi-lis'tines, What *do* these He'-brews *here?* And A'chish said unto the princes of the Phi-lis'tines, *Is* not this Da'vid, the servant of Saul the king of Is'ra-el, which hath been with me these days, or these

years, and I have found no fault in him since he fell *unto me* unto this day?

4 And the princes of the Phi-lis'tines were wroth with him; and the princes of the Phi-lis'tines said unto him, Make this fellow return, that he may go again to his place which thou hast appointed him, and let him not go down with us to battle, lest in the battle he be an adversary to us: for wherewith should he reconcile himself unto his master? *should it* not *be* with the heads of these men?

5 *Is* not this Da'vid, of whom they sang one to another in dances, saying, Saul slew his thousands, and Da'vid his ten thousands?

6 Then A'chish called Da'vid, and said unto him, Surely, *as* the Lord liveth, thou hast been upright, and thy going out and thy coming in with me in the host *is* good in my sight: for I have not found evil in thee since the day of thy coming unto me unto this day: nevertheless the lords favour thee not.

7 Wherefore now return, and go in peace, that thou displease not the lords of the Phi-lis'tines.

8 And Da'vid said unto A'chish, But what have I done? and what hast thou found in thy servant so long as I have been with thee unto this day, that I may not go fight against the enemies of my lord the king?

9 And A'chish answered and said to Da'vid, I know that thou *art* good in my sight, as an angel of God: notwithstanding the princes of the Phi-lis'tines have said, He shall not go up with us to the battle.

10 Wherefore now rise up early in the morning with thy master's servants that are come with thee:

God Intervenes

171

and as soon as ye be up early in the morning, and have light, depart.

11 So Da'vid and his men rose up early to depart in the morning, to return into the land of the Phi-lis'tines. And the Phi-lis'tines went up to Jez're-el.

David's Time of Rescue

30 AND IT came to pass, when Da'vid and his men were come to Zik'lag on the third day, that the Am'a-lek-ites had invaded the south, and Zik'lag, and smitten Zik'lag, and burned it with fire;

2 And had taken the women captives, that *were* therein: they slew not any, either great or small, but carried *them* away, and went on their way.

3 So Da'vid and his men came to the city, and, behold, *it was* burned with fire; and their wives, and their sons, and their daughters, were taken captives.

4 Then Da'vid and the people that *were* with him lifted up their voice and wept, until they had no more power to weep.

5 And Da'vid's two wives were taken captives, A-hin'o-am the Jez're-el-it-ess, and Ab'i-gail the wife of Na'bal the Car'mel-ite.

6 And Da'vid was greatly distressed; for the people spake of stoning him, because the soul of all the people was grieved, every man for his sons and for his daughters: but Da'vid encouraged himself in the LORD his God.

7 And Da'vid said to A-bi'a-thar the priest, A-him'e-lech's son, I pray thee, bring me hither the ephod. And A-bi'a-thar brought thither the ephod to Da'vid.

8 And Da'vid enquired at the LORD, saying, Shall I pursue after this troop? shall I overtake them?

And he answered him, Pursue: for thou shalt surely overtake *them,* and without fail recover *all.*

9 So Da'vid went, he and the six hundred men that *were* with him, and came to the brook Be'-sor, where those that were left behind stayed.

10 But Da'vid pursued, he and four hundred men: for two hundred abode behind, which were so faint that they could not go over the brook Be'sor.

11 And they found an E-gyp'tian in the field, and brought him to Da'vid, and gave him bread, and he did eat; and they made him drink water;

12 And they gave him a piece of a cake of figs, and two clusters of raisins: and when he had eaten, his spirit came again to him: for he had eaten no bread, nor drunk *any* water, three days and three nights.

13 And Da'vid said unto him, To whom *belongest* thou? and whence *art* thou? And he said, I *am* a young man of E'gypt, servant to an Am'a-lek-ite; and my master left me, because three days agone I fell sick.

14 We made an invasion *upon* the south of the Cher'eth-ites, and upon *the coast* which *belongeth* to Ju'dah, and upon the south of Ca'leb; and we burned Zik'lag with fire.

15 And Da'vid said to him, Canst thou bring me down to this company? And he said, Swear unto me by God, that thou wilt neither kill me, nor deliver me into the hands of my master, and I will bring thee down to this company.

16 And when he had brought him down, behold, *they were* spread abroad upon all the earth, eating and drinking, and dancing, because of all the great spoil that they had taken out of the land of the Phi-lis'tines, and out of the land of Ju'dah.

17 And Da'vid smote them from the twilight even unto the evening of the next day: and there escaped not a man of them, save four hundred young men, which rode upon camels, and fled.

18 And Da'vid recovered all that the Am'a-lek-ites had carried away: and Da'vid rescued his two wives.

19 And there was nothing lacking to them, neither small nor great, neither sons nor daughters, neither spoil, nor any *thing* that they had taken to them: Da'vid recovered all.

20 And Da'vid took all the flocks and the herds, *which* they drave before those *other* cattle, and said, This *is* Da'vid's spoil.

Generosity in Victory

21 And Da'vid came to the two hundred men, which were so faint that they could not follow Da'vid, whom they had made also to abide at the brook Be'sor: and they went forth to meet Da'vid, and to meet the people that *were* with him: and when Da'vid came near to the people, he saluted them.

22 Then answered all the wicked men and *men* of Be'li-al, of those that went with Da'vid, and said, Because they went not with us, we will not give them *ought* of the spoil that we have recovered, save to every man his wife and his children, that they may lead *them* away, and depart.

23 Then said Da'vid, Ye shall not do so, my brethren, with that which the LORD hath given us, who hath preserved us, and delivered the company that came against us into our hand.

24 For who will hearken unto you in this matter? but as his part *is* that goeth down to the battle, so *shall* his part *be* that tarrieth by the stuff: they shall part alike.

25 And it was *so* from that day forward, that he made it a statute and an ordinance for Is'ra-el unto this day.

26 And when Da'vid came to Zik'lag, he sent of the spoil unto the elders of Ju'dah, *even* to his friends, saying, Behold a present for you of the spoil of the enemies of the LORD;

27 To *them* which *were* in Beth'-el, and to *them* which *were* in south Ra'moth, and to *them* which *were* in Jat'tir,

28 And to *them* which *were* in Ar'o-er, and to *them* which *were* in Siph'moth, and to *them* which *were* in Esh-te-mo'a,

29 And to *them* which *were* in Ra'chal, and to *them* which *were* in the cities of the Je-rah'me-el-ites, and to *them* which *were* in the cities of the Ken'ites,

30 And to *them* which *were* in Hor'mah, and to *them* which *were* in Chor-a'shan, and to *them* which *were* in A'thach,

31 And to *them* which *were* in He'bron, and to all the places where Da'vid himself and his men were wont to haunt.

31 NOW THE Phi-lis'tines fought against Is'ra-el: and the men of Is'ra-el fled from before the Phi-lis'tines, and fell down slain in mount Gil-bo'a.

2 And the Phi-lis'tines followed hard upon Saul and upon his sons; and the Phi-lis'tines slew Jon'a-than, and A-bin'a-dab, and Mel'chi-shu'a, Saul's sons.

3 And the battle went sore against Saul, and the archers hit him; and he was sore wounded of the archers.

Loyal to the End (31:1–13)

Saul's Death

_____

_____

_____

_____

_____

_____

_____

_____

_____

_____

The Aftermath of the Battle

_____

A Sad and Tragic Story

_____

_____

_____

_____

_____

_____

_____

_____

_____

4 Then said Saul unto his armourbearer, Draw thy sword, and thrust me through therewith; lest these uncircumcised come and thrust me through, and abuse me. But his armourbearer would not; for he was sore afraid. Therefore Saul took a sword, and fell upon it.

5 And when his armourbearer saw that Saul was dead, he fell likewise upon his sword, and died with him.

6 So Saul died, and his three sons, and his armourbearer, and all his men, that same day together.

7 And when the men of Is'ra-el that *were* on the other side of the valley, and *they* that *were* on the other side Jor'dan, saw that the men of Is'ra-el fled, and that Saul and his sons were dead, they forsook the cities, and fled; and the Phi-lis'tines came and dwelt in them.

8 And it came to pass on the morrow, when the Phi-lis'tines came to strip the slain, that they found Saul and his three sons fallen in mount Gil-bo'a.

9 And they cut off his head, and stripped off his armour, and sent into the land of the Phi-lis'tines round about, to publish *it in* the house of their idols, and among the people.

10 And they put his armour in the house of Ash'ta-roth: and they fastened his body to the wall of Beth'-shan.

11 And when the inhabitants of Ja'besh-gil'e-ad heard of that which the Phi-lis'tines had done to Saul;

12 All the valiant men arose, and went all night, and took the body of Saul and the bodies of his sons from the wall of Beth'-shan, and came to Ja'-besh, and burnt them there.

13 And they took their bones, and buried *them* under a tree at Ja'besh, and fasted seven days.

LESSON 7

2 SAMUEL 1:1–10:19
Service That Leads to Greatness

Loving Both Friends and Enemies (1:1–27)

_____
_____
_____
_____
_____
_____
_____
_____
_____
_____
_____
_____
_____
_____
_____
_____
_____

1 NOW IT came to pass after the death of Saul, when Da'vid was returned from the slaughter of the Am'a-lek-ites, and Da'vid had abode two days in Zik'lag;

2 It came even to pass on the third day, that, behold, a man came out of the camp from Saul with his clothes rent, and earth upon his head: and *so* it was, when he came to Da'vid, that he fell to the earth, and did obeisance.

3 And Da'vid said unto him, From whence comest thou? And he said unto him, Out of the camp of Is'ra-el am I escaped.

4 And Da'vid said unto him, How went the matter? I pray thee, tell me. And he answered, That the people are fled from the battle, and many of the people also are fallen and dead; and Saul and Jon'a-than his son are dead also.

5 And Da'vid said unto the young man that told him, How knowest thou that Saul and Jon'a-than his son be dead?

6 And the young man that told him said, As I happened by chance upon mount Gil-bo'a, behold, Saul leaned upon his spear; and, lo, the chariots and horsemen followed hard after him.

7 And when he looked behind him, he saw me, and called unto me. And I answered, Here *am* I.

8 And he said unto me, Who *art* thou? And I answered him, I *am* an Am'a-lek-ite.

9 He said unto me again, Stand, I pray thee, upon me, and slay me: for anguish is come upon me, because my life *is* yet whole in me.

10 So I stood upon him, and slew him, because I was sure that he could not live after that he was fallen: and I took the crown that *was* upon his head, and the bracelet that *was* on his arm, and have brought them hither unto my lord.

11 Then Da'vid took hold on his clothes, and rent them; and likewise all the men that *were* with him:

12 And they mourned, and wept, and fasted until even, for Saul, and for Jon'a-than his son, and for the people of the LORD, and for the house of Is'ra-el; because they were fallen by the sword.

13 And Da'vid said unto the young man that told him, Whence *art* thou? And he answered, I *am* the son of a stranger, an Am'a-lek-ite.

14 And Da'vid said unto him, How wast thou not afraid to stretch forth thine hand to destroy the LORD's anointed?

15 And Da'vid called one of the young men, and said, Go near, *and* fall upon him. And he smote him that he died.

16 And Da'vid said unto him, Thy blood *be* upon thy head; for thy mouth hath testified against thee, saying, I have slain the LORD's anointed.

17 And Da'vid lamented with this lamentation over Saul and over Jon'a-than his son:

18 (Also he bade them teach the children of Ju'dah *the use of* the bow: behold, *it is* written in the book of Ja'sher.)

Respect for the Lord's Anointed

The Song of Grief

179

19 The beauty of Is'ra-el is slain upon thy high places: how are the mighty fallen!

20 Tell *it* not in Gath, publish *it* not in the streets of As'ke-lon; lest the daughters of the Phi-lis'tines rejoice, lest the daughters of the uncircumcised triumph.

21 Ye mountains of Gil-bo'a, *let there be* no dew, neither *let there be* rain, upon you, nor fields of offerings: for there the shield of the mighty is vilely cast away, the shield of Saul, *as though he had* not *been* anointed with oil.

22 From the blood of the slain, from the fat of the mighty, the bow of Jon'a-than turned not back, and the sword of Saul returned not empty.

23 Saul and Jon'a-than *were* lovely and pleasant in their lives, and in their death they were not divided: they were swifter than eagles, they were stronger than lions.

24 Ye daughters of Is'ra-el, weep over Saul, who clothed you in scarlet, with *other* delights, who put on ornaments of gold upon your apparel.

25 How are the mighty fallen in the midst of the battle! O Jon'a-than, *thou wast* slain in thine high places.

26 I am distressed for thee, my brother Jon'a-than: very pleasant hast thou been unto me: thy love to me was wonderful, passing the love of women.

27 How are the mighty fallen, and the weapons of war perished!

Snatching Defeat from Victory (2:1–32)

2 AND IT came to pass after this, that Da'vid enquired of the LORD, saying, Shall I go up into any of the cities of Ju'dah? And the LORD said unto

him, Go up. And Da'vid said, Whither shall I go up? And he said, Unto He'-bron.

2 So Da'vid went up thither, and his two wives also, A-hin'o-am the Jez're-el-it-ess, and Ab'i-gail Na'bal's wife the Car'mel-ite.

3 And his men that *were* with him did Da'vid bring up, every man with his household: and they dwelt in the cities of He'bron.

4 And the men of Ju'dah came, and there they anointed Da'vid king over the house of Ju'dah. And they told Da'vid, saying, *That* the men of Ja'-besh-gil'e-ad *were they* that buried Saul.

5 And Da'vid sent messengers unto the men of Ja'besh-gil'e-ad, and said unto them, Blessed *be* ye of the LORD, that ye have shewed this kindness unto your lord, *even* unto Saul, and have buried him.

6 And now the LORD shew kindness and truth unto you: and I also will requite you this kindness, because ye have done this thing.

7 Therefore now let your hands be strengthened, and be ye valiant: for your master Saul is dead, and also the house of Ju'-dah have anointed me king over them.

8 But Ab'ner the son of Ner, captain of Saul's host, took Ish-bo'sheth the son of Saul, and brought him over to Ma-ha-na'im;

9 And made him king over Gil'e-ad, and over the Ash'ur-ites, and over Jez're-el, and over E'phra-im, and over Ben'ja-min, and over all Is'ra-el.

10 Ish-bo'sheth Saul's son *was* forty years old when he began to reign over Is'ra-el, and reigned two years. But the house of Ju'dah followed Da'vid.

David Is Made King Over Judah

Israel Has a New King

181

11 And the time that Da'vid was king in He'-bron over the house of Ju'dah was seven years and six months.

12 And Ab'ner the son of Ner, and the servants of Ish-bo'sheth the son of Saul, went out from Ma-ha-na'im to Gib'e-on.

13 And Jo'ab the son of Zer-u-i'ah, and the servants of Da'-vid, went out, and met together by the pool of Gib'e-on: and they sat down, the one on the one side of the pool, and the other on the other side of the pool.

14 And Ab'ner said to Jo'ab, Let the young men now arise, and play before us. And Jo'ab said, Let them arise.

15 Then there arose and went over by number twelve of Ben'ja-min, which *pertained* to Ish-bo'sheth the son of Saul, and twelve of the servants of Da'vid.

16 And they caught every one his fellow by the head, and *thrust* his sword in his fellow's side; so they fell down together: wherefore that place was called Hel'kath-haz'zu-rim, which *is* in Gib'e-on.

17 And there was a very sore battle that day; and Ab'ner was beaten, and the men of Is'ra-el, before the servants of Da'vid.

18 And there were three sons of Zer-u-i'ah there, Jo'ab, and A-bish'a-i, and A'sa-hel: and A'sa-hel *was as* light of foot as a wild roe.

19 And A'sa-hel pursued after Ab'ner; and in going he turned not to the right hand nor to the left from following Ab'ner.

20 Then Ab'ner looked behind him, and said, *Art* thou A'sa-hel? And he answered, I *am.*

21 And Ab'ner said to him, Turn thee aside to thy right hand or to thy left, and lay thee hold on

one of the young men, and take thee his armour. But A'sa-hel would not turn aside from following of him.

22 And Ab'ner said again to A'sa-hel, Turn thee aside from following me: wherefore should I smite thee to the ground? how then should I hold up my face to Jo'ab thy brother?

23 How be it he refused to turn aside: wherefore Ab'ner with the hinder end of the spear smote him under the fifth *rib,* that the spear came out behind him; and he fell down there, and died in the same place: and it came to pass, *that* as many as came to the place where A'sa-hel fell down and died stood still.

24 Jo'ab also and A-bish'a-i pursued after Ab'ner: and the sun went down when they were come to the hill of Am'mah, that *lieth* before Gi'ah by the way of the wilderness of Gib'e-on.

25 And the children of Ben'ja-min gathered themselves together after Ab'ner, and became one troop, and stood on the top of an hill.

26 Then Ab'ner called to Jo'ab, and said, Shall the sword devour for ever? knowest thou not that it will be bitterness in the latter end? how long shall it be then, ere thou bid the people return from following their brethren?

27 And Jo'ab said, *As* God liveth, unless thou hadst spoken, surely then in the morning the people had gone up every one from following his brother.

28 So Jo'ab blew a trumpet, and all the people stood still, and pursued after Is'ra-el no more, neither fought they any more.

29 And Ab'ner and his men walked all that night through the plain, and passed over Jor'dan, and

went through all Bith'ron, and they came to Ma-ha-na'im.

30 And Jo'ab returned from following Ab'ner: and when he had gathered all the people together, there lacked of Da'vid's servants nineteen men and A'sa-hel.

31 But the servants of Da'vid had smitten of Ben'ja-min, and of Ab'ner's men, *so that* three hundred and threescore men died.

32 And they took up A'sa-hel, and buried him in the sepulchre of his father, which *was in* Beth'-le-hem. And Jo'ab and his men went all night, and they came to He'bron at break of day.

Dealing with Conflict (3:1–4:12)

The Ongoing Confrontation David's Family

3 NOW THERE was long war between the house of Saul and the house of Da'vid: but Da'vid waxed stronger and stronger, and the house of Saul waxed weaker and weaker.

2 And unto Da'vid were sons born in He'bron: and his firstborn was Am'non, of A-hin'o-am the Jez're-el-it-ess;

3 And his second, Chil'e-ab, of Ab'i-gail the wife of Na'bal the Car'mel-ite; and the third, Ab'sa-lom the son of Ma'a-cah the daughter of Tal'mai king of Ge'shur;

4 And the fourth, Ad-o-ni'jah the son of Hag'-gith; and the fifth, Sheph-a-ti'ah the son of Ab'i-tal;

5 And the sixth, Ith're-am, by Eg'lah Da'vid's wife. These were born to Da'vid in He'bron.

6 And it came to pass, while there was war between the house of Saul and the house of Da'vid, that Ab'ner made himself strong for the house of Saul.

7 And Saul had a concubine, whose name *was* Riz'pah, the daughter of A-i'ah: and *Ish-bo'sheth* said to Ab'ner, Wherefore hast thou gone in unto my father's concubine?

8 Then was Ab'ner very wroth for the words of Ish-bo'sheth, and said, *Am* I a dog's head, which against Ju'dah do shew kindness this day unto the house of Saul thy father, to his brethren, and to his friends, and have not delivered thee into the hand of Da'vid, that thou chargest me to day with a fault concerning this woman?

9 So do God to Ab'ner, and more also, except, as the LORD hath sworn to Da'vid, even so I do to him;

10 To translate the kingdom from the house of Saul, and to set up the throne of Da'vid over Is'ra-el and over Ju'dah, from Dan even to Be'er-she'ba.

11 And he could not answer Ab'ner a word again, because he feared him.

12 And Ab'ner sent messengers to Da'vid on his behalf, saying, Whose *is* the land? saying *also,* Make thy league with me, and, behold, my hand *shall be* with thee, to bring about all Is'ra-el unto thee.

13 And he said, Well; I will make a league with thee: but one thing I require of thee, that is, Thou shalt not see my face, except thou first bring Mi'-chal Saul's daughter, when thou comest to see my face.

14 And Da'vid sent messengers to Ish-bo'sheth Saul's son, saying, Deliver *me* my wife Mi'-chal, which I espoused to me for an hundred foreskins of the Phi-lis'tines.

15 And Ish-bo'sheth sent, and took her from *her* husband, *even* from Phal'ti-el the son of La'ish.

16 And her husband went with her along weep-

An Attempt to Deliver the Kingdom to David

ing behind her to Ba-hu'rim. Then said Ab'ner unto him, Go, return. And he returned.

17 And Ab'ner had communication with the elders of Is'ra-el, saying, Ye sought for Da'vid in times past *to be* king over you:

18 Now then do *it:* for the LORD hath spoken of Da'vid, saying, By the hand of my servant Da'vid I will save my people Is'ra-el out of the hand of the Phi-lis'tines, and out of the hand of all their enemies.

19 And Ab'ner also spake in the ears of Ben'ja-min: and Ab'-ner went also to speak in the ears of Da'vid in He'bron all that seemed good to Is'ra-el, and that seemed good to the whole house of Ben'ja-min.

20 So Ab'ner came to Da'vid to He'bron, and twenty men with him. And Da'vid made Ab'ner and the men that *were* with him a feast.

21 And Ab'ner said unto Da'vid, I will arise and go, and will gather all Is'ra-el unto my lord the king, that they may make a league with thee, and that thou mayest reign over all that thine heart desireth. And Da'vid sent Ab'ner away; and he went in peace.

Abner Murdered

22 And, behold, the servants of Da'vid and Jo'ab came from *pursuing* a troop, and brought in a great spoil with them: but Ab'ner *was* not with Da'vid in He'bron; for he had sent him away, and he was gone in peace.

23 When Jo'ab and all the host that *was* with him were come, they told Jo'ab, saying, Ab'ner the son of Ner came to the king, and he hath sent him away, and he is gone in peace.

24 Then Jo'ab came to the king, and said, What hast thou done? behold, Ab'ner came unto thee;

why *is* it *that* thou hast sent him away, and he is quite gone?

25 Thou knowest Ab'ner the son of Ner, that he came to deceive thee, and to know thy going out and thy coming in, and to know all that thou doest.

26 And when Jo'ab was come out from Da'vid, he sent messengers after Ab'ner, which brought him again from the well of Si'-rah: but Da'vid knew *it* not.

27 And when Ab'ner was returned to He'bron, Jo'ab took him aside in the gate to speak with him quietly, and smote him there under the fifth *rib,* that he died, for the blood of A'sa-hel his brother.

28 And afterward when Da'vid heard *it,* he said, I and my kingdom *are* guiltless before the Lord for ever, from the blood of Ab'ner the son of Ner:

29 Let it rest on the head of Jo'ab, and on all his father's house; and let there not fail from the house of Jo'ab one that hath an issue, or that is a leper, or that leaneth on a staff, or that falleth on the sword, or that lacketh bread.

30 So Jo'ab and A-bish'a-i his brother slew Ab'ner, because he had slain their brother A'sa-hel at Gib'e-on in the battle.

31 And Da'vid said to Jo'ab, and to all the people that *were* with him, Rend your clothes, and gird you with sackcloth, and mourn before Ab'ner. And king Da'vid *himself* followed the bier.

32 And they buried Ab'ner in He'bron: and the king lifted up his voice, and wept at the grave of Ab'ner; and all the people wept.

33 And the king lamented over Ab'ner, and said, Died Ab'-ner as a fool dieth?

34 Thy hands *were* not bound, nor thy feet put into fetters: as a man falleth before wicked men,

so fellest thou. And all the people wept again over him.

35 And when all the people came to cause Da'vid to eat meat while it was yet day, Da'vid sware, saying, So do God to me, and more also, if I taste bread, or ought else, till the sun be down.

36 And all the people took notice *of it,* and it pleased them: as whatsoever the king did pleased all the people.

37 For all the people and all Is'ra-el understood that day that it was not of the king to slay Ab'ner the son of Ner.

38 And the king said unto his servants, Know ye not that there is a prince and a great man fallen this day in Is'ra-el?

39 And I *am* this day weak, though anointed king; and these men the sons of Zer-u-i'ah *be* too hard for me: the LORD shall reward the doer of evil according to his wickedness.

The Contagion of Violence

4 AND WHEN Saul's son heard that Ab'ner was dead in He'bron, his hands were feeble, and all the Is'ra-el-ites were troubled.

2 And Saul's son had two men *that were* captains of bands: the name of the one *was* Ba'a-nah, and the name of the other Re'-chab, the sons of Rim'-mon a Be-e'roth-ite, of the children of Ben'ja-min: (for Be-e'roth also was reckoned to Ben'ja-min.

3 And the Be-e'roth-ites fled to Git'ta-im, and were sojourners there until this day.)

4 And Jon'a-than, Saul's son, had a son *that was* lame of *his* feet. He was five years old when the tidings came of Saul and Jon'a-than out of Jez're-el, and his nurse took him up, and fled: and it came to

pass, as she made haste to flee, that he fell, and became lame. And his name *was* Me-phib'o-sheth.

5 And the sons of Rim'mon the Be-e'roth-ite, Re'chab and Ba'a-nah, went, and came about the heat of the day to the house of Ish-bo'sheth, who lay on a bed at noon.

6 And they came thither into the midst of the house, *as though* they would have fetched wheat; and they smote him under the fifth *rib:* and Re'-chab and Ba'a-nah his brother escaped.

7 For when they came into the house, he lay on his bed in his bedchamber, and they smote him, and slew him, and beheaded him, and took his head, and gat them away through the plain all night.

8 And they brought the head of Ish-bo'sheth unto Da'vid to He'bron, and said to the king, Behold the head of Ish-bo'sheth the son of Saul thine enemy, which sought thy life; and the LORD hath avenged my lord the king this day of Saul, and of his seed.

9 And Da'vid answered Re'chab and Ba'a-nah his brother, the sons of Rim'mon the Be-e'roth-ite, and said unto them, As the LORD liveth, who hath redeemed my soul out of all adversity,

10 When one told me, saying, Behold, Saul is dead, thinking to have brought good tidings, I took hold of him, and slew him in Zik'lag, who *thought* that I would have given him a reward for his tidings:

11 How much more, when wicked men have slain a righteous person in his own house upon his bed? shall I not therefore now require his blood of your hand, and take you away from the earth?

12 And Da'vid commanded his young men, and they slew them, and cut off their hands and their

feet, and hanged *them* up over the pool in He'bron. But they took the head of Ish-bo'sheth, and buried *it* in the sepulchre of Ab'ner in He'bron.

Victories in Service (5:1–25)

King at Last!

5 THEN CAME all the tribes of Is'ra-el to Da'vid unto He'bron, and spake, saying, Behold, we *are* thy bone and thy flesh.

2 Also in time past, when Saul was king over us, thou wast he that leddest out and broughtest in Is'ra-el: and the LORD said to thee, Thou shalt feed my people Is'ra-el, and thou shalt be a captain over Is'ra-el.

3 So all the elders of Is'ra-el came to the king to He'bron; and king Da'vid made a league with them in He'bron before the LORD: and they anointed Da'vid king over Is'ra-el.

4 Da'vid *was* thirty years old when he began to reign, *and* he reigned forty years.

5 In He'bron he reigned over Ju'dah seven years and six months: and in Je-ru'sa-lem he reigned thirty and three years over all Is'ra-el and Ju'dah.

The Capture of Jerusalem

6 And the king and his men went to Je-ru'sa-lem unto the Jeb'u-sites, the inhabitants of the land: which spake unto Da'vid, saying, Except thou take away the blind and the lame, thou shalt not come in hither: thinking, Da'vid cannot come in hither.

7 Nevertheless Da'vid took the strong hold of Zi'on: the same *is* the city of Da'vid.

8 And Da'vid said on that day, Whosoever getteth up to the gutter, and smiteth the Jeb'u-sites, and the lame and the blind, *that are* hated of Da'vid's soul, *he shall be chief and captain.* Wherefore they said, The blind and the lame shall not come into the house.

9 So Da'vid dwelt in the fort, and called it the city of Da'vid. And Da'vid built round about from Mil'lo and inward.

10 And Da'vid went on, and grew great, and the LORD God of hosts *was* with him.

Acting Like a King

11 And Hi'ram king of Tyre sent messengers to Da'vid, and cedar trees, and carpenters, and masons: and they built Da'vid an house.

12 And Da'vid perceived that the LORD had established him king over Is'ra-el, and that he had exalted his kingdom for his people Is'ra-el's sake.

13 And Da'vid took *him* more concubines and wives out of Je-ru'sa-lem, after he was come from He'bron: and there were yet sons and daughters born to Da'vid.

14 And these *be* the names of those that were born unto him in Je-ru'sa-lem; Sham-mu'ah, and Sho'bab, and Na'than, and Sol'o-mon,

15 Ib'har also, and El-i-shu'a, and Ne'pheg, and Ja-phi'a,

16 And E-lish'a-ma, and E-li'a-da, and E-liph'a-let.

Victory Over the Philistines

17 But when the Phi-lis'-tines heard that they had anointed Da'vid king over Is'ra-el, all the Phi-lis'tines came up to seek Da'vid; and Da'vid heard *of it,* and went down to the hold.

18 The Phi-lis'tines also came and spread themselves in the valley of Reph'a-im.

19 And Da'vid enquired of the LORD, saying, Shall I go up to the Phi-lis'tines? wilt thou deliver them into mine hand? And the LORD said unto Da'vid, Go up: for I will doubtless deliver the Phi-lis'tines into thine hand.

20 And Da'vid came to Ba'al-per'a-zim, and Da'vid smote them there, and said, The LORD hath

191

broken forth upon mine enemies before me, as the breach of waters. Therefore he called the name of that place Ba'al-per'a-zim.

21 And there they left their images, and Da'vid and his men burned them.

A New Day in Israel

22 And the Phi-lis'tines came up yet again, and spread themselves in the valley of Re-ph'a-im.

23 And when Da'vid enquired of the LORD, he said, Thou shalt not go up; *but* fetch a compass behind them, and come upon them over against the mulberry trees.

24 And let it be, when thou hearest the sound of a going in the tops of the mulberry trees, that then thou shalt bestir thyself: for then shall the LORD go out before thee, to smite the host of the Phi-lis'-tines.

25 And Da'vid did so, as the LORD had commanded him; and smote the Phi-lis'tines from Ge'ba until thou come to Ga'zer.

Worship As a Way of Life
(6:1–7:29)

6 AGAIN, DA'VID gathered together all *the* chosen *men* of Is'ra-el, thirty thousand.

2 And Da'vid arose, and went with all the people that *were* with him from Ba'a-le of Ju'dah, to bring up from thence the ark of God, whose name is called by the name of the LORD of hosts that dwelleth *between* the cherubims.

The Ark of the Covenant Starts
Toward Jerusalem

3 And they set the ark of God upon a new cart, and brought it out of the house of A-bin'a-dab that *was* in Gib'e-ah: and Uz'zah and A-hi'o, the sons of A-bin'a-dab, drave the new cart.

4 And they brought it out of the house of A-bin'a-dab which *was* at Gib'e-ah, accompanying the ark of God: and A-hi'o went before the ark.

5 And Da'vid and all the house of Is'ra-el played before the LORD on all manner of *instruments made of* fir wood, even on harps, and on psalteries, and on timbrels, and on cornets, and on cymbals.

6 And when they came to Na'chon's threshing-floor, Uz'zah put forth *his hand* to the ark of God, and took hold of it; for the oxen shook *it.*

7 And the anger of the LORD was kindled against Uz'zah; and God smote him there for *his* error; and there he died by the ark of God.

8 And Da'vid was displeased, because the LORD had made a breach upon Uz'zah: and he called the name of the place Pe'rez-uz'zah to this day.

9 And Da'vid was afraid of the LORD that day, and said, How shall the ark of the LORD come to me?

10 So Da'vid would not remove the ark of the LORD unto him into the city of Da'vid: but Da'vid carried it aside into the house of O'bed-e'dom the Git'-tite.

11 And the ark of the LORD continued in the house of O'bed-e'dom the Git'tite three months: and the LORD blessed O'bed-e'dom, and all his household.

12 And it was told king Da'vid, saying, The LORD hath blessed the house of O'bed-e'dom, and all that *pertaineth* unto him, because of the ark of God. So Da'vid went and brought up the ark of God from the house of O'bed-e'dom into the city of Da'vid with gladness.

13 And it was *so,* that when they that bare the ark of the LORD had gone six paces, he sacrificed oxen and fatlings.

14 And Da'vid danced before the LORD with all *his* might; and Da'vid *was* girded with a linen ephod.

The Uzzah Lesson

A Joyous Celebration

193

15 So Da'vid and all the house of Is'ra-el brought up the ark of the LORD with shouting, and with the sound of the trumpet.

16 And as the ark of the LORD came into the city of Da'vid, Mi'chal Saul's daughter looked through a window, and saw king Da'vid leaping and dancing before the LORD; and she despised him in her heart.

17 And they brought in the ark of the LORD, and set it in his place, in the midst of the tabernacle that Da'vid had pitched for it: and Da'vid offered burnt offerings and peace offerings before the LORD.

18 And as soon as Da'vid had made an end of offering burnt offerings and peace offerings, he blessed the people in the name of the LORD of hosts.

19 And he dealt among all the people, *even* among the whole multitude of Is'ra-el, as well to the women as men, to every one a cake of bread, and a good piece *of flesh,* and a flagon *of wine.* So all the people departed every one to his house.

A Sour Note

20 Then Da'vid returned to bless his household. And Mi'chal the daughter of Saul came out to meet Da'vid, and said, How glorious was the king of Is'ra-el to day, who uncovered himself to day in the eyes of the handmaids of his servants, as one of the vain fellows shamelessly uncovereth himself!

21 And Da'vid said unto Mi'chal, *It was* before the LORD, which chose me before thy father, and before all his house, to appoint me ruler over the people of the LORD, over Is'ra-el: therefore will I play before the LORD.

22 And I will yet be more vile than thus, and will be base in mine own sight: and of the maid-servants which thou hast spoken of, of them shall I be had in honour.

23 Therefore Mi'chal the daughter of Saul had no child unto the day of her death.

7 AND IT came to pass, when the king sat in his house, and the LORD had given him rest round about from all his enemies;

David Wants to Honor God

2 That the king said unto Na'than the prophet, See now, I dwell in an house of cedar, but the ark of God dwelleth within curtains.

3 And Na'than said to the king, Go, do all that *is* in thine heart; for the LORD *is* with thee.

4 And it came to pass that night, that the word of the LORD came unto Na'than, saying,

David Is Honored by God

5 Go and tell my servant Da'vid, Thus saith the LORD, Shalt thou build me an house for me to dwell in?

6 Whereas I have not dwelt in *any* house since the time that I brought up the children of Is'ra-el out of E'gypt, even to this day, but have walked in a tent and in a tabernacle.

7 In all *the places* wherein I have walked with all the children of Is'ra-el spake I a word with any of the tribes of Is'ra-el, whom I commanded to feed my people Is'ra-el, saying, Why build ye not me an house of cedar?

8 Now therefore so shalt thou say unto my servant Da'vid, Thus saith the LORD of hosts, I took thee from the sheepcote, from following the sheep, to be ruler over my people, over Is'ra-el:

9 And I was with thee whithersoever thou wentest, and have cut off all thine enemies out of thy sight, and have made thee a great name, like unto the name of the great *men* that *are* in the earth.

10 Moreover I will appoint a place for my people Is'ra-el, and will plant them, that they may dwell

in a place of their own, and move no more; neither shall the children of wickedness afflict them any more, as beforetime,

11 And as since the time that I commanded judges *to be* over my people Is'ra-el, and have caused thee to rest from all thine enemies. Also the LORD telleth thee that he will make thee an house.

12 And when thy days be fulfilled, and thou shalt sleep with thy fathers, I will set up thy seed after thee, which shall proceed out of thy bowels, and I will establish his kingdom.

13 He shall build an house for my name, and I will stablish the throne of his kingdom for ever.

14 I will be his father, and he shall be my son. If he commit iniquity, I will chasten him with the rod of men, and with the stripes of the children of men:

15 But my mercy shall not depart away from him, as I took *it* from Saul, whom I put away before thee.

16 And thine house and thy kingdom shall be established for ever before thee: thy throne shall be established for ever.

17 According to all these words, and according to all this vision, so did Na'than speak unto Da'vid.

18 Then went king Da'vid in, and sat before the LORD, and he said, Who *am* I, O Lord GOD? and what *is* my house, that thou hast brought me hitherto?

19 And this was yet a small thing in thy sight, O Lord GOD; but thou hast spoken also of thy servant's house for a great while to come. And *is* this the manner of man, O Lord GOD?

20 And what can Da'vid say more unto thee? for thou, Lord GOD, knowest thy servant.

21 For thy word's sake, and according to thine own heart, hast thou done all these great things, to make thy servant know *them.*

22 Wherefore thou art great, O Lord God: for *there is* none like thee, neither *is there any* God beside thee, according to all that we have heard with our ears.

23 And what one nation in the earth *is* like thy people, *even* like Is'ra-el, whom God went to redeem for a people to himself, and to make him a name, and to do for you great things and terrible, for thy land, before thy people, which thou redeemedst to thee from E'gypt, *from* the nations and their gods?

24 For thou hast confirmed to thyself thy people Is'ra-el *to be* a people unto thee for ever: and thou, Lord, art become their God.

25 And now, O Lord God, the word that thou hast spoken concerning thy servant, and concerning his house, establish *it* for ever, and do as thou hast said.

26 And let thy name be magnified for ever, saying, The Lord of hosts *is* the God over Is'ra-el: and let the house of thy servant Da'vid be established before thee.

27 For thou, O Lord of hosts, God of Is'ra-el, hast revealed to thy servant, saying, I will build thee an house: therefore hath thy servant found in his heart to pray this prayer unto thee.

28 And now, O Lord God, thou *art* that God, and thy words be true, and thou hast promised this goodness unto thy servant:

29 Therefore now let it please thee to bless the house of thy servant, that it may continue for ever before thee: for thou, O Lord God, hast spoken *it:*

and with thy blessing let the house of thy servant be blessed for ever.

Victory As a Way of Life

Defeating the Enemies of the People of God

8 AND AFTER this it came to pass, that Da'vid smote the Phi-lis'-tines, and subdued them: and Da'vid took Me'theg-am'mah out of the hand of the Phi-lis'-tines.

2 And he smote Mo'ab, and measured them with a line, casting them down to the ground; even with two lines measured he to put to death, and with one full line to keep alive. And *so* the Mo'ab-ites became Da'vid's servants, *and* brought gifts.

3 Da'vid smote also Had-ad-e'zer, the son of Re'hob, king of Zo'bah, as he went to recover his border at the river Eu-phra'tes.

4 And Da'vid took from him a thousand *chariots,* and seven hundred horsemen, and twenty thousand footmen: and Da'vid houghed all the chariot *horses,* but reserved of them *for* an hundred chariots.

5 And when the Syr'i-ans of Da-mas'cus came to succour Had-ad-e'zer king of Zo'bah, Da'vid slew of the Syr'i-ans two and twenty thousand men.

6 Then Da'vid put garrisons in Syr'i-a of Da-mas'cus: and the Syr'i-ans became servants to Da'vid, *and* brought gifts. And the LORD preserved Da'vid whithersoever he went.

7 And Da'vid took the shields of gold that were on the servants of Had-ad-e'zer, and brought them to Je-ru'sa-lem.

8 And from Be'tah, and from Ber'o-thai, cities of Had-ad-e'zer, king Da'vid took exceeding much brass.

9 When To'i king of Ha'-math heard that Da'vid had smitten all the host of Had-ad-e'zer,

10 Then To'i sent Jo'ram his son unto king Da'vid, to salute him, and to bless him, because he had fought against Had-ad-e'zer, and smitten him: for Had-ad-e'zer had wars with To'i. And *Jo'ram* brought with him vessels of silver, and vessels of gold, and vessels of brass:

11 Which also king Da'vid did dedicate unto the Lord, with the silver and gold that he had dedicated of all nations which he subdued;

12 Of Syr'i-a, and of Mo'ab, and of the children of Am'mon, and of the Phi-lis'tines, and of Am'a-lek, and of the spoil of Had-ad-e'zer, son of Re'hob, king of Zo'bah.

13 And Da'vid gat *him* a name when he returned from smiting of the Syr'i-ans in the valley of salt, *being* eighteen thousand *men*.

14 And he put garrisons in E'dom; throughout all E'dom put he garrisons, and all they of E'dom became Da'vid's servants. And the Lord preserved Da'vid whithersoever he went.

15 And Da'vid reigned over all Is'ra-el; and Da'vid executed judgment and justice unto all his people.

16 And Jo'ab the son of Zer-u-i'ah *was* over the host; and Je-hosh'a-phat the son of A-hi'lud *was* recorder;

17 And Za'dok the son of A-hi'tub, and A-him'e-lech the son of A-bi'a-thar, *were* the priests; and Ser-a-i'ah *was* the scribe;

18 And Be-na'iah the son of Je-hoi'a-da *was over* both the Cher'eth-ites and the Pe'leth-ites; and Da'vid's sons were chief rulers.

The Consolidation Process

David and Mephibosheth

_____
_____
_____
_____
_____
_____
_____
_____
_____
_____
_____
_____
_____
_____
_____
_____
_____
_____
_____
_____
_____
_____
_____

9 AND DA'VID said, Is there yet any that is left of the house of Saul, that I may shew him kindness for Jon'a-than's sake?

2 And *there was* of the house of Saul a servant whose name *was* Zi'ba. And when they had called him unto Da'vid, the king said unto him, *Art* thou Zi'ba? And he said, Thy servant *is he.*

3 And the king said, *Is* there not yet any of the house of Saul, that I may shew the kindness of God unto him? And Zi'ba said unto the king, Jon'a-than hath yet a son, *which is* lame on *his* feet.

4 And the king said unto him, Where *is* he? And Zi'ba said unto the king, Behold, he *is* in the house of Ma'chir, the son of Am'mi-el, in Lo-de'bar.

5 Then king Da'vid sent, and fetched him out of the house of Ma'chir, the son of Am'mi-el, from Lo-de'bar.

6 Now when Me-phib'o-sheth, the son of Jon'a-than, the son of Saul, was come unto Da'vid, he fell on his face, and did reverence. And Da'vid said, Me-phib'o-sheth. And he answered, Behold thy servant!

7 And Da'vid said unto him, Fear not: for I will surely shew thee kindness for Jon'a-than thy father's sake, and will restore thee all the land of Saul thy father; and thou shalt eat bread at my table continually.

8 And he bowed himself, and said, What *is* thy servant, that thou shouldest look upon such a dead dog as I *am?*

9 Then the king called to Zi'ba, Saul's servant, and said unto him, I have given unto thy master's son all that pertained to Saul and to all his house.

10 Thou therefore, and thy sons, and thy servants, shall till the land for him, and thou shalt bring

200

in *the fruits,* that thy master's son may have food to eat: but Me-phib'o-sheth thy master's son shall eat bread alway at my table. Now Zi'ba had fifteen sons and twenty servants.

11 Then said Zi'ba unto the king, According to all that my lord the king hath commanded his servant, so shall thy servant do. As for Me-phib'o-sheth, *said the king,* he shall eat at my table, as one of the king's sons.

12 And Me-phib'o-sheth had a young son, whose name *was* Mi'cha. And all that dwelt in the house of Zi'ba *were* servants unto Me-phib'o-sheth.

13 So Me-phib'o-sheth dwelt in Je-ru'sa-lem: for he did eat continually at the king's table; and was lame on both his feet.

10 AND IT came to pass after this, that the king of the children of Am'mon died, and Ha'nun his son reigned in his stead.

2 Then said Da'vid, I will shew kindness unto Ha'nun the son of Na'hash, as his father shewed kindness unto me. And Da'vid sent to comfort him by the hand of his servants for his father. And Da'vid's servants came into the land of the children of Am'mon.

3 And the princes of the children of Am'mon said unto Ha'-nun their lord, Thinkest thou that Da'vid doth honour thy father, that he hath sent comforters unto thee? hath not Da'vid *rather* sent his servants unto thee, to search the city, and to spy it out, and to overthrow it?

4 Wherefore Ha'nun took Da'vid's servants, and shaved off the one half of their beards, and cut off their garments in the middle, *even* to their buttocks, and sent them away.

The War with Ammon

5 When they told *it* unto Da'vid, he sent to meet them, because the men were greatly ashamed: and the king said, Tarry at Jer'i-cho until your beards be grown, and *then* return.

6 And when the children of Am'mon saw that they stank before Da'vid, the children of Am'mon sent and hired the Syr'i-ans of Beth-re'hob, and the Syr'i-ans of Zo'ba, twenty thousand footmen, and of king Ma'a-cah a thousand men, and of Ish'-tob twelve thousand men.

7 And when Da'vid heard of *it,* he sent Jo'ab, and all the host of the mighty men.

8 And the children of Am'-mon came out, and put the battle in array at the entering in of the gate: and the Syr'i-ans of Zo'ba, and of Re'hob, and Ish'-tob, and Ma'a-cah, *were* by themselves in the field.

9 When Jo'ab saw that the front of the battle was against him before and behind, he chose of all the choice *men* of Is'ra-el, and put *them* in array against the Syr'i-ans:

10 And the rest of the people he delivered into the hand of A-bish'-a-i his brother, that he might put *them* in array against the children of Am'mon.

11 And he said, If the Syr'i-ans be too strong for me, then thou shalt help me: but if the children of Am'mon be too strong for thee, then I will come and help thee.

12 Be of good courage, and let us play the men for our people, and for the cities of our God: and the LORD do that which seemeth him good.

13 And Jo'ab drew nigh, and the people that *were* with him, unto the battle against the Syr'i-ans: and they fled before him.

14 And when the children of Am'mon saw that the Syr'i-ans were fled, then fled they also before

A-bish'a-i, and entered into the city. So Jo'ab returned from the children of Am'mon, and came to Je-ru'sa-lem.

15 And when the Syr'i-ans saw that they were smitten before Is'ra-el, they gathered themselves together.

16 And Had-ar-e'zer sent, and brought out the Syr'i-ans that *were* beyond the river: and they came to He'lam; and Sho'bach the captain of the host of Had-ar-e'zer *went* before them.

17 And when it was told Da'vid, he gathered all Is'ra-el together, and passed over Jor'dan, and came to He'lam. And the Syr'i-ans set themselves in array against Da'vid, and fought with him.

18 And the Syr'i-ans fled before Is'ra-el; and Da'vid slew *the men of* seven hundred chariots of the Syr'i-ans, and forty thousand horsemen, and smote Sho'bach the captain of their host, who died there.

19 And when all the kings *that were* servants to Had-ar-e'zer saw that they were smitten before Is'ra-el, they made peace with Is'ra-el, and served them. So the Syr'i-ans feared to help the children of Am'mon any more.

LESSON 8

2 SAMUEL 11:1–24:25
Sin That Leads to Tragedy

The Ways of Sin

_____

_____

_____

The Time and Opportunity for
Sin

_____

_____

_____

_____

_____

Panic in the Face of Guilt

_____

_____

_____

_____

11 AND IT came to pass, after the year was expired, at the time when kings go forth *to battle,* that Da'vid sent Jo'ab, and his servants with him, and all Is'ra-el; and they destroyed the children of Am'mon, and besieged Rab'bah. But Da'vid tarried still at Je-ru'sa-lem.

2 And it came to pass in an eveningtide, that Da'vid arose from off his bed, and walked upon the roof of the king's house: and from the roof he saw a woman washing herself; and the woman *was* very beautiful to look upon.

3 And Da'vid sent and enquired after the woman. And *one* said, *Is* not this Bath'-she-ba, the daughter of E-li'am, the wife of U-ri'ah the Hit'-tite?

4 And Da'vid sent messengers, and took her; and she came in unto him, and he lay with her; for she was purified from her uncleanness: and she returned unto her house.

5 And the woman conceived, and sent and told Da'vid, and said, I *am* with child.

6 And Da'vid sent to Jo'ab, *saying,* Send me U-ri'ah the Hit'-tite. And Jo'ab sent U-ri'ah to Da'vid.

7 And when U-ri'ah was come unto him, Da'vid demanded *of him* how Jo'ab did, and how the people did, and how the war prospered.

8 And Da'vid said to U-ri'ah, Go down to thy house, and wash thy feet. And U-ri'ah departed out of the king's house, and there followed him a mess *of meat* from the king.

9 But U-ri'ah slept at the door of the king's house, with all the servants of his lord, and went not down to his house.

10 And when they had told Da'vid, saying, U-ri'ah went not down unto his house, Da'vid said unto U-ri'ah, Camest thou not from *thy* journey? why *then* didst thou not go down unto thine house?

11 And U-ri'ah said unto Da'vid, The ark, and Is'ra-el, and Ju'dah, abide in tents; and my lord Jo'ab, and the servants of my lord, are encamped in the open fields; shall I then go into mine house, to eat and to drink, and to lie with my wife? *as* thou livest, and *as* thy soul liveth, I will not do this thing.

12 And Da'vid said to U-ri'ah, Tarry here to day also, and to morrow I will let thee depart. So U-ri'ah abode in Je-ru'sa-lem that day, and the morrow.

13 And when Da'vid had called him, he did eat and drink before him; and he made him drunk: and at even he went out to lie on his bed with the servants of his lord, but went not down to his house.

14 And it came to pass in the morning, that Da'vid wrote a letter to Jo'ab, and sent *it* by the hand of U-ri'ah.

15 And he wrote in the letter, saying, Set ye U-ri'ah in the forefront of the hottest battle, and retire ye from him, that he may be smitten, and die.

16 And it came to pass, when Jo'ab observed the city, that he assigned U-ri'ah unto a place where he knew that valiant men *were.*

_____
_____
_____
_____
_____

When Sin Appears to Be
Hidden

_____
_____
_____
_____
_____
_____
_____
_____
_____
_____
_____
_____
_____
_____
_____

17 And the men of the city went out, and fought with Jo'ab: and there fell *some* of the people of the servants of Da'vid; and U-ri'ah the Hit'tite died also.

18 Then Jo'ab sent and told Da'vid all the things concerning the war;

19 And charged the messenger, saying, When thou hast made an end of telling the matters of the war unto the king,

20 And if so be that the king's wrath arise, and he say unto thee, Wherefore approached ye so nigh unto the city when ye did fight? knew ye not that they would shoot from the wall?

21 Who smote A-bim'e-lech the son of Je-rub'be-sheth? did not a woman cast a piece of a millstone upon him from the wall, that he died in The'bez? why went ye nigh the wall? then say thou, Thy servant U-ri'ah the Hit'tite is dead also.

22 So the messenger went, and came and shewed Da'vid all that Jo'ab had sent him for.

23 And the messenger said unto Da'vid, Surely the men prevailed against us, and came out unto us into the field, and we were upon them even unto the entering of the gate.

24 And the shooters shot from off the wall upon thy servants; and *some* of the king's servants be dead, and thy servant U-ri'ah the Hit'tite is dead also.

25 Then Da'vid said unto the messenger, Thus shalt thou say unto Jo'ab, Let not this thing displease thee, for the sword devoureth one as well as another: make thy battle more strong against the city, and overthrow it: and encourage thou him.

26 And when the wife of U-ri'ah heard that U-ri'ah her husband was dead, she mourned for her husband.

27 And when the mourning was past, Da'vid sent and fetched her to his house, and she became his wife, and bare him a son. But the thing that Da'vid had done displeased the Lord.

12 AND THE Lord sent Na'than unto Da'vid. And he came unto him, and said unto him, There were two men in one city; the one rich, and the other poor.

The Wages of Sin

2 The rich *man* had exceeding many flocks and herds:

3 But the poor *man* had nothing, save one little ewe lamb, which he had bought and nourished up: and it grew up together with him, and with his children; it did eat of his own meat, and drank of his own cup, and lay in his bosom, and was unto him as a daughter.

Nathan's Strange Parable

4 And there came a traveller unto the rich man, and he spared to take of his own flock and of his own herd, to dress for the wayfaring man that was come unto him; but took the poor man's lamb, and dressed it for the man that was come to him.

5 And Da'vid's anger was greatly kindled against the man; and he said to Na'than, As the Lord liveth, the man that hath done this *thing* shall surely die:

6 And he shall restore the lamb fourfold, because he did this thing, and because he had no pity.

7 And Na'than said to Da'vid, Thou *art* the man. Thus saith the Lord God of Is'ra-el, I anointed thee king over Is'ra-el, and I delivered thee out of the hand of Saul;

Thou Art the Man

8 And I gave thee thy master's house, and thy master's wives into thy bosom, and gave thee the house of Is'ra-el and of Ju'dah; and if *that had been*

too little, I would moreover have given unto thee such and such things.

9 Wherefore hast thou despised the commandment of the Lord, to do evil in his sight? thou hast killed U-ri'ah the Hit'-tite with the sword, and hast taken his wife *to be* thy wife, and hast slain him with the sword of the children of Am'mon.

10 Now therefore the sword shall never depart from thine house; because thou hast despised me, and hast taken the wife of U-ri'ah the Hit'tite to be thy wife.

11 Thus saith the Lord, Behold, I will raise up evil against thee out of thine own house, and I will take thy wives before thine eyes, and give *them* unto thy neighbour, and he shall lie with thy wives in the sight of this sun.

12 For thou didst *it* secretly: but I will do this thing before all Is'ra-el, and before the sun.

I Have Sinned

13 And Da'vid said unto Na'-than, I have sinned against the Lord. And Na'than said unto Da'vid, The Lord also hath put away thy sin; thou shalt not die.

14 Howbeit, because by this deed thou hast given great occasion to the enemies of the Lord to blaspheme, the child also *that is* born unto thee shall surely die.

Grief and Comfort

15 And Na'than departed unto his house. And the Lord struck the child that U-ri'ah's wife bare unto Da'vid, and it was very sick.

16 Da'vid therefore besought God for the child; and Da'vid fasted, and went in, and lay all night upon the earth.

17 And the elders of his house arose, *and went* to him, to raise him up from the earth: but he would not, neither did he eat bread with them.

18 And it came to pass on the seventh day, that the child died. And the servants of Da'vid feared to tell him that the child was dead: for they said, Behold, while the child was yet alive, we spake unto him, and he would not hearken unto our voice: how will he then vex himself, if we tell him that the child is dead?

19 But when Da'vid saw that his servants whispered, Da'vid perceived that the child was dead: therefore Da'vid said unto his servants, Is the child dead? And they said, He is dead.

20 Then Da'vid arose from the earth, and washed, and anointed *himself,* and changed his apparel, and came into the house of the LORD, and worshipped: then he came to his own house; and when he required, they set bread before him, and he did eat.

21 Then said his servants unto him, What thing *is* this that thou hast done? thou didst fast and weep for the child, *while it was* alive; but when the child was dead, thou didst rise and eat bread.

22 And he said, While the child was yet alive, I fasted and wept: for I said, Who can tell *whether* GOD will be gracious to me, that the child may live?

23 But now he is dead, wherefore should I fast? can I bring him back again? I shall go to him, but he shall not return to me.

24 And Da'vid comforted Bath'-she-ba his wife, and went in unto her, and lay with her: and she bare a son, and he called his name Sol'o-mon: and the LORD loved him.

25 And he sent by the hand of Na'than the prophet; and he called his name Jed-i-di'ah, because of the LORD.

26 And Jo'ab fought against Rab'bah of the children of Am'mon, and took the royal city.

The Battle of Rabbath-Ammon Concluded

27 And Jo'ab sent messengers to Da'vid, and said, I have fought against Rab'bah, and have taken the city of waters.

28 Now therefore gather the rest of the people together, and encamp against the city, and take it: lest I take the city, and it be called after my name.

29 And Da'vid gathered all the people together, and went to Rab'bah, and fought against it, and took it.

30 And he took their king's crown from off his head, the weight whereof *was* a talent of gold with the precious stones: and it was *set* on Da'vid's head. And he brought forth the spoil of the city in great abundance.

31 And he brought forth the people that *were* therein, and put *them* under saws, and under harrows of iron, and under axes of iron, and made them pass through the brickkiln: and thus did he unto all the cities of the children of Am'mon. So Da'vid and all the people returned unto Je-ru'sa-lem.

Sin Is Contagious

Amnon's Lust and the Rape of Tamar

13 AND IT came to pass after this, that Ab'salom the son of Da'vid had a fair sister, whose name *was* Ta'mar; and Am'non the son of Da'vid loved her.

2 And Am'non was so vexed, that he fell sick for his sister Ta'mar; for she *was* a virgin; and Am'non thought it hard for him to do any thing to her.

3 But Am'non had a friend, whose name *was* Jon'a-dab, the son of Shim'e-ah Da'vid's brother: and Jon'a-dab *was* a very subtil man.

4 And he said unto him, Why *art* thou, *being* the king's son, lean from day to day? wilt thou not tell

me? And Am'non said unto him, I love Ta'mar, my brother Ab'sa-lom's sister.

5 And Jon'a-dab said unto him, Lay thee down on thy bed, and make thyself sick: and when thy father cometh to see thee, say unto him, I pray thee, Let my sister Ta'mar come, and give me meat, and dress the meat in my sight, that I may see *it*, and eat *it* at her hand.

6 So Am'non lay down, and made himself sick: and when the king was come to see him, Am'non said unto the king, I pray thee, let Ta'mar my sister come, and make me a couple of cakes in my sight, that I may eat at her hand.

7 Then Da'vid sent home to Ta'mar, saying, Go now to thy brother Am'non's house, and dress him meat.

8 So Ta'mar went to her brother Am'non's house; and he was laid down. And she took flour, and kneaded *it*, and made cakes in his sight, and did bake the cakes.

9 And she took a pan, and poured *them* out before him; but he refused to eat. And Am'non said, Have out all men from me. And they went out every man from him.

10 And Am'non said unto Ta'mar, Bring the meat into the chamber, that I may eat of thine hand. And Ta'mar took the cakes which she had made, and brought *them* into the chamber to Am'non her brother.

11 And when she had brought *them* unto him to eat, he took hold of her, and said unto her, Come lie with me, my sister.

12 And she answered him, Nay, my brother, do not force me; for no such thing ought to be done in Is'ra-el: do not thou this folly.

13 And I, whither shall I cause my shame to go? and as for thee, thou shalt be as one of the fools in Is'ra-el. Now therefore, I pray thee, speak unto the king; for he will not withhold me from thee.

14 Howbeit he would not hearken unto her voice: but, being stronger than she, forced her, and lay with her.

15 Then Am'non hated her exceedingly; so that the hatred wherewith he hated her *was* greater than the love wherewith he had loved her. And Am'non said unto her, Arise, be gone.

16 And she said unto him, *There is* no cause: this evil in sending me away *is* greater than the other that thou didst unto me. But he would not hearken unto her.

17 Then he called his servant that ministered unto him, and said, Put now this *woman* out from me, and bolt the door after her.

18 And *she had* a garment of divers colours upon her: for with such robes were the king's daughters *that were* virgins apparelled. Then his servant brought her out, and bolted the door after her.

19 And Ta'mar put ashes on her head, and rent her garment of divers colours that *was* on her, and laid her hand on her head, and went on crying.

20 And Ab'sa-lom her brother said unto her, Hath Am'non thy brother been with thee? but hold now thy peace, my sister: he *is* thy brother; regard not this thing. So Ta'mar remained desolate in her brother Ab'sa-lom's house.

21 But when king Da'vid heard of all these things, he was very wroth.

Revenge

22 And Ab'sa-lom spake unto his brother Am'non neither good nor bad: for Ab'sa-lom hated Am'non, because he had forced his sister Ta'mar.

23 And it came to pass after two full years, that Ab'sa-lom had sheepshearers in Ba'al-ha'zor, which *is* beside E'phra-im: and Ab'sa-lom invited all the king's sons.

24 And Ab'sa-lom came to the king, and said, Behold now, thy servant hath sheepshearers; let the king, I beseech thee, and his servants go with thy servant.

25 And the king said to Ab'sa-lom, Nay, my son, let us not all now go, lest we be chargeable unto thee. And he pressed him: howbeit he would not go, but blessed him.

26 Then said Ab'sa-lom, If not, I pray thee, let my brother Am'non go with us. And the king said unto him, Why should he go with thee?

27 But Ab'sa-lom pressed him, that he let Am'non and all the king's sons go with him.

28 Now Ab'sa-lom had commanded his servants, saying, Mark ye now when Am'non's heart is merry with wine, and when I say unto you, Smite Am'-non; then kill him, fear not: have not I commanded you? be courageous, and be valiant.

29 And the servants of Ab'sa-lom did unto Am'non as Ab'sa-lom had commanded. Then all the king's sons arose, and every man gat him up upon his mule, and fled.

30 And it came to pass, while they were in the way, that tidings came to Da'vid, saying, Ab'sa-lom hath slain all the king's sons, and there is not one of them left.

31 Then the king arose, and tare his garments, and lay on the earth; and all his servants stood by with their clothes rent.

32 And Jon'a-dab, the son of Shim'e-ah Da'vid's brother, answered and said, Let not my lord sup-

The Amnon-Absalom Lesson

213

pose *that* they have slain all the young men the king's sons; for Am'non only is dead: for by the appointment of Ab'sa-lom this hath been determined from the day that he forced his sister Ta'mar.

33 Now therefore let not my lord the king take the thing to his heart, to think that all the king's sons are dead: for Am'non only is dead.

34 But Ab'sa-lom fled. And the young man that kept the watch lifted up his eyes, and looked, and, behold, there came much people by the way of the hill side behind him.

35 And Jon'a-dab said unto the king, Behold, the king's sons come: as thy servant said, so it is.

36 And it came to pass, as soon as he had made an end of speaking, that, behold, the king's sons came, and lifted up their voice and wept: and the king also and all his servants wept very sore.

37 But Ab'sa-lom fled, and went to Tal'mai, the son of Am-mi'hud, king of Ge'shur. And *Da'vid* mourned for his son every day.

38 So Ab'sa-lom fled, and went to Ge'shur, and was there three years.

39 And *the soul of* king Da'vid longed to go forth unto Ab'sa-lom: for he was comforted concerning Am'non, seeing he was dead.

Unforgiving Forgiveness

14 NOW JO'AB the son of Zer-u-i'ah perceived that the king's heart *was* toward Ab'sa-lom.

David's Dilemma

2 And Jo'ab sent to Te-ko'ah, and fetched thence a wise woman, and said unto her, I pray thee, feign thyself to be a mourner, and put on now mourning apparel, and anoint not thyself with oil,

but be as a woman that had a long time mourned for the dead:

3 And come to the king, and speak on this manner unto him. So Jo'ab put the words in her mouth.

Joab Calls for Help

4 And when the woman of Te-ko'ah spake to the king, she fell on her face to the ground, and did obeisance, and said, Help, O king.

5 And the king said unto her, What aileth thee? And she answered, I *am* indeed a widow woman, and mine husband is dead.

6 And thy handmaid had two sons, and they two strove together in the field, and *there was* none to part them, but the one smote the other, and slew him.

7 And, behold, the whole family is risen against thine handmaid, and they said, Deliver him that smote his brother, that we may kill him, for the life of his brother whom he slew; and we will destroy the heir also: and so they shall quench my coal which is left, and shall not leave to my husband *neither* name nor remainder upon the earth.

8 And the king said unto the woman, Go to thine house, and I will give charge concerning thee.

9 And the woman of Te-ko'ah said unto the king, My lord, O king, the iniquity *be* on me, and on my father's house: and the king and his throne *be* guiltless.

10 And the king said, Whosoever saith *ought* unto thee, bring him to me, and he shall not touch thee any more.

Absalom Is Completely Forgiven

11 Then said she, I pray thee, let the king remember the LORD thy God, that thou wouldest not suffer the revengers of blood to destroy any more, lest they destroy my son. And he said, *As* the LORD liveth, there shall not one hair of thy son fall to the earth.

12 Then the woman said, Let thine handmaid, I pray thee, speak *one* word unto my lord the king. And he said, Say on.

13 And the woman said, Wherefore then hast thou thought such a thing against the people of God? for the king doth speak this thing as one which is faulty, in that the king doth not fetch home again his banished.

14 For we must needs die, and *are* as water spilt on the ground, which cannot be gathered up again; neither doth God respect *any* person: yet doth he devise means, that his banished be not expelled from him.

15 Now therefore that I am come to speak of this thing unto my lord the king, *it is* because the people have made me afraid: and thy handmaid said, I will now speak unto the king; it may be that the king will perform the request of his handmaid.

16 For the king will hear, to deliver his handmaid out of the hand of the man *that would* destroy me and my son together out of the inheritance of God.

17 Then thine handmaid said, The word of my lord the king shall now be comfortable: for as an angel of God, so *is* my lord the king to discern good and bad: therefore the Lord thy God will be with thee.

18 Then the king answered and said unto the woman, Hide not from me, I pray thee, the thing that I shall ask thee. And the woman said, Let my lord the king now speak.

19 And the king said, *Is not* the hand of Jo'ab with thee in all this? And the woman answered and said, *As* thy soul liveth, my lord the king, none can turn to the right hand or to the left from ought that my lord the king hath spoken: for thy servant

Jo'ab, he bade me, and he put all these words in the mouth of thine handmaid:

20 To fetch about this form of speech hath thy servant Jo'ab done this thing: and my lord *is* wise, according to the wisdom of an angel of God, to know all *things* that *are* in the earth.

21 And the king said unto Jo'ab, Behold now, I have done this thing: go therefore, bring the young man Ab'sa-lom again.

22 And Jo'ab fell to the ground on his face, and bowed himself, and thanked the king: and Jo'ab said, To day thy servant knoweth that I have found grace in thy sight, my lord, O king, in that the king hath fulfilled the request of his servant.

23 So Jo'ab arose and went to Ge'shur, and brought Ab'sa-lom to Je-ru'sa-lem.

24 And the king said, Let him turn to his own house, and let him not see my face. So Ab'sa-lom returned to his own house, and saw not the king's face.

25 But in all Is'ra-el there was none to be so much praised as Ab'sa-lom for his beauty: from the sole of his foot even to the crown of his head there was no blemish in him.

26 And when he polled his head, (for it was at every year's end that he polled *it:* because *the hair* was heavy on him, therefore he polled it:) he weighed the hair of his head at two hundred she-kels after the king's weight.

27 And unto Ab'sa-lom there were born three sons, and one daughter, whose name *was* Ta'mar: she was a woman of a fair countenance.

28 So Ab'sa-lom dwelt two full years in Je-ru'sa-lem, and saw not the king's face.

29 Therefore Ab'sa-lom sent for Jo'ab, to have

sent him to the king; but he would not come to him: and when he sent again the second time, he would not come.

30 Therefore he said unto his servants, See, Jo'ab's field is near mine, and he hath barley there; go and set it on fire. And Ab'sa-lom's servants set the field on fire.

31 Then Jo'ab arose, and came to Ab'sa-lom unto *his* house, and said unto him, Wherefore have thy servants set my field on fire?

32 And Ab'sa-lom answered Jo'ab, Behold, I sent unto thee, saying, Come hither, that I may send thee to the king, to say, Wherefore am I come from Ge'-shur? *it had been* good for me *to have been* there still: now therefore let me see the king's face; and if there be *any* iniquity in me, let him kill me.

33 So Jo'ab came to the king, and told him: and when he had called for Ab'sa-lom, he came to the king, and bowed himself on his face to the ground before the king: and the king kissed Ab'sa-lom.

Sin's Costly Consequences

15 AND IT came to pass after this, that Ab'sa-lom prepared him chariots and horses, and fifty men to run before him.

Conspiracy Against the King

2 And Ab'sa-lom rose up early, and stood beside the way of the gate: and it was *so,* that when any man that had a controversy came to the king for judgment, then Ab'sa-lom called unto him, and said, Of what city *art* thou? And he said, Thy servant *is* of one of the tribes of Is'ra-el.

3 And Ab'sa-lom said unto him, See, thy matters *are* good and right; but *there is* no man *deputed* of the king to hear thee.

4 Ab'sa-lom said moreover, Oh that I were made judge in the land, that every man which hath any

suit or cause might come unto me, and I would do him justice!

5 And it was *so,* that when any man came nigh *to him* to do him obeisance, he put forth his hand, and took him, and kissed him.

6 And on this manner did Ab'sa-lom to all Is'ra-el that came to the king for judgment: so Ab'sa-lom stole the hearts of the men of Is'ra-el.

7 And it came to pass after forty years, that Ab'sa-lom said unto the king, I pray thee, let me go and pay my vow, which I have vowed unto the Lord, in He-'bron.

8 For thy servant vowed a vow while I abode at Ge'shur in Syr'i-a, saying, If the Lord shall bring me again indeed to Je-ru'sa-lem, then I will serve the Lord.

9 And the king said unto him, Go in peace. So he arose, and went to He'bron.

10 But Ab'sa-lom sent spies throughout all the tribes of Is'ra-el, saying, As soon as ye hear the sound of the trumpet, then ye shall say, Ab'sa-lom reigneth in He'bron.

11 And with Ab'sa-lom went two hundred men out of Je-ru'sa-lem, *that were* called; and they went in their simplicity, and they knew not any thing.

12 And Ab'sa-lom sent for A-hith'o-phel the Gi'lo-nite, Da-'vid's counsellor, from his city, *even* from Gi'loh, while he offered sacrifices. And the conspiracy was strong; for the people increased continually with Ab'sa-lom.

13 And there came a messenger to Da'vid, saying, The hearts of the men of Is'ra-el are after Ab'sa-lom.

14 And Da'vid said unto all his servants that *were* with him at Je-ru'sa-lem, Arise, and let us flee; for

David Leaves Jerusalem

219

we shall not *else* escape from Ab'sa-lom: make speed to depart, lest he overtake us suddenly, and bring evil upon us, and smite the city with the edge of the sword.

15 And the king's servants said unto the king, Behold, thy servants *are ready to do* whatsoever my lord the king shall appoint.

16 And the king went forth, and all his household after him. And the king left ten women, *which were* concubines, to keep the house.

17 And the king went forth, and all the people after him, and tarried in a place that was far off.

18 And all his servants passed on beside him; and all the Cher'-eth-ites, and all the Pe'leth-ites, and all the Git'tites, six hundred men which came after him from Gath, passed on before the king.

19 Then said the king to It'ta-i the Git'tite, Wherefore goest thou also with us? return to thy place, and abide with the king: for thou *art* a stranger, and also an exile.

20 Whereas thou camest *but* yesterday, should I this day make thee go up and down with us? seeing I go whither I may, return thou, and take back thy brethren: mercy and truth *be* with thee.

21 And It'ta-i answered the king, and said, *As* the LORD liveth, and *as* my lord the king liveth, surely in what place my lord the king shall be, whether in death or life, even there also will thy servant be.

22 And Da'vid said to It'ta-i, Go and pass over. And It'ta-i the Git'tite passed over, and all his men, and all the little ones that *were* with him.

23 And all the country wept with a loud voice, and all the people passed over: the king also himself passed over the brook Kid'ron, and all the people passed over, toward the way of the wilderness.

24 And lo Za'dok also, and all the Le'vites *were* with him, bearing the ark of the covenant of God: and they set down the ark of God; and A-bi'a-thar went up, until all the people had done passing out of the city.

25 And the king said unto Za'dok, Carry back the ark of God into the city: if I shall find favour in the eyes of the LORD, he will bring me again, and shew me *both* it, and his habitation:

26 But if he thus say, I have no delight in thee; behold, *here am* I, let him do to me as seemeth good unto him.

27 The king said also unto Za'dok the priest, *Art not* thou a seer? return into the city in peace, and your two sons with you, A-him'a-az thy son, and Jon'a-than the son of A-bi'a-thar.

28 See, I will tarry in the plain of the wilderness, until there come word from you to certify me.

29 Za'dok therefore and A-bi'a-thar carried the ark of God again to Je-ru'sa-lem: and they tarried there.

30 And Da'vid went up by the ascent of *mount* Ol'i-vet, and wept as he went up, and had his head covered, and he went barefoot: and all the people that *was* with him covered every man his head, and they went up, weeping as they went up.

31 And *one* told Da'vid, saying, A-hith'o-phel *is* among the conspirators with Ab'sa-lom. And Da'vid said, O LORD, I pray thee, turn the counsel of A-hith'o-phel into foolishness.

32 And it came to pass, that *when* Da'vid was come to the top *of the mount,* where he worshipped God, behold, Hu'shai the Ar'chite came to meet him with his coat rent, and earth upon his head:

33 Unto whom Da'vid said, If thou passest on with me, then thou shalt be a burden unto me:

Hushai and Ahithophel

34 But if thou return to the city, and say unto Ab'sa-lom, I will be thy servant, O king; *as I have been* thy father's servant hitherto, so *will* I now also *be* thy servant: then mayest thou for me defeat the counsel of A-hith'o-phel.

35 And *hast thou* not there with thee Za'dok and A-bi'a-thar the priests? therefore it shall be, *that* what thing soever thou shalt hear out of the king's house, thou shalt tell *it* to Za'dok and A-bi'a-thar the priests.

36 Behold, *they have* there with them their two sons, A-him'a-az Za'dok's *son,* and Jon'a-than A-bi'a-thar's *son;* and by them ye shall send unto me every thing that ye can hear.

37 So Hu'shai Da'vid's friend came into the city, and Ab'sa-lom came into Je-ru'sa-lem.

Questionable Loyalty and
Blatant Hostility

16 AND WHEN Da'vid was a little past the top *of the hill,* behold, Zi'ba the servant of Me-phib'o-sheth met him, with a couple of asses saddled, and upon them two hundred *loaves* of bread, and an hundred bunches of raisins, and an hundred of summer fruits, and a bottle of wine.

2 And the king said unto Zi'ba, What meanest thou by these? And Zi'ba said, The asses *be* for the king's household to ride on; and the bread and summer fruit for the young men to eat; and the wine, that such as be faint in the wilderness may drink.

3 And the king said, And where *is* thy master's son? And Zi'ba said unto the king, Behold, he abideth at Je-ru'sa-lem: for he said, To day shall the house of Is'ra-el restore me the kingdom of my father.

4 Then said the king to Zi'ba, Behold, thine *are* all that *pertained* unto Me-phib'o-sheth. And Zi'ba

said, I humbly beseech thee *that* I may find grace in thy sight, my lord, O king.

5 And when king Da'vid came to Ba-hu'rim, behold, thence came out a man of the family of the house of Saul, whose name *was* Shim'e-i, the son of Ge'ra: he came forth, and cursed still as he came.

6 And he cast stones at Da'-vid, and at all the servants of king Da'vid: and all the people and all the mighty men *were* on his right hand and on his left.

7 And thus said Shim'e-i when he cursed, Come out, come out, thou bloody man, and thou man of Be'li-al:

8 The Lord hath returned upon thee all the blood of the house of Saul, in whose stead thou hast reigned; and the Lord hath delivered the kingdom into the hand of Ab'sa-lom thy son: and, behold, thou *art taken* in thy mischief, because thou *art* a bloody man.

9 Then said A-bish'a-i the son of Zer-u-i'ah unto the king, Why should this dead dog curse my lord the king? let me go over, I pray thee, and take off his head.

10 And the king said, What have I to do with you, ye sons of Zer-u-i'ah? so let him curse, because the Lord hath said unto him, Curse Da'vid. Who shall then say, Wherefore hast thou done so?

11 And Da'vid said to A-bish'a-i, and to all his servants, Behold, my son, which came forth of my bowels, seeketh my life: how much more now *may this* Ben'ja-mite *do it?* let him alone, and let him curse; for the Lord hath bidden him.

12 It may be that the Lord will look on mine affliction, and that the Lord will requite me good for his cursing this day.

223

13 And as Da'vid and his men went by the way, Shim'e-i went along on the hill's side over against him, and cursed as he went, and threw stones at him, and cast dust.

14 And the king, and all the people that *were* with him, came weary, and refreshed themselves there.

15 And Ab'sa-lom, and all the people the men of Is'ra-el, came to Je-ru'sa-lem, and A-hith'o-phel with him.

16 And it came to pass, when Hu'shai the Ar'ch-ite, Da'vid's friend, was come unto Ab'sa-lom, that Hu'shai said unto Ab'sa-lom, God save the king, God save the king.

17 And Ab'sa-lom said to Hu'shai, *Is* this thy kindness to thy friend? why wentest thou not with thy friend?

18 And Hu'shai said unto Ab'sa-lom, Nay; but whom the LORD, and this people, and all the men of Is'ra-el, choose, his will I be, and with him will I abide.

19 And again, whom should I serve? *should I* not *serve* in the presence of his son? as I have served in thy father's presence, so will I be in thy presence.

20 Then said Ab'sa-lom to A-hith'o-phel, Give counsel among you what we shall do.

21 And A-hith'o-phel said unto Ab'sa-lom, Go in unto thy father's concubines, which he hath left to keep the house; and all Is'ra-el shall hear that thou art abhorred of thy father: then shall the hands of all that *are* with thee be strong.

22 So they spread Ab'sa-lom a tent upon the top of the house; and Ab'sa-lom went in unto his father's concubines in the sight of all Is'ra-el.

23 And the counsel of A-hith'o-phel, which he

counselled in those days, *was* as if a man had en-quired at the oracle of God: so *was* all the counsel of A-hith'o-phel both with Da'vid and with Ab'sa-lom.

17 MOREOVER A-HITH'O-PHEL said unto Ab'sa-lom, Let me now choose out twelve thousand men, and I will arise and pursue after Da'vid this night:

2 And I will come upon him while he *is* weary and weak handed, and will make him afraid: and all the people that *are* with him shall flee; and I will smite the king only:

3 And I will bring back all the people unto thee: the man whom thou seekest *is* as if all returned: *so* all the people shall be in peace.

4 And the saying pleased Ab'sa-lom well, and all the elders of Is'ra-el.

5 Then said Ab'sa-lom, Call now Hu'shai the Ar'chite also, and let us hear likewise what he saith.

6 And when Hu'shai was come to Ab'sa-lom, Ab'sa-lom spake unto him, saying, A-hith'o-phel hath spoken after this manner: shall we do *after* his saying? if not; speak thou.

7 And Hu'shai said unto Ab'sa-lom, The coun-sel that A-hith'o-phel hath given *is* not good at this time.

8 For, said Hu'shai, thou knowest thy father and his men, that they *be* mighty men, and they *be* chafed in their minds, as a bear robbed of her whelps in the field: and thy father *is* a man of war, and will not lodge with the people.

9 Behold, he is hid now in some pit, or in some *other* place: and it will come to pass, when some of

Good Advice Not Taken

225

them be overthrown at the first, that whosoever heareth it will say, There is a slaughter among the people that follow Ab'sa-lom.

10 And he also *that is* valiant, whose heart *is* as the heart of a lion, shall utterly melt: for all Is'ra-el knoweth that thy father *is* a mighty man, and *they* which *be* with him *are* valiant men.

11 Therefore I counsel that all Is'ra-el be generally gathered unto thee, from Dan even to Be'er-she'ba, as the sand that *is* by the sea for multitude; and that thou go to battle in thine own person.

12 So shall we come upon him in some place where he shall be found, and we will light upon him as the dew falleth on the ground: and of him and of all the men that *are* with him there shall not be left so much as one.

13 Moreover, if he be gotten into a city, then shall all Is'ra-el bring ropes to that city, and we will draw it into the river, until there be not one small stone found there.

14 And Ab'sa-lom and all the men of Is'ra-el said, The counsel of Hu'shai the Ar'chite *is* better than the counsel of A-hith'o-phel. For the Lord had appointed to defeat the good counsel of A-hith'o-phel, to the intent that the Lord might bring evil upon Ab'sa-lom.

15 Then said Hu'shai unto Za'dok and to A-bi'a-thar the priests, Thus and thus did A-hith'o-phel counsel Ab'sa-lom and the elders of Is'ra-el; and thus and thus have I counselled.

16 Now therefore send quickly, and tell Da'vid, saying, Lodge not this night in the plains of the wilderness, but speedily pass over; lest the king be swallowed up, and all the people that *are* with him.

17 Now Jon'a-than and A-him'a-az stayed by

En-ro'gel; for they might not be seen to come into the city: and a wench went and told them; and they went and told king Da'vid.

18 Nevertheless a lad saw them, and told Ab'sa-lom: but they went both of them away quickly, and came to a man's house in Ba-hu'rim, which had a well in his court; whither they went down.

19 And the woman took and spread a covering over the well's mouth, and spread ground corn thereon; and the thing was not known.

20 And when Ab'sa-lom's servants came to the woman to the house, they said, Where *is* A-him'a-az and Jon'a-than? And the woman said unto them, They be gone over the brook of water. And when they had sought and could not find *them,* they returned to Je-ru'sa-lem.

21 And it came to pass, after they were departed, that they came up out of the well, and went and told king Da'vid, and said unto Da'vid, Arise, and pass quickly over the water: for thus hath A-hi-th'o-phel counselled against you.

22 Then Da'vid arose, and all the people that *were* with him, and they passed over Jor'dan: by the morning light there lacked not one of them that was not gone over Jor'dan.

23 And when A-hith'o-phel saw that his counsel was not followed, he saddled *his* ass, and arose, and gat him home to his house, to his city, and put his household in order, and hanged himself, and died, and was buried in the sepulchre of his father.

24 Then Da'vid came to Ma-ha-na'im. And Ab'sa-lom passed over Jor'dan, he and all the men of Is'ra-el with him.

25 And Ab'sa-lom made Am'a-sa captain of the host instead of Jo'ab: which Am'a-sa *was* a man's

Ahithophel's Suicide

The Death of Absalom

227

son, whose name *was* Ith'ra an Is'ra-el-ite, that went in to Ab'i-gail the daughter of Na'-hash, sister to Zer-u-i'ah Jo'ab's mother.

26 So Is'ra-el and Ab'sa-lom pitched in the land of Gil'e-ad.

27 And it came to pass, when Da'vid was come to Ma-ha-na'im, that Sho'bi the son of Na'hash of Rab'bah of the children of Am'mon, and Ma'chir the son of Am'mi-el of Lo-de'bar, and Bar-zil'la-i the Gil'e-ad-ite of Ro-ge'lim,

28 Brought beds, and basons, and earthen vessels, and wheat, and barley, and flour, and parched *corn,* and beans, and lentiles, and parched *pulse,*

29 And honey, and butter, and sheep, and cheese of kine, for Da'vid, and for the people that *were* with him, to eat: for they said, The people *is* hungry, and weary, and thirsty, in the wilderness.

18 AND DA'VID numbered the people that *were* with him, and set captains of thousands and captains of hundreds over them.

2 And Da'vid sent forth a third part of the people under the hand of Jo'ab, and a third part under the hand of A-bish'a-i the son of Zer-u-i'ah, Jo'ab's brother, and a third part under the hand of It'ta-i the Git'tite. And the king said unto the people, I will surely go forth with you myself also.

3 But the people answered, Thou shalt not go forth: for if we flee away, they will not care for us; neither if half of us die, will they care for us: but now *thou art* worth ten thousand of us: therefore now *it is* better that thou succour us out of the city.

4 And the king said unto them, What seemeth you best I will do. And the king stood by the gate

side, and all the people came out by hundreds and by thousands.

5 And the king commanded Jo'ab and A-bish'a-i and It'ta-i, saying, *Deal* gently for my sake with the young man, *even* with Ab'sa-lom. And all the people heard when the king gave all the captains charge concerning Ab'sa-lom.

6 So the people went out into the field against Is'ra-el: and the battle was in the wood of E'phra-im;

7 Where the people of Is'ra-el were slain before the servants of Da'vid, and there was there a great slaughter that day of twenty thousand *men.*

8 For the battle was there scattered over the face of all the country: and the wood devoured more people that day than the sword devoured.

9 And Ab'sa-lom met the servants of Da'vid. And Ab'sa-lom rode upon a mule, and the mule went under the thick boughs of a great oak, and his head caught hold of the oak, and he was taken up between the heaven and the earth; and the mule that *was* under him went away.

10 And a certain man saw *it,* and told Jo'ab, and said, Behold, I saw Ab'sa-lom hanged in an oak.

11 And Jo'ab said unto the man that told him, And, behold, thou sawest *him,* and why didst thou not smite him there to the ground? and I would have given thee ten *shekels* of silver, and a girdle.

12 And the man said unto Jo'ab, Though I should receive a thousand *shekels* of silver in mine hand, *yet* would I not put forth mine hand against the king's son: for in our hearing the king charged thee and A-bish'a-i and It'ta-i, saying, Beware that none *touch* the young man Ab'sa-lom.

13 Otherwise I should have wrought falsehood against mine own life: for there is no matter hid from the king, and thou thyself wouldest have set thyself against *me.*

14 Then said Jo'ab, I may not tarry thus with thee. And he took three darts in his hand, and thrust them through the heart of Ab'sa-lom, while he *was* yet alive in the midst of the oak.

15 And ten young men that bare Jo'ab's armour compassed about and smote Ab'sa-lom, and slew him.

16 And Jo'ab blew the trumpet, and the people returned from pursuing after Is'ra-el: for Jo'ab held back the people.

17 And they took Ab'sa-lom, and cast him into a great pit in the wood, and laid a very great heap of stones upon him: and all Is'ra-el fled every one to his tent.

18 Now Ab'sa-lom in his lifetime had taken and reared up for himself a pillar, which *is* in the king's dale: for he said, I have no son to keep my name in remembrance: and he called the pillar after his own name: and it is called unto this day, Ab'sa-lom's place.

19 Then said A-him'a-az the son of Za'dok, Let me now run, and bear the king tidings, how that the LORD hath avenged him of his enemies.

20 And Jo'ab said unto him, Thou shalt not bear tidings this day, but thou shalt bear tidings another day: but this day thou shalt bear no tidings, because the king's son is dead.

21 Then said Jo'ab to Cu'shi, Go tell the king what thou hast seen. And Cu'shi bowed himself unto Jo'ab, and ran.

22 Then said A-him'a-az the son of Za'dok yet again to Jo'ab, But howsoever, let me, I pray thee,

also run after Cu'shi. And Jo'ab said, Wherefore wilt thou run, my son, seeing that thou hast no tidings ready?

23 But howsoever, *said he,* let me run. And he said unto him, Run. Then A-him'a-az ran by the way of the plain, and overran Cu'shi.

24 And Da'vid sat between the two gates: and the watchman went up to the roof over the gate unto the wall, and lifted up his eyes, and looked, and behold a man running alone.

25 And the watchman cried, and told the king. And the king said, If he *be* alone, *there is* tidings in his mouth. And he came apace, and drew near.

26 And the watchman saw another man running: and the watchman called unto the porter, and said, Behold *another* man running alone. And the king said, He also bringeth tidings.

27 And the watchman said, Me thinketh the running of the foremost is like the running of A-him'a-az the son of Za'dok. And the king said, He *is* a good man, and cometh with good tidings.

28 And A-him'a-az called, and said unto the king, All is well. And he fell down to the earth upon his face before the king, and said, Blessed *be* the LORD thy God, which hath delivered up the men that lifted up their hand against my lord the king.

29 And the king said, Is the young man Ab'salom safe? And A-him'a-az answered, When Jo'ab sent the king's servant, and *me* thy servant, I saw a great tumult, but I knew not what *it was.*

30 And the king said *unto him,* Turn aside, *and* stand here. And he turned aside, and stood still.

31 And, behold, Cu'shi came; and Cu'shi said, Tidings, my lord the king: for the LORD hath

avenged thee this day of all them that rose up against thee.

32 And the king said unto Cu'shi, *Is* the young man Ab'sa-lom safe? And Cu'shi answered, The enemies of my lord the king, and all that rise against thee to do *thee* hurt, be as *that* young man *is*.

33 And the king was much moved, and went up to the chamber over the gate, and wept: and as he went, thus he said, O my son Ab'sa-lom, my son, my son Ab'sa-lom! would God I had died for thee, O Ab'sa-lom, my son, my son!

War and Intrigue Continue (19:1–20:26)

David Restored to the Kingdom

19 AND IT was told Jo'ab, Behold, the king weepeth and mourneth for Ab'sa-lom.

2 And the victory that day was *turned* into mourning unto all the people: for the people heard say that day how the king was grieved for his son.

3 And the people gat them by stealth that day into the city, as people being ashamed steal away when they flee in battle.

4 But the king covered his face, and the king cried with a loud voice, O my son Ab'sa-lom, O Ab'sa-lom, my son, my son!

5 And Jo'ab came into the house to the king, and said, Thou hast shamed this day the faces of all thy servants, which this day have saved thy life, and the lives of thy sons and of thy daughters, and the lives of thy wives, and the lives of thy concubines;

6 In that thou lovest thine enemies, and hatest thy friends. For thou hast declared this day, that thou regardest neither princes nor servants: for this day I perceive, that if Ab'sa-lom had lived, and all we had died this day, then it had pleased thee well.

7 Now therefore arise, go forth, and speak comfortably unto thy servants: for I swear by the LORD, if thou go not forth, there will not tarry one with thee this night: and that will be worse unto thee than all the evil that befell thee from thy youth until now.

8 Then the king arose, and sat in the gate. And they told unto all the people, saying, Behold, the king doth sit in the gate. And all the people came before the king: for Is'ra-el had fled every man to his tent.

9 And all the people were at strife throughout all the tribes of Is'ra-el, saying, The king saved us out of the hand of our enemies, and he delivered us out of the hand of the Phi-lis'tines; and now he is fled out of the land for Ab'sa-lom.

10 And Ab'sa-lom, whom we anointed over us, is dead in battle. Now therefore why speak ye not a word of bringing the king back?

11 And king Da'vid sent to Za'dok and to A-bi'a-thar the priests, saying, Speak unto the elders of Ju'dah, saying, Why are ye the last to bring the king back to his house? seeing the speech of all Is'ra-el is come to the king, *even* to his house.

12 Ye *are* my brethren, ye *are* my bones and my flesh: wherefore then are ye the last to bring back the king?

13 And say ye to Am'a-sa, *Art* thou not of my bone, and of my flesh? God do so to me, and more also, if thou be not captain of the host before me continually in the room of Jo'ab.

14 And he bowed the heart of all the men of Ju'dah, even as *the heart of* one man; so that they sent *this word* unto the king, Return thou, and all thy servants.

15 So the king returned, and came to Jor'dan. And Ju'dah came to Gil'gal, to go to meet the king, to conduct the king over Jor'dan.

16 And Shim'e-i the son of Ge'ra, a Ben'ja-mite, which *was* of Ba-hu'rim, hasted and came down with the men of Ju'dah to meet king Da'vid.

17 And *there were* a thousand men of Ben'ja-min with him, and Zi'ba the servant of the house of Saul, and his fifteen sons and his twenty servants with him; and they went over Jor'dan before the king.

18 And there went over a ferry boat to carry over the king's household, and to do what he thought good. And Shim'e-i the son of Ge'ra fell down before the king, as he was come over Jor'dan;

19 And said unto the king, Let not my lord impute iniquity unto me, neither do thou remember that which thy servant did perversely the day that my lord the king went out of Je-ru'sa-lem, that the king should take it to his heart.

20 For thy servant doth know that I have sinned: therefore, behold, I am come the first this day of all the house of Jo'seph to go down to meet my lord the king.

21 But A-bish'a-i the son of Zer-u-i'ah answered and said, Shall not Shim'e-i be put to death for this, because he cursed the LORD's anointed?

22 And Da'vid said, What have I to do with you, ye sons of Zer-u-i'ah, that ye should this day be adversaries unto me? shall there any man be put to death this day in Is'ra-el? for do not I know that I *am* this day king over Is'ra-el?

23 Therefore the king said unto Shim'e-i, Thou shalt not die. And the king sware unto him.

24 And Me-phib'o-sheth the son of Saul came down to meet the king, and had neither dressed his

feet, nor trimmed his beard, nor washed his clothes, from the day the king departed until the day he came *again* in peace.

25 And it came to pass, when he was come to Je-ru'sa-lem to meet the king, that the king said unto him, Wherefore wentest not thou with me, Me-phib'o-sheth?

26 And he answered, My lord, O king, my servant deceived me: for thy servant said, I will saddle me an ass, that I may ride thereon, and go to the king; because thy servant *is* lame.

27 And he hath slandered thy servant unto my lord the king; but my lord the king *is* as an angel of God: do therefore *what is* good in thine eyes.

28 For all *of* my father's house were but dead men before my lord the king: yet didst thou set thy servant among them that did eat at thine own table. What right therefore have I yet to cry any more unto the king?

29 And the king said unto him, Why speakest thou any more of thy matters? I have said, Thou and Zi'ba divide the land.

30 And Me-phib'o-sheth said unto the king, Yea, let him take all, forasmuch as my lord the king is come again in peace unto his own house.

31 And Bar-zil'la-i the Gil'e-ad-ite came down from Ro-ge'lim, and went over Jor'dan with the king, to conduct him over Jor'dan.

32 Now Bar-zil'la-i was a very aged man, *even* fourscore years old: and he had provided the king of sustenance while he lay at Ma-ha-na'im; for he *was* a very great man.

33 And the king said unto Bar-zil'la-i, Come thou over with me, and I will feed thee with me in Je-ru'sa-lem.

34 And Bar-zil'la-i said unto the king, How long have I to live, that I should go up with the king unto Je-ru'sa-lem?

35 I *am* this day fourscore years old: *and* can I discern between good and evil? can thy servant taste what I eat or what I drink? can I hear any more the voice of singing men and singing women? wherefore then should thy servant be yet a burden unto my lord the king?

36 Thy servant will go a little way over Jor'dan with the king: and why should the king recompense it me with such a reward?

37 Let thy servant, I pray thee, turn back again, that I may die in mine own city, *and be buried* by the grave of my father and of my mother. But behold thy servant Chim'ham; let him go over with my lord the king; and do to him what shall seem good unto thee.

38 And the king answered, Chim'ham shall go over with me, and I will do to him that which shall seem good unto thee: and whatsoever thou shalt require of me, *that* will I do for thee.

39 And all the people went over Jor'dan. And when the king was come over, the king kissed Bar-zil'la-i, and blessed him; and he returned unto his own place.

40 Then the king went on to Gil'gal, and Chim'-ham went on with him: and all the people of Ju'dah conducted the king, and also half the people of Is'ra-el.

41 And, behold, all the men of Is'ra-el came to the king, and said unto the king, Why have our brethren the men of Ju'dah stolen thee away, and have brought the king, and his household, and all Da'vid's men with him, over Jor'dan?

42 And all the men of Ju'dah answered the men of Is'ra-el, Because the king *is* near of kin to us: wherefore then be ye angry for this matter? have we eaten at all of the king's *cost?* or hath he given us any gift?

43 And the men of Is'ra-el answered the men of Ju'dah, and said, We have ten parts in the king, and we have also more *right* in Da'vid than ye: why then did ye despise us, that our advice should not be first had in bringing back our king? And the words of the men of Ju'dah were fiercer than the words of the men of Is'ra-el.

20 AND THERE happened to be there a man of Be'li-al, whose name *was* She'ba, the son of Bich'ri, a Ben'ja-mite: and he blew a trumpet, and said, We have no part in Da'vid, neither have we inheritance in the son of Jes'se: every man to his tents, O Is'ra-el.

Problems within the Kingdom

2 So every man of Is'ra-el went up from after Da'vid, *and* followed She'ba the son of Bich'ri: but the men of Ju'dah clave unto their king, from Jor'-dan even to Je-ru'sa-lem.

3 And Da'vid came to his house at Je-ru'sa-lem; and the king took the ten women *his* concubines, whom he had left to keep the house, and put them in ward, and fed them, but went not in unto them. So they were shut up unto the day of their death, living in widowhood.

4 Then said the king to Am'a-sa, Assemble me the men of Ju'dah within three days, and be thou here present.

5 So Am'a-sa went to assemble *the men of* Ju'dah: but he tarried longer than the set time which he had appointed him.

6 And Da'vid said to A-bish'a-i, Now shall She'ba the son of Bich'ri do us more harm than *did* Ab'sa-lom: take thou thy lord's servants, and pursue after him, lest he get him fenced cities, and escape us.

7 And there went out after him Jo'ab's men, and the Cher'eth-ites, and the Pe'leth-ites, and all the mighty men: and they went out of Je-ru'sa-lem, to pursue after She'ba the son of Bich'ri.

8 When they *were* at the great stone which *is* in Gib'e-on, Am'a-sa went before them. And Jo'ab's garment that he had put on was girded unto him, and upon it a girdle *with* a sword fastened upon his loins in the sheath thereof; and as he went forth it fell out.

9 And Jo'ab said to Am'a-sa, *Art* thou in health, my brother? And Jo'ab took Am'a-sa by the beard with the right hand to kiss him.

10 But Am'a-sa took no heed to the sword that *was* in Jo'ab's hand: so he smote him therewith in the fifth *rib,* and shed out his bowels to the ground, and struck him not again; and he died. So Jo'ab and A-bish'a-i his brother pursued after She'ba the son of Bich'ri.

11 And one of Jo'ab's men stood by him, and said, He that favoureth Jo'ab, and he that *is* for Da'vid, *let him go* after Jo'ab.

12 And Am'a-sa wallowed in blood in the midst of the highway. And when the man saw that all the people stood still, he removed Am'a-sa out of the highway into the field, and cast a cloth upon him, when he saw that every one that came by him stood still.

13 When he was removed out of the highway, all the people went on after Jo'ab, to pursue after She'ba the son of Bich'ri.

14 And he went through all the tribes of Is'ra-el unto A'bel, and to Beth-ma'a-chah, and all the Be'rites: and they were gathered together, and went also after him.

15 And they came and besieged him in A'bel of Beth-ma'a-chah, and they cast up a bank against the city, and it stood in the trench: and all the people that *were* with Jo'ab battered the wall, to throw it down.

16 Then cried a wise woman out of the city, Hear, hear; say, I pray you, unto Jo'ab, Come near hither, that I may speak with thee.

17 And when he was come near unto her, the woman said, *Art* thou Jo'ab? And he answered, I *am he.* Then she said unto him, Hear the words of thine handmaid. And he answered, I do hear.

18 Then she spake, saying, They were wont to speak in old time, saying, They shall surely ask *counsel* at A'bel: and so they ended *the matter.*

19 I *am one of them that are* peaceable *and* faithful in Is'ra-el: thou seekest to destroy a city and a mother in Is'ra-el: why wilt thou swallow up the inheritance of the LORD?

20 And Jo'ab answered and said, Far be it, far be it from me, that I should swallow up or destroy.

21 The matter *is* not so: but a man of mount E'phra-im, She'ba the son of Bich'ri by name, hath lifted up his hand against the king, *even* against Da'vid: deliver him only, and I will depart from the city. And the woman said unto Jo'ab, Behold, his head shall be thrown to thee over the wall.

22 Then the woman went unto all the people in her wisdom. And they cut off the head of She'ba the son of Bich'ri, and cast *it* out to Jo'ab. And he blew a trumpet, and they retired from the city,

every man to his tent. And Jo'ab returned to Je-ru'sa-lem unto the king.

23 Now Jo'ab *was* over all the host of Is'ra-el: and Be-na'iah the son of Je-hoi'a-da *was* over the Cher'eth-ites and over the Pe'leth-ites:

24 And A-do'ram *was* over the tribute: and Je-hosh'a-phat the son of A-hi'lud *was* recorder:

25 And She'va *was* scribe: and Za'dok and A-bi'a-thar *were* the priests:

26 And I'ra also the Ja'ir-ite was a chief ruler about Da'vid.

The Long, Long Whimper

Famine and War, Death and Destruction

21 THEN THERE was a famine in the days of Da'vid three years, year after year; and Da'vid enquired of the LORD. And the LORD answered, *It is* for Saul, and for *his* bloody house, because he slew the Gib'e-on-ites.

2 And the king called the Gib'e-on-ites, and said unto them; (now the Gib'e-on-ites *were* not of the children of Is'ra-el, but of the remnant of the Am'or-ites; and the children of Is'ra-el had sworn unto them: and Saul sought to slay them in his zeal to the children of Is'ra-el and Ju'dah.)

3 Wherefore Da'vid said unto the Gib'e-on-ites, What shall I do for you? and wherewith shall I make the atonement, that ye may bless the inheritance of the LORD?

4 And the Gib'e-on-ites said unto him, We will have no silver nor gold of Saul, nor of his house; neither for us shalt thou kill any man in Is'ra-el. And he said, What ye shall say, *that* will I do for you.

5 And they answered the king, The man that consumed us, and that devised against us *that* we

240

should be destroyed from remaining in any of the coasts of Is'ra-el,

6 Let seven men of his sons be delivered unto us, and we will hang them up unto the LORD in Gib'e-ah of Saul, *whom* the LORD did choose. And the king said, I will give *them.*

7 But the king spared Me-phib'o-sheth, the son of Jon'a-than the son of Saul, because of the LORD's oath that *was* between them, between Da'vid and Jon'a-than the son of Saul.

8 But the king took the two sons of Riz'pah the daughter of A-i'ah, whom she bare unto Saul, Ar-mo'ni and Me-phib'o-sheth; and the five sons of Mi'chal the daughter of Saul, whom she brought up for A'dri-el the son of Bar-zil'la-i the Me-hol'ath-ite:

9 And he delivered them into the hands of the Gib'e-on-ites, and they hanged them in the hill before the LORD: and they fell *all* seven together, and were put to death in the days of harvest, in the first *days,* in the beginning of barley harvest.

10 And Riz'pah the daughter of A-i'ah took sackcloth, and spread it for her upon the rock, from the beginning of harvest until water dropped upon them out of heaven, and suffered neither the birds of the air to rest on them by day, nor the beasts of the field by night.

11 And it was told Da'vid what Riz'pah the daughter of A-i'ah, the concubine of Saul, had done.

12 And Da'vid went and took the bones of Saul and the bones of Jon'a-than his son from the men of Ja'besh-gil'e-ad, which had stolen them from the street of Beth'-shan, where the Phi-lis'tines had hanged them, when the Phi-lis'tines had slain Saul in Gil-bo'a:

241

13 And he brought up from thence the bones of Saul and the bones of Jon'a-than his son; and they gathered the bones of them that were hanged.

14 And the bones of Saul and Jon'a-than his son buried they in the country of Ben'ja-min in Ze'lah, in the sepulchre of Kish his father: and they performed all that the king commanded. And after that God was intreated for the land.

15 Moreover the Phi-lis'-tines had yet war again with Is'ra-el; and Da'vid went down, and his servants with him, and fought against the Phi-lis'tines: and Da'vid waxed faint.

16 And Ish'bi-be'nob, which *was* of the sons of the giant, the weight of whose spear *weighed* three hundred *shekels* of brass in weight, he being girded with a new *sword,* thought to have slain Da'vid.

17 But A-bish'a-i the son of Zer-u-i'ah succoured him, and smote the Phi-lis'tine, and killed him. Then the men of Da'vid sware unto him, saying, Thou shalt go no more out with us to battle, that thou quench not the light of Is'ra-el.

18 And it came to pass after this, that there was again a battle with the Phi-lis'tines at Gob: then Sib'be-chai the Hu'shath-ite slew Saph, which *was* of the sons of the giant.

19 And there was again a battle in Gob with the Phi-lis'tines, where El-ha'nan the son of Ja-ar'e-or'e-gim, a Beth'-le-hem-ite, slew *the brother of* Go-li'ath the Git'tite, the staff of whose spear *was* like a weaver's beam.

20 And there was yet a battle in Gath, where was a man of *great* stature, that had on every hand six fingers, and on every foot six toes, four and twenty in number; and he also was born to the giant.

21 And when he defied Is'ra-el, Jon'a-than the son of Shim'e-ah the brother of Da'vid slew him.

22 These four were born to the giant in Gath, and fell by the hand of Da'vid, and by the hand of his servants.

22 AND DA'VID spake unto the LORD the words of this song in the day *that* the LORD had delivered him out of the hand of all his enemies, and out of the hand of Saul:

2 And he said, The LORD *is* my rock, and my fortress, and my deliverer;

3 The God of my rock; in him will I trust: *he is* my shield, and the horn of my salvation, my high tower, and my refuge, my saviour; thou savest me from violence.

4 I will call on the LORD, *who is* worthy to be praised: so shall I be saved from mine enemies.

5 When the waves of death compassed me, the floods of ungodly men made me afraid;

6 The sorrows of hell compassed me about; the snares of death prevented me;

7 In my distress I called upon the LORD, and cried to my God: and he did hear my voice out of his temple, and my cry *did enter* into his ears.

8 Then the earth shook and trembled; the foundations of heaven moved and shook, because he was wroth.

9 There went up a smoke out of his nostrils, and fire out of his mouth devoured: coals were kindled by it.

10 He bowed the heavens also, and came down; and darkness *was* under his feet.

Gratitude in the Song of David

243

11 And he rode upon a cherub, and did fly: and he was seen upon the wings of the wind.

12 And he made darkness pavilions round about him, dark waters, *and* thick clouds of the skies.

13 Through the brightness before him were coals of fire kindled.

14 The Lord thundered from heaven, and the most High uttered his voice.

15 And he sent out arrows, and scattered them; lightning, and discomfited them.

16 And the channels of the sea appeared, the foundations of the world were discovered, at the rebuking of the Lord, at the blast of the breath of his nostrils.

17 He sent from above, he took me; he drew me out of many waters;

18 He delivered me from my strong enemy, *and* from them that hated me: for they were too strong for me.

19 They prevented me in the day of my calamity: but the Lord was my stay.

20 He brought me forth also into a large place: he delivered me, because he delighted in me.

21 The Lord rewarded me according to my righteousness: according to the cleanness of my hands hath he recompensed me.

22 For I have kept the ways of the Lord, and have not wickedly departed from my God.

23 For all his judgments *were* before me: and *as for* his statutes, I did not depart from them.

24 I was also upright before him, and have kept myself from mine iniquity.

25 Therefore the Lord hath recompensed me ac-

cording to my righteousness; according to my cleanness in his eye sight.

26 With the merciful thou wilt shew thyself merciful, *and* with the upright man thou wilt shew thyself upright.

27 With the pure thou wilt shew thyself pure; and with the froward thou wilt shew thyself un-savoury.

28 And the afflicted people thou wilt save: but thine eyes *are* upon the haughty, *that* thou mayest bring *them* down.

29 For thou *art* my lamp, O LORD: and the LORD will lighten my darkness.

30 For by thee I have run through a troop: by my God have I leaped over a wall.

31 *As for* God, his way *is* perfect; the word of the LORD *is* tried: he *is* a buckler to all them that trust in him.

32 For who *is* God, save the LORD? and who *is* a rock, save our God?

33 God *is* my strength *and* power: and he maketh my way perfect.

34 He maketh my feet like hinds' *feet:* and setteth me upon my high places.

35 He teacheth my hands to war; so that a bow of steel is broken by mine arms.

36 Thou hast also given me the shield of thy salvation: and thy gentleness hath made me great.

37 Thou hast enlarged my steps under me; so that my feet did not slip.

38 I have pursued mine enemies, and destroyed them; and turned not again until I had consumed them.

39 And I have consumed them, and wounded them, that they could not arise: yea, they are fallen under my feet.

40 For thou hast girded me with strength to battle: them that rose up against me hast thou subdued under me.

41 Thou hast also given me the necks of mine enemies, that I might destroy them that hate me.

42 They looked, but *there was* none to save; *even* unto the LORD, but he answered them not.

43 Then did I beat them as small as the dust of the earth, I did stamp them as the mire of the street, *and* did spread them abroad.

44 Thou also hast delivered me from the strivings of my people, thou hast kept me *to be* head of the heathen: a people *which* I knew not shall serve me.

45 Strangers shall submit themselves unto me: as soon as they hear, they shall be obedient unto me.

46 Strangers shall fade away, and they shall be afraid out of their close places.

47 The LORD liveth; and blessed *be* my rock; and exalted be the God of the rock of my salvation.

48 It *is* God that avengeth me, and that bringeth down the people under me,

49 And that bringeth me forth from mine enemies: thou also hast lifted me up on high above them that rose up against me: thou hast delivered me from the violent man.

50 Therefore I will give thanks unto thee, O LORD, among the heathen, and I will sing praises unto thy name.

51 *He is* the tower of salvation for his king: and

sheweth mercy to his anointed, unto Da'vid, and to his seed for evermore.

23 NOW THESE *be* the last words of Da'vid. Da'vid the son of Jes'se said, and the man *who was* raised up on high, the anointed of the God of Ja'cob, and the sweet psalmist of Is'ra-el, said,

2 The Spirit of the LORD spake by me, and his word *was* in my tongue.

3 The God of Is'ra-el said, the Rock of Is'ra-el spake to me, He that ruleth over men *must be* just, ruling in the fear of God.

4 And *he shall be* as the light of the morning, *when* the sun riseth, *even* a morning without clouds; *as* the tender grass *springing* out of the earth by clear shining after rain.

5 Although my house *be* not so with God; yet he hath made with me an everlasting covenant, ordered in all *things,* and sure: for *this is* all my salvation, and all *my* desire, although he make *it* not to grow.

6 But *the sons* of Be'li-al *shall be* all of them as thorns thrust away, because they cannot be taken with hands:

7 But the man *that* shall touch them must be fenced with iron and the staff of a spear; and they shall be utterly burned with fire in the *same* place.

8 These *be* the names of the mighty men whom Da'vid had: The Tach'mo-nite that sat in the seat, chief among the captains; the same *was* Ad'i-no the Ez'nite: *he lift up his spear* against eight hundred, whom he slew at one time.

9 And after him *was* E-le-a'zar the son of Do'do the A-ho'hite, *one* of the three mighty men with

David's Last Words

_____

_____

_____

_____

_____

_____

_____

_____

_____

_____

_____

_____

Acknowledgment of Indebtedness

_____

_____

_____

_____

247

Da'vid, when they defied the Phi-lis'tines *that* were there gathered together to battle, and the men of Is'ra-el were gone away:

10 He arose, and smote the Phi-lis'tines until his hand was weary, and his hand clave unto the sword: and the Lord wrought a great victory that day; and the people returned after him only to spoil.

11 And after him *was* Sham'-mah the son of Ag'e-e the Ha'ra-rite. And the Phi-lis'tines were gathered together into a troop, where was a piece of ground full of lentiles: and the people fled from the Phi-lis'tines.

12 But he stood in the midst of the ground, and defended it, and slew the Phi-lis'tines: and the Lord wrought a great victory.

13 And three of the thirty chief went down, and came to Da'vid in the harvest time unto the cave of A-dul'lam: and the troop of the Phi-lis'tines pitched in the valley of Reph'a-im.

14 And Da'vid *was* then in an hold, and the garrison of the Phi-lis'tines *was* then *in* Beth'-le-hem.

15 And Da'vid longed, and said, Oh that one would give me drink of the water of the well of Beth'-le-hem, which *is* by the gate!

16 And the three mighty men brake through the host of the Phi-lis'tines, and drew water out of the well of Beth'-le-hem, that *was* by the gate, and took *it,* and brought *it* to Da'vid: nevertheless he would not drink thereof, but poured it out unto the Lord.

17 And he said, Be it far from me, O Lord, that I should do this: *is not this* the blood of the men that went in jeopardy of their lives? therefore he would not drink it. These things did these three mighty men.

18 And A-bish′a-i, the brother of Jo′ab, the son of Zer-u-i′ah, was chief among three. And he lifted up his spear against three hundred, *and* slew *them*, and had the name among three.

19 Was he not most honourable of three? therefore he was their captain: howbeit he attained not unto the *first* three.

20 And Be-na′iah the son of Je-hoi′a-da, the son of a valiant man, of Kab′ze-el, who had done many acts, he slew two lionlike men of Mo′ab: he went down also and slew a lion in the midst of a pit in time of snow:

21 And he slew an E-gyp′tian, a goodly man: and the E-gyp′tian had a spear in his hand; but he went down to him with a staff, and plucked the spear out of the E-gyp′tian's hand, and slew him with his own spear.

22 These *things* did Be-na′iah the son of Je-hoi′a-da, and had the name among three mighty men.

23 He was more honourable than the thirty, but he attained not to the *first* three. And Da′vid set him over his guard.

24 A′sa-hel the brother of Jo′ab *was* one of the thirty; El-ha′nan the son of Do′do of Beth′-le-hem,

25 Sham′mah the Ha′rod-ite, El′i-ka the Ha′rod-ite,

26 He′lez the Pal′tite, I′ra the son of Ik′kesh the Te-ko′ite,

27 A-bi-e′zer the An′e-thoth-ite, Me-bun′nai the Hu′shath-ite,

28 Zal′mon the A-ho′hite, Ma-har′a-i the Ne-toph′a-thite,

29 He′leb the son of Ba′a-nah, a Ne-toph′a-thite, It′ta-i the son of Ri′bai out of Gib′e-ah of the children of Ben′ja-min,

249

30 Be-na'iah the Pir'a-thon-ite, Hid'da-i of the brooks of Ga'ash,

31 A'bi-al'bon the Ar'bath-ite, Az'ma-veth the Bar-hu'mite,

32 E-li'ah-ba the Sha-al'bo-nite, of the sons of Ja'shen, Jon'a-than,

33 Sham'mah the Ha'ra-rite, A-hi'am the son of Sha'rar the Ha'ra-rite,

34 E-liph'e-let the son of A-has'ba-i, the son of the Ma-ach'a-thite, E-li'am the son of A-hith'o-phel the Gi'lo-nite,

35 Hez'ra-i the Car'mel-ite, Pa'a-rai the Ar'bite,

36 I'gal the son of Na'than of Zo'bah, Ba'ni the Gad'ite,

37 Ze'lek the Am'mon-ite, Na'ha-ri the Be-e'roth-ite, armourbearer to Jo'ab the son of Zer-u-i'ah,

38 I'ra an Ith'rite, Ga'reb an Ith'rite,

39 U-ri'ah the Hit'tite: thirty and seven in all.

David's Census and the Epidemic

24 AND AGAIN the anger of the LORD was kindled against Is'ra-el, and he moved Da'vid against them to say, Go, number Is'ra-el and Ju'dah.

2 For the king said to Jo'ab the captain of the host, which *was* with him, Go now through all the tribes of Is'ra-el, from Dan even to Be'er-she'ba, and number ye people, that I may know the number of the people.

3 And Jo'ab said unto the king, Now the LORD thy God add unto the people, how many soever they be, an hundredfold, and that the eyes of my lord the king may see *it:* but why doth my lord the king delight in this thing?

4 Notwithstanding the king's word prevailed against Jo'ab, and against the captains of the host. And Jo'ab and the captains of the host went out from the presence of the king, to number the people of Is'ra-el.

5 And they passed over Jor'dan, and pitched in Ar'o-er, on the right side of the city that *lieth* in the midst of the river of Gad, and toward Ja'zer:

6 Then they came to Gil'e-ad, and to the land of Tah'tim-hod'shi; and they came to Dan-ja'an, and about to Zi'don,

7 And came to the strong hold of Tyre, and to all the cities of the Hi'vites, and of the Ca'naan-ites: and they went out to the south of Ju'dah, *even* to Be'er-she'ba.

8 So when they had gone through all the land, they came to Je-ru'sa-lem at the end of nine months and twenty days.

9 And Jo'ab gave up the sum of the number of the people unto the king: and there were in Is'ra-el eight hundred thousand vailant men that drew the sword; and the men of Ju'dah *were* five hundred thousand men.

10 And Da'vid's heart smote him after that he had numbered the people. And Da'-vid said unto the Lord, I have sinned greatly in that I have done: and now, I beseech thee, O Lord, take away the iniquity of thy servant; for I have done very foolishly.

11 For when Da'vid was up in the morning, the word of the Lord came unto the prophet Gad, Da'vid's seer, saying,

12 Go and say unto Da'vid, Thus saith the Lord, I offer thee three *things;* choose thee one of them, that I may *do it* unto thee.

251

13 So Gad came to Da'vid, and told him, and said unto him, Shall seven years of famine come unto thee in thy land? or wilt thou flee three months before thine enemies, while they pursue thee? or that there be three days' pestilence in thy land? now advise, and see what answer I shall return to him that sent me.

14 And Da'vid said unto Gad, I am in a great strait: let us fall now into the hand of the LORD; for his mercies *are* great: and let me not fall into the hand of man.

15 So the LORD sent a pestilence upon Is'ra-el from the morning even to the time appointed: and there died of the people from Dan even to Be'er-she'ba seventy thousand men.

16 And when the angel stretched out his hand upon Je-ru'sa-lem to destroy it, the LORD repented him of the evil, and said to the angel that destroyed the people, It is enough: stay now thine hand. And the angel of the LORD was by the threshingplace of A-rau'nah the Jeb'u-site.

17 And Da'vid spake unto the LORD when he saw the angel that smote the people, and said, Lo, I have sinned, and I have done wickedly: but these sheep, what have they done? let thine hand, I pray thee, be against me, and against my father's house.

18 And Gad came that day to Da'vid, and said unto him, Go up, rear an altar unto the LORD in the threshingfloor of A-rau'nah the Jeb'u-site.

19 And Da'vid, according to the saying of Gad, went up as the LORD commanded.

20 And A-rau'nah looked, and saw the king and his servants coming on toward him: and A-rau'nah went out, and bowed himself before the king on his face upon the ground.

21 And A-rau'nah said, Wherefore is my lord the king come to his servant? And Da'vid said, To buy the threshingfloor of thee, to build an altar unto the LORD, that the plague may be stayed from the people.

22 And A-rau'nah said unto Da'vid, Let my lord the king take and offer up what *seemeth* good unto him: behold, *here be* oxen for burnt sacrifice, and threshing instruments and *other* instruments of the oxen for wood.

23 All these *things* did A-rau'nah, *as* a king, give unto the king. And A-rau'nah said unto the king, The LORD thy God accept thee.

24 And the king said unto A-rau'nah, Nay; but I will surely buy *it* of thee at a price: neither will I offer burnt offerings unto the LORD my God of that which doth cost me nothing. So Da'vid bought the threshingfloor and the oxen for fifty shekels of silver.

25 And Da'vid built there an altar unto the LORD, and offered burnt offerings and peace offerings. So the LORD was intreated for the land, and the plague was stayed from Is'ra-el.